The Young Count

Bilbury

Vernon Coleman

Bilbury Village is the fifth of Vernon Coleman's books about Bilbury. If you enjoy the Bilbury books you may enjoy other books by the same author including `*Mr Henry Mulligan*' and `*Mrs Caldicot's Cabbage War*'. For full details of over 100 books by Vernon Coleman please see his author page on Amazon or www.vernoncoleman.com

To Donna Antoinette

Wherever I am with you
I will always be at home.
You will always have my love
You will never be alone.

CHAPTER 1

I had forgotten how much blood there is in the human body and how much of it can be lost without the heart and brain shutting down completely. And I had forgotten that a few pints of blood can look like gallons when they're out of the arteries and veins through which they I once flowed.

The human body contains eight pints of blood. It contains eight pints because that's what it needs to move oxygen from the lungs to the tissues and organs.

There wasn't eight pints left in the man in the car. The stuff had been pumping out of him at quite a rate. An artery had been severed and the man's blood was squirting out like a fountain. Fortunately, it wasn't a big artery and so it wasn't a big fountain.

It's easy to tell whether it's a vein or an artery that's been severed. Blood comes slowly out of a leaking vein. The pressure is so low that unless a major vein is completely severed the blood loss is more of a mess than an emergency.

But when an artery is cut the blood comes out under pressure. When I was a medical student, and we were being taught how to perform venipunctures by practising on one another, one of my colleagues asked the tutor how she'd know if she'd hit an artery instead of a vein. 'You'll know,' said the tutor. 'The syringe will come whistling back past your ear.' It may have been a slight exaggeration but the keyword is 'slight' and not 'exaggeration'.

Normally, the human heart pumps eight pints of blood through the arteries every minute of every day. But the amount of blood the organs and tissues need varies from minute to minute. In an emergency-when the body's organs need extra supplies-the heart can pump fifty pints of blood a minute to give the muscles extra power and strength.

Anyone who loses a lot of blood will faint. This is a deliberate technique used to ensure that the brain gets a good supply of food.
When standing, blood has to travel upwards to reach the brain.

Someonewhofaintsautomaticallyliesdown andthismakeiteasier forblood togettothebrain-themostimportantorgan.

* * *

Themaninsidethecarwasalongwayfromproducingscartissue buthewaslosingbloodfroma cutinhis wrist.Hisradialarteryhad beenslicedintwo. Ihadnoideawhat hadcausedthecutbut the insideofthecarwasbadlysmashedupandtherewereseveralsharp edgedpiecesofplasticaround whichcouldhavedone thedamage. Judgingbythestickinessinthecarhehadlostfarmore blood than wasentirely good forhim.He wasunconscious,thoughwhether thiswasbecausehehadfaintedorbecauseofsomethingelseIhad noidea.MyonlyconcernwastodoeverythingIcouldtokeephim alive.Making aformaldiagnosisandinitiating treatmentwouldbe someoneelse'sresponsibility.AllIwasinterestedinwasgettinghim tohospitalandkeeping himaliveuntilIgothimthere.

Thereare many ways in which peopleare preparedfor emergencies. From time totime theauthoritieshavepractice emergencydays.Accidentsarestagedonarailwaylineorinalarge factory and civil servants, politicians, administratorsand others arerehearsed inanattempt toshow them how theyshould react. Allthisis,ofcourse, utterly useless. Inarealemergencythose memories aresuppressed;overtaken byfear,panicand thereality ofthemoment.

Similarly,firstaiderswhopractiseina villagehallorschool gymnasiummaythinkthattheyare preparingthemselvesforan emergencybut,sadly,theyaredoingnothingofthesort.They may becomeproficient inavillagehallorschoolgymnasium butwhen faced with arealsituation virtually everythingthey have learned willbeforgotten.Therewillbenoinstinctive musclememoriesto helpthembecausetheonlyway toprepareyourselftoreactinan emergencyistofindyourselfinemergencysituations sooften that you automaticallyknowwhat todo.

FortunatelyIhad,beforecomingtowork ingeneral practicein Bilbury, workedlong hours, long weeks, long monthsinseveral busycasualtydepartments.Ihadseen enoughemergenciesnot to panic.Dealingwithemergenciesneverbecomesroutine,andnever should, but thepracticalities canbecomeinstinctive sothatthere is timeforthebrain totelltherestofthebody whatithastodo.

* * *

The car was lying on its side in a deep ditch. It looked like a complete wreck. The man wasn't the only occupant in the car. Wriggling down into the car to attend to the man I had found a woman in the car too. I guessed that she had been the passenger and he had been driving. She was lying underneath the man and she too was unconscious. The water in the car had risen several inches in the few minutes I'd been in there with them. She was still alive but if I didn't get her out quickly she would drown. When it had crashed into the ditch the car had tipped onto its side. The windscreen and nearside windows had smashed and water from the ditch had flooded into the car. As the rain continued to pour down so the water level in the ditch rose—and as the water level in the ditch rose so the water level in the car rose too. I gently moved the woman's head as much as I could and tried to wedge her in such a way that her head was as far as possible above the water.

I clambered out of the car and the torch beam that had been shining into the car followed me out. Thumper Robinson had used orange baler twine to tie the car door on the driver's side to the car's front bumper in order to keep it open. The rain was getting heavier. It was like standing under a huge tap. Living on the North Devon coast I'd got accustomed to storms and strong winds. South Devon is all sunshine and gentle breezes. North Devon is more gale force winds and horizontal rain. But this was bad even for our part of the coastline. I thought the force of the water and the wind was going to knock me over. Apart from whatever happened to be lit by the torch I couldn't see anything. The night was pitch black. If there was a moon I couldn't see it. The wind must have been close to hurricane levels.

'Are they dead?' asked the man with the torch.

'No,' I said rather too sharply. 'They're both still alive. But we need to get them out of there fast. He's bleeding from a cut artery and I think he's fractured his left ankle. His foot is certainly pointing in the wrong direction. She's badly cut and has a broken arm.' Those were the injuries I'd been able to find. There were, I suspected, almost certainly more.

'The petrol tank is ruptured,' said Thumper. 'Petrol is coming out. I can't see it but I can smell it.'

I sighed. Something else to worry about. Somehow I didn't really care. You reach a point where there isn't any brain left for worrying. Besides, I had plenty of other things to think about.

7

I'd taken offmycoattoenablemetowriggleinto thecarand thewind wastearingatmyshirt.Iwassoakingwet andshivering almostuncontrollably. Itriedtotearthesleeveoutofmyshirtbut failedeventobreakthestitching.Itmusthavebeenagoodshirt.In themoviespeoplealwaysmanagetoripupshirtswith ease.Inreal lifeit'smore difficult.Itookmypenknifeoutofmytrouserpocket andmanaged tocutinto thematerialandthen tearoffasleeve.

'Shouldn'tweleavethem where theyareuntil the emergency servicesgethere?'askedafemalevoice.'Patientsshouldn'tbemoved when theyhavespinalinjuries,'sheadded.

'Ifwedon'tmovethembothquicklythewomandown therewill drown,'Itoldher.'She'sunconsciousandshe'strapped underneath theman. The waterlevelisrisingfastandherheadisabout three inches above thewaterlevel-oratleastitwaswhen Iwaslastin there.They'vebothgotheadinjuries.Howlongwillthefirebrigade andtheambulance be?'

'Theycan't gethere,' saidThumperRobinson.

Thumperwasmyoldestandbestfriendin Bilbury. Thoughwe werethesameagewewerethepro verbial chalkandcheese.Ihad spentmostofmyearlylifeatschool,studyingbooks. Hehadspent most of his early life playing truant from school, studying cars, animals and the countryside. He'd certainly never been to university. I had 'O' level Latin, knew who Pythagoras was and could tell you the names of all the small bones in the human wrist. Thumper could catch a trout with his bare hands, could build a stout and serviceable chair from a couple of fallen tree branches, could skin a rabbit quicker than any butcher, could change a car engine and could tell you, with certainty, which mushrooms were edible and which would kill you. In short my learning had largely theoretical value while Thumper's learning was exclusively practical.

Thumper,however, wasnotadoctor. Iwas,andassuchIwas expected tobeabletosavethelivesofthetwopeoplewho were trappedintheircar.

'The mainroadisclosedabouthalfamile fromhere,'explained Thumper. 'Thestreamhasfloodedtheroadandtheywon't beable togetthrough. Notevenwithanambulance.'

'Can theygetacrossthefields?'

Thewindwassofiercethatwehadtoshouttomakeourselves heard.IwishedI'dputonsomethingwarmer.Ishivered.

'It's far too wet,' replied Thumper. 'The ground is soaking. The nearest an ambulance can get is probably the spot where the A39 passes the end of Southcombe Wood and crosses Lower Kentisbury Ford.'

'Then we have to get them out of the car,' I said, making the decision. 'And if the ambulance can't get to them then we have to get them to an ambulance. But first I need to put a tourniquet on the man's arm. He's losing a lot of blood. And then I need something to make a couple of splints with.'

'I thought tourniquets were considered too dangerous,' said the woman. 'They can result in tissue damage. Shouldn't we apply direct pressure?'

I peered through the darkness. 'Are you a doctor?'

'I'm a social worker and a fully qualified first aider.'

I was getting rather tetchy. 'Do you want him to bleed to death?'

'No, of course not.'

'Then I need to put on a tourniquet.'

I climbed back into the car. Just before I disappeared back into the sticky blackness I turned back and called to Nick Houghton, who'd been holding the torch. 'Go and ask your Dad to drive over here with his tractor,' I said. 'He'll need to bring a trailer. Something we can put these two on. And while he brings the tractor you stay there and ring 999. Ask for an ambulance and tell them I need one to meet us where the road from Barnstaple to Lynton passes the end of Southcombe Wood and crosses Lower Kentisbury Ford.'

I wanted Nick's father to drive the tractor because I knew no one in Devon who handled a tractor more skilfully in tricky conditions. In addition to running a large farm Samuel had a contract with the local authority to keep the local roads clear of snow. He would fix a huge snow-moving attachment to the front of his ancient red monster of a tractor and drive serenely through anything. Whatever the weather, however cold, he always did it wearing a rusty brown tweed jacket with a length of baler twine around his waist. He never wore an overcoat of any kind.

I had often wondered how I would feel if I started practising medicine again. Would I panic and forget what to do? A doctor, more than any other professional, needs to know how to look and sound calm whatever his inner feelings. I was relieved to discover that I didn't feel in the slightest bit panicky. And I knew what I had to do. But I had been reminded, with a shocking suddenness, that the responsibilities of a country general practitioner are awesome. The real measure of responsibility is just how big a mistake you can make before someone stops you and at that moment I couldn't think of a job I could be doing that would carry more direct responsibility. I don't suppose either highly paid civil servants or corporate executives paid millions for their decision-making are faced with many split-second life or death decisions.

* * *

Forty minutes earlier I'd been fast asleep in bed. Warm, dry and cosy. I don't know how long the telephone had been ringing when I woke but it couldn't have been long. I'd been a general practitioner long enough to wake almost instantly at the first ring of a telephone bell.

'Is that the doctor?' demanded a frantic sounding voice which I didn't recognise.

'Well, yes, sort of,' I replied warily, instantly awake but puzzled. 'I am a doctor but I don't practise any more.' I had been a GP in Bilbury but I'd retired a year or two earlier when the authorities had decided that Bilbury wasn't a big enough village to have its own doctor. Medical services were now provided by a practice in Barnstaple

'You're needed urgently,' said the voice. 'There's been an accident. In the lane just beyond Softly's Bottom. On the Parracombe road. About a quarter of a mile past the turn to the Henshaw's farm.' The words came out so quickly that I had difficulty understanding what I was being told.

'Slow down,' I said. I sat up in bed and turned on the bedside light on the small oak table that stood at my side of the bed. Emily and Sophie, our two cats who were sleeping on the bed, didn't budge. Ben, the Welsh sheepdog who always slept on the carpet next to my slippers, was awake. She looked up, ears pricked, but didn't make a sound. Patsy slept on undisturbed.

'Thumper asked me to call you,' said the voice.

'Thumper? Is he OK? Is Thumper hurt?'

'No. Thumper is fine. But he's at the accident. He was driving past and saw the car in the ditch. There are two people in there. He thinks they're seriously injured and daren't move them.'

'What's your name?'

'Michael Houghton. I'm Samuel's son. We've played cricket together a few times.'

I knew Samuel Houghton. He was a local farmer. And I knew his, sons. Michael was a good batsman and a competent medium pace bowler when he didn't try to bowl too quickly.

'Have you telephoned for an ambulance?' I asked him.

'They can't get through. The road from Barnstaple is blocked. The storm has brought down trees all over the place and the road is flooded in several places.'

'So the doctors can't get through from Barnstaple?'

'No. Thumper says you're the only doctor who can get here.

He said to say he's sorry to have to ring you. He came to our house because we're the nearest. My brother Nick and his girlfriend have gone with him. They told me to ring you.'

'I'll be there as soon as I can,' I said. I put the phone back on its rest, pulled back the covers and started to climb out of bed. Ben looked excited. I shook my head at her to tell her she wasn't going with me. She looked crestfallen.

'Who was that?' asked a sleepy Patsy.

'There's been an accident,' I told her. 'No one can get through from Barnstaple so I'm the only doctor around.'

I looked around the bedroom. When I'd been practising as a GP I'd always kept my clothes ready by the bed so that I could get dressed quickly and be out of the house in minutes.

'Shall I get your bag out of the old surgery?' asked Patsy. Although it had been some time since I'd practised medicine we'd left the old surgery just as it was.

I thought for a moment. 'I don't think there's anything in it that will be much use,' I told her. 'But there's a first aid kit in the car.' Little did I know as I spoke that a stethoscope would have been about as much use as the box of sticking plasters the first aid kit contained.

* * *

Using my shirt sleeve as a tourniquet I'd managed to stop the man bleeding to death. And then, inch by inch, I had, with Thumper's help, succeeded in dragging the two people out of their crashed car.

Once they were out in the open it was possible to see that they were both very young. He was wearing a thin blue suit. She was wearing a mini dress. They looked as if they had been out to a party somewhere. I found a rug in the boot of my car. I wrapped it around them both to try and keep them warm.

'Do you know them?' I asked Thumper.

He shook his head. 'Will they make it?'

'I think so,' I said. Neither of them had been wearing seat belts and they'd both been bashed around quite a bit in the crash. They were both still unconscious.

'Do you recognise them?' Thumper asked Nick's girlfriend. I still didn't know her name. She had stayed behind in case the unconscious girl woke up and needed comforting.

She nodded.

'The man is George Willoughby,' she said. 'He lives in Lynton. The girl is Enid something. I don't know her second name. She lives in Lynton too.' She turned to me. 'Are they going to be OK?'

'I think so,' I told her quietly.

'He's only eighteen,' said Nick's girlfriend. 'It's his Dad's car. He always drives too bloody fast.'

I didn't say anything.

'I'd just like to apologise for being a bit bossy,' she said. I could tell it wasn't easy for her to say 'sorry'. But she said it anyway.

'That's OK,' I said. 'Forget it.' I smiled at her. 'I was a bit irritable,' I apologised. 'We didn't have much time. You're quite right about tourniquets by the way. But under the circumstances...'

'Under the circumstances you obviously did the right thing,' said Nick's girlfriend.

The rain was now coming down harder than ever. And the wind was still howling. It was an evil night. The wind was making so much noise that we saw the lights of Samuel's tractor before we heard it. I have never in my life been so pleased to see a piece of farm machinery. It was strangely comforting to see that Samuel was, as always, wearing his rusty brown tweed jacket with baler twine around the waist. Some things never change and it is those things which give us stability and strength.

Forty minutes later, after getting stuck twice and nearly overturning more times than I can remember, we met the ambulance at the pre-arranged spot on the Barnstaple road. Since I had no morphine I wasn't too unhappy that they were both still unconscious. They were both breathing well and their pulse rates were good. The ambulance then drove the two accident victims to Barnstaple. It was a relief to see them driven away in safe, professional hands

.

CHAPTER 2

'I heard the car come into the drive,' said Patsy when I walked into the kitchen. Outside the sun was corning up and the storm was subsiding. 'The kettle is boiling. I've put some muffins in the toaster.'

'Great,' I said. 'Then I need a hot bath.' I reached down and rubbed Ben's head. She sniffed at me. I could see the puzzlement in her eyes. I was soaked in ditch water and blood. I probably didn't smell anything like me.

Patsy came closer. 'You're drenched!' she said. 'You'd better get out of those wet clothes.'

I put two hands on the back of a kitchen chair and lent on it. I was almost too exhausted to move. It had been a difficult and tiring few hours. Almost as difficult physically as it had been mentally. Gently, Patsy unfastened my jacket and helped me undress. She tossed my waterproof jacket, my sweater, shirt and trousers onto the floor by the side of the Aga. I took off the rest of my clothes myself. Even my socks were dripping wet. Patsy handed me a huge cream coloured towel which was warming on a rack above the Aga. I wrapped the towel round me. It was soft, fluffy and warm. It felt wonderful.

'Is this blood?' Patsy asked, pointing to a huge dark stain on my discarded trousers.

I nodded.

'Not yours?'

I shook my head.

'Was it bad?'

'Pretty bad.'

Patsy plucked a small towel from a rail in front of the Aga and began to rub my hair.

'You've got blood on your face.' She wiped the blood away with a comer of the towel.

'An artery was squirting blood everywhere.'

'Is Thumper OK?'

'Thumper is fine. He's gone home for a bath and something to eat. He was brilliant.'

The kettle started to boil. Patsy poured hot water into two mugs which already contained granules of instant coffee. 'Do you want some whisky in yours?'

'Just a splash.'

She opened a cupboard, took out a bottle and added half an inch of whisky to one of the mugs.

I inhaled the steaming vapour, then put the mug down on the kitchen table and flopped in to one of the chairs.

While she took muffins out of the toaster I explained what had happened and why I had been called. She sliced two of the muffins in half, buttered them and put the four halves on a plate. She put the plate in front of me. The muffins were hot and the butter was melting into the soft dough. I managed to pick up one of the halved muffins all by myself.

'Do you think they'll both be all right?'

I chewed and thought hard before answering. 'I think they've got a good chance,' I said. 'They were lucky.'

'Lucky they had you.'

'Lucky that Thumper happened to drive by. He doesn't usually go down there but the lane past Withydown Farm was flooded. If he hadn't seen them they would have certainly died. He and Nick Houghton, one of Samuel Houghton's sons were there. Plus Nick's girlfriend.'

'Did the ambulance get through in the end?'

I shook my head. 'Samuel Houghton took the two of them on a trailer we hitched on the back of his tractor. We went across the fields and met the ambulance on the main road. I'd had to put a tourniquet on the man's arm. I needed to tell one of the ambulance men to unfasten it every few minutes. Then Sam took Thumper and me back to our cars.'

Patsy hesitated. There was something else she wanted to ask me. I knew what it was.

'Was it difficult?' she asked me at last.

'You mean, not having done it for a while?' It was two years since I'd retired from medical practice. Two years since I'd picked up a stethoscope. Two years since I'd seen someone else's blood.

'Being a doctor again.'

'No. It wasn't difficult.' I smiled at her. 'Fortunately, it seems that doctoring is a bit like riding a bicycle,' I said. I grinned at her. 'Luckily, it all came back to me.'

I had always thought that a doctor's instinct is derived not so much from medical school training (that simply provides the framework for learning) as from an accumulation of experiences. Now I was sure I was right about that.

Patsy wanted to ask me something else. I knew what it was and so I answered the unasked question. 'It felt good,' I told her. 'It felt good being able to help someone. Maybe help save a life.'

'It was awful that they made you close the practice,' Patsy said quietly.

I shrugged. 'Nothing we can do about it. Nothing we could have done about it.'

'You've missed it haven't you?'

I didn't answer.

'We could move somewhere else. You could start a practice or get a job as a partner somewhere else.'

'Leave Bilbury?' She nodded.

I shook my head without hesitation. 'I do sometimes miss medicine,' I admitted. 'But I wouldn't - couldn't - leave Bilbury. This is our home. And it always will be.'

I knew what leaving Bilbury would have meant to her. Bilbury is the village everyone dreams of living in. It's a village where people speak to strangers and are kind to each other, it's a village where doors are left open during the day and at night and when they are shut (rather than bolted) it is merely to keep out the cold and the neighbours' cats. It's a village where children play on the village green without mothers hovering constantly nearby, alert for dangerous strangers in long overcoats.

Villagers in Bilbury leave their doors open when they pop to the shop so that unexpected visitors can make themselves a cup of tea. Living rooms have log fires, the pub has a piano and no one knows what a window lock is. I knew of nowhere in the world quite like Bilbury.

She put an arm around me. I put an arm around her. We stayed like that for a while. Despite the warmth of the Aga and the hot towel I still felt cold. I shivered. She felt the involuntary movement.

'I'll run you a bath,' she said. 'Finish your coffee and eat the last of the muffins.'

I did as I was told.

* * *

Forty minutes later I clambered out of the bath, got dressed and went downstairs. Patsy was in the kitchen baking. The smell, as always, was wonderful.

'What are you making?'

'An iced sponge cake, some of those buns you like and another tray of fudge.'

'Great!' I said, with genuine enthusiasm. 'When will they be ready?'

'Aren't you going back to bed?' Patsy asked.

I shook my head, took a teaspoon from the cutlery drawer and helped myself to a taste of the mixture in the bowl she was working on. 'Terrific,' I said.

'You've just got an awfully sweet tooth.'

'No, no,' I protested. 'Your icing is much better than anyone else's.'

She raised an eyebrow.

I once complained to my friend Patchy Fogg, a local antique dealer that I was putting on weight.

'Could there be a link between that fact and the fact that Patsy is a brilliant cook?' Patchy had asked. He had been right, of course.

'I thought I'd do some work on the latest Bilbury book,' I told her. 'I'm a bit bogged down at the moment.' The last book in my series about the village had been well received and I'd received an encouraging number of letters from readers wanting more.

Curiously, the only complaint had come from the friend upon whom I had based the character Thumper Robinson. My friend had wanted to know why I had called him by the name 'Thumper Robinson' in the books, rather than using his real name.

'Everyone knows that the person you are writing about is me,' he'd said.

I'd explained that I'd given him another name so that I could, if I wanted to, make him do things in the book that he didn't do in real life.

'But Thumper is me!' he'd protested. 'And if you want me to do something else, all you have to do is say!'

'How did the writing go?' asked Patsy, when I went downstairs two hours later.

'Not bad.'

'Thumper telephoned and left a message for you while you were working.' As she spoke she opened the door to the Aga cooker and put a hand just inside to check the air temperature. Satisfied, she closed the door.

'Did he sound OK?'

'He was a bit shook up, I think,' said Patsy. 'He said the two families are very grateful. The hospital doctor told them that the couple would have both died if you hadn't been there. He said the boy has got a broken ankle and a broken clavicle. The girl had a fractured skull and a broken arm. But they're both going to be OK.'

'That's good,' I said. 'I completely missed the broken clavicle and the skull fracture.'

'I suspect it was easier to spot them in a dry, well-lit ward,' said Patsy.

'Probably,' I admitted.

'Thumper wanted to know if we could go to a meeting in the Duck and Puddle tonight,' said Patsy.

The Duck and Puddle is Bilbury's local public house and the unofficial centre of village life.

'A meeting?' I said, with some surprise. Thumper wasn't the sort of person who usually went to meetings. I'd certainly never known him to organise one.

'He said he was ringing round and trying to get as many people there as he could.'

'Do you know what the meeting is about?'

Patsy shook her head. 'He didn't say. He just said it was important. And that we should get there at half past nine.'

'Then we'd better go,' I said. I frowned as I realised what Patsy had said. 'Half past nine is a bit late to start a meeting,' I said.

'That's what I thought,' agreed Patsy. 'But he was quite definite about the time.' She started running hot water into the sink, ready to wash up the dishes she'd been using. 'Oh, and I've got to pop into Barnstaple this afternoon.'

'OK,' I said, surprised. It was unusual for either of us to go into Barnstaple by ourselves. We usually went in together and had a pub lunch in the Regent Hotel. 'Problem?'

'Oh, no, just something I need to do.'

I kissed her on the cheek, and went back upstairs to my study to struggle with the book I was writing.

'Lunch will be in half an hour!' called Patsy.

'Great,' I called back. 'I'm starving.'

CHAPTER 3

It was just over two years since health service administrators had forced me to close down my medical practice in Bilbury.

A miserable, mean-spirited Health Service administrator called Perkins, a bureaucrat who worked for the National Health Service's local Planning and Rationalisation Department (a branch of the NHS that was so badly thought of by those whose lives were touched by it that those who worked for it did everything they could to remain secret) had decided that Bilbury was too small to have its own general practitioner. Perkins, who spoke with an annoying, whining voice which suited him perfectly, had invoked Government regulations and used his powers to cancel my contract with the Secretary of State and to put all my patients into the care of a practice in Barnstaple. It was, he had told me, in a long and almost incomprehensible letter, part of a Government plan to 'maximise resource utilisation'. For the health service it was the equivalent to Dr Beeching's savage cuts of the nation's railway system. To me, and to everyone in Bilbury it seemed to be as socially destructive as Beeching's cuts threatened to be. It was, we felt sure, a foolish decision that would undoubtedly produce short-term savings but, equally certainly, do long-term damage to the village and to the health of those who lived in it.

And so, as a result of Government policy, the health care of the villagers of Bilbury had officially become the responsibility of a modem group practice in Barnstaple. One of the senior partners there was young Dr Brownlow, the son of Bilbury's previous GP.

When my practice had been closed down I had been forced to choose between applying for a job elsewhere, and leaving Bilbury, or taking early retirement and trying to earn my living as a writer.

It wasn't a difficult decision to make.

I'd enjoyed being a village doctor. I could have imagined spending my life that way. I enjoyed being a part of a small, tight-knit community and feeling that I was making a small contribution to the safety of the village.

'Being a village doctor is like being responsible for the health of a large family,' my predecessor Dr Brownlow once told me. 'As a GP in a village you'll see your patients grow old with you. You'll deliver babies, attend their weddings and then look after them when they have children.'

But when my practice was closed I didn't want to leave Bilbury. And I knew that my wife Patsy didn't want to leave the village either. Friends and relatives who had visited used to write and say how much they loved the place. 'I like to consider myself an honorary Bilburian,' wrote one friend who told me that it was only dreaming of life in Bilbury that he managed to get through the darker days of his life.

Most of the people who lived in Bilbury had lived there for years. Very few people moved there and then moved away. I knew several people in the village who had only ever been as far as Lynmouth to the east, Bideford to the west and Exeter to the south and who, indeed, regarded trips to any of these places as expeditions rather than mere excursions. A visit to Barnstaple, on the other hand, was considered to be simply an excursion requiring little more than a few days advance planning.

'Why would I want to go further?' asked one. 'I've talked to people who have travelled and I've seen the television. Nothing seems better than here.'

I found it difficult to argue with this viewpoint.

And so in 1972, when the Government had closed down my practice, I'd chosen to stay in Bilbury, to hang up my stethoscope, and to earn my living with my typewriter.

* * *

The Duck and Puddle was packed for the meeting to which Patsy and I had been invited. It was immediately clear that Thumper had done an excellent job at convening a meeting at such short notice.

Patchy Fogg welcomed Patsy and me to the meeting. 'It has been decided that we've survived long enough without a resident doctor in the village,' he said. There was much murmuring of approval response to this. 'A real village,' he went on, 'needs a pub, a shop, a church, a school and a doctor. We've got four of those. We need - and we intend to have - the fifth. How can you have a village without a doctor?'

21

'Without a doctor the very survival of Bilbury is threatened,' said Thumper. 'Without a doctor people will leave the village and no one will want to come here. The village will die.'

'Without enough people living here the Duck and Puddle and my shop will have to close,' said Peter Marshall. 'House prices will collapse,' he added after a short pause.

'Would you be willing to reopen your practice here in Bilbury?' asked Thumper.

The question wasn't a complete surprise, of course. Patsy and I had guessed that this could well be the purpose of the meeting. But I didn't know whether I should or could reopen my practice. It had been a couple of years since I'd last wielded a stethoscope in earnest. In particular I worried that the instincts I'd acquired as a GP might have left me.

My experience at the road accident had, in hindsight, not done my self-assurance any good at all. The small oasis of confidence I'd had had vanished and had been replaced by an endless, arid desert of doubt. A village GP, the only doctor around for miles, has to have belief in himself and has to be able to transmit that belief and faith to his patients without them feeling that he is arrogant or reckless. At the same time he needs to know, probably more than any other type of doctor, when he doesn't know and what he doesn't know. A village doctor works alone and must rely entirely on his own resources.

Could I still do it?

I'd thought long and hard about it.

Conscious that everyone was looking at me, waiting to hear my response, I picked my words with care.

'I'm very flattered that you'd like me to reopen the surgery,' I said. 'But it's really not down to me.' I paused. 'I'm afraid I don't think the bureaucrats will let me reopen my practice,' I went on. 'When they forced me to close the surgery they were quite certain about it. And they quoted some very official sounding regulations which gave them the authority to do it.'

'But when the weather is bad the doctors in Barnstaple can't always get out here,' said Patchy Fogg.

'As happened last night,' added another villager. I didn't see who it was.

'If you hadn't still been living here there would have been no one to help that couple in the car,' said Anne Thwaites, Thumper's long-standing girlfriend.

'I suspect the bureaucrats will just say that last night was exceptional,' I said.

I was dodging the important question and putting everything in the hands of the bureaucrats. It was, I suppose, my way of letting fate make the decision.

'The village has been cut off at least three times in the last twelve months,' pointed out Frank Parsons, the landlord of the Duck and Puddle. 'If anyone in the village needs a doctor when we're cut off what are we supposed to do? The authorities have to let us have our own doctor.'

'It's not as if we're asking them to build a new health centre,' said Gilly, Frank's wife. 'We just want them to let the doctor reopen his surgery at Bilbury Grange. A village needs five things to be a proper village: a shop, a church, a school, a doctor and a pub. We've got a pub. We've got a shop. We've got a church and a school. We need a doctor.'

There was loud murmuring of support for this point of view.

'If he wants to,' added Frank quickly, looking at me.

'If he wants to,' agreed Gilly.

'I never wanted to close the practice,' I told them truthfully. 'But the closure was forced on me. And whatever we decide we want won't matter a jot if the bureaucrats won't give us permission to reopen the surgery.'

'But if they gave permission you might be willing to do it?'

I looked at Patsy. 'Patsy and I would have to talk about it,' I said. 'It's a big decision which would, of course, affect us both a great deal.'

'But you might say yes?' said Patchy.

I looked at Patsy again. She smiled and, almost imperceptibly, she nodded. 'Yes,' I agreed. 'We might say 'yes'.'

'That's all we wanted to hear,' said Thumper. 'I think we can get the authorities to approve a reopening of your surgery.'

He said this with such certainty that I looked around. 'Is there something going on here that we don't know about?' I asked.

'Definitely,' laughed Frank.

'What?' I asked.

'We think it's better that you don't know,' smiled Thumper.

* * *

It was a cold but clear, moonlit and starry evening. We had walked to the Duck and Puddle and taken Ben with us. By the time the three of us had walked back to Bilbury Grange it was half past eleven. Ben loved night-time walks. From a dog's point of view there always seems to be far more going on at night than there is during the daytime. Several times we had to stop and wait for her while she scrambled through hedges and raced across nearby fields.

'How did you get on in Barnstaple?' I asked as we stood waiting for Ben to return.

'Fine,' said Patsy.

There was something in her voice. I looked at her. 'Are you all right?'

'I'm very definitely all right,' she said.

I looked at her. 'Is there something you should tell me?'

'I was going to keep it until tomorrow,' she said. 'It's been a busy day.'

'Keep what for tomorrow?'

'I'll tell you in the morning.'

I looked at her. 'You can't do that! Tell me now. What is it? Is there are a problem? Are you OK? You're not sick?'

She laughed. 'No, I'm not sick. I'm very healthy.'

Suddenly, I don't know why, I realised where she'd been. 'You went to see the doctor?'

She nodded. 'That nice lady doctor in Barnstaple.'

'But...why didn't you say something? What's wrong? What did you think was wrong? We're not supposed to have secrets from one another.'

Patsy laughed out loud. 'There's nothing at all wrong,' she said.

'At least I don't think there is.' She paused and bent down to pat Ben who had returned. She was soaking wet and muddy. 'And I hope you won't.'

I put my hands on her shoulders. 'Patsy, what is it?' I asked her.

'I think we should consider redecorating the small bedroom next to ours,' she said. 'Nice pretty wallpaper.'

'Don't change the subject!' I told her, pulling her towards me.

'Tell me why you went to see the doctor.' Ben wriggled and wriggled and managed to squeeze between us. She really was soaking wet.

'They've got some lovely pink and blue striped wallpaper in Hutchins,' she said, mentioning a smart store in Barnstaple. 'We could get Thumper to put it up.'

'I can put up wallpaper,' I said.

'Oh, why not lct Thumper do it,' she said.

'That stuff I put up in the dining room is still on the wall isn't it?.
'

'Most of it,' she agreed with a laugh. 'I had to get some more paste for two pieces. And the pattern doesn't quite match.'

She was being kind. The patterned wallpaper I had put up didn't match at all. And it had taken me days to do that.

'OK,' I said, feeling exasperated. 'We'll decorate the small bedroom and we'll get Thumper to do it. Will you please forget about wallpaper and tell me why you went to Barnstaple!'

'The beauty of it being pink and blue is that you don't have to worry about getting it wrong,' she said. 'And, despite all the clever things they can do with technology, I'd rather it was a surprise wouldn't you?'

'We'll paper the room purple and yellow if you like,' I said. 'But why did you go and see the doctor in Barnstaple?'

'Oh no, it's got to be pink and blue,' said Patsy.

I thought about this for a moment. Ben had now run off again and I could hear her barking at something. 'We really need a spare bathroom. If we're going to all this trouble wouldn't it be more sensible to see how much it would cost to have another bathroom put in?'

Patsy started to giggle. 'You really haven't guessed?'

'No! Guessed what?' I was genuinely getting confused.

'And maybe we could get Peter Marshall to make us a cradle. He made a beautiful one for the young Henshaws.'

'What on earth do we want...' I began.

It was only then that I realised exactly what Patsy had been trying to tell me. And suddenly, at long last, I understood. There wasn't much point in having a nursery or getting Peter Marshall to make a cradle if there wasn't going to be a baby to put in them.

And so, suddenly I understood.

'You're having...' She corrected me.

'*We're* having a baby.'

I hugged her, kissed and let out a great cry of joy. Ben, assuming that I was calling her came hurtling back across the field and through the hedge. She hurled herself up at me. I held onto her and felt her rough tongue licking my cheek. The three of us stood there in the dark. A small family about to grow a little larger.

CHAPTER 4

The morning after the meeting at the Duck and Puddle I went to see Dr Brownlow.

Dr Brownlow was the reason I was living in Bilbury. He was the reason I was married to Patsy and the reason I had, before the bureaucrats closed it down, been a general practitioner in the village

Now Dr Brownlow looked more like a ghost than the man I had met when I'd first arrived in Bilbury. He weighed less than half he had done a year earlier. And the weight loss wasn't the result of dieting.

For the last few weeks he'd been my only, entirely unofficial patient.

It had started, as so many things do, with a telephone call.

* * *

He rang me one Thursday morning and asked me to pop round when I had a moment. He wouldn't say what it was for. When I arrived at his home the door was, as usual, opened by Bradshaw, Dr Brownlow's long-standing butler, valet and factotum.

Bradshaw looked no different now to how he'd looked when I first met him. He wore a black frock coat, black trousers, a white shirt and a black bow tie. Wizened, tiny and frail he had looked at least eighty when I'd first met him. He looked no younger now. On the other hand he looked no older either.

'Dr Brownlow is expecting you,' said Bradshaw, with an almost imperceptible bow of his head. He led the way to the drawing room. Dr Brownlow was sitting in a leather armchair beside a roaring log fire. He nodded to the chair opposite me. I sat down. The chair had long since lost its springs. It was like sitting on a marshmallow.

'Shall I make tea, sir?' asked Bradshaw.

Dr Brownlow looked at me. I shook my head. 'No thank you.'

'No thanks, Bradshaw,' said Dr Brownlow. He watched as the butler shuffled out of the room, closing the door behind him.

'Get me a whisky will you?' said Dr Brownlow, when we were alone.

There was a tray on a table beside Dr Brownlow's chair. There was a whisky bottle on the tray, together with a jug of water and two cut glass tumblers.

I got up, poured him about two fingers of whisky and looked across at him. He raised a hand to suggest I added more. I poured another two fingers worth. 'Water?'

He shook his head.

I handed him the glass and sat down again.

'Are you not having one?'

'No thanks,' I said. 'Maybe later.'

He took a sip, closed his eyes and savoured the flavour of the whisky. He held it in his mouth for a long time before he swallowed.

'How is everything?' I asked.

'Did you know that the Porters had left?'

I nodded. 'I heard,' I said. Frank Porter had been Dr Brownlow's gardener. His wife Ethel had been Dr Brownlow's housekeeper and cook.

'Frank inherited a chip shop in Lancashire,' said Dr Brownlow. 'He and Ethel have gone up there.'

'Have you got someone else?' I asked, though from the state of the garden I knew he hadn't.

He shook his head. 'And the dogs have both gone.'

'I know,' I said quietly. 'Thumper told me.' Dr Brownlow had had two Doberman Pinschers. They had terrified the life out of me, and most other people too.

'Thumper buried them for me,' said Dr Brownlow. I nodded. I knew that too.

Dr Brownlow shook his head. 'Are you still on the medical register?' he asked me suddenly.

Puzzled, I nodded.

'You can still write prescriptions and sign certificates?'

'Yes. I suppose so. But I don't have any patients.'

'Will you accept me as a patient? A private patient.'

'Yes, of course,' I replied, without having to think about the answer.

But then I thought about the question.

'Why?' I asked him. 'I don't understand. Is there something wrong with you? Why me? The Barnstaple practice looks after everyone in Bilbury.'

'I don't want them looking after me,' said Dr Brownlow. He started to say something but changed his mind. 'I don't want them looking after me,' he repeated.

His son was a senior partner at the practice which had taken over my former Bilbury practice. Clearly Dr Brownlow didn't want his son looking after him. 'We don't get on,' he told me bluntly, though this was no surprise.

'What's wrong with you?' I asked him, quictly. 'Why do you need a doctor?'

'Cancer,' he said bluntly. 'Pancreas.' He took a big sip of his whisky. This time he just swallowed it.

Shocked, disbelieving, I looked at him. 'How do you know? What tests have you had? Are you sure? When did you find out?' The questions were queuing up to be asked.

'I made the diagnosis a couple of months ago,' he said. 'I went up to London and saw a couple of chaps there. They did some prodding and some tests.'

'And they were certain?'

'No question of it.'

'Can they operate?'

Dr Brownlow shook his head.

'Drugs?'

'Just painkillers,' he said. 'That's where you come in.' He sipped at the whisky again. 'Three months. Probably less. No more.'

'I'll have that whisky if you don't mind,' I said. I stood up, walked the couple of paces to the whisky bottle and poured myself a stiff drink. I offered Dr Brownlow the bottle. He nodded. I added another good slug of whisky to his glass. He sat quite still, staring into space. Then, slowly, his eyes closed. For a moment I thought he had died and then I realised that he had just fallen asleep. I reached for his wrist. His pulse was fine. His eyelids fluttered but didn't open. I sat down and sipped at my whisky. It was, as always, a good malt. It was Dr Brownlow who had first introduced me to malt whisky. He'd insisted that I should know how it was made if I was going to drink it. 'You let the barley grains start to grow,' he said, 'until they're shoots an inch or so long. Then they're called malts. You smoke them over burning peat until they pick up the flavours of the peat and the smoke and have become nice and crisp. Then you make a mash of the malts with water - river or beck water not the stuff that comes out of the tap - and you let the stuff ferment. Then you distil it and you put the distillation into wooden casks to age it for several years. That's malt whisky. And there are enough different flavours and tastes and smells of malt whisky to suit every palate and to keep a man going through his life testing and tasting. In wooden casks the spirit develops and grows. You need to keep it in the wood for at least three years. Ten or fifteen years is better.'

I remembered I'd asked him what the difference was between malt whisky and ordinary grain whisky. He said that for ordinary grain whisky they just made the barley into a mash without the other stages. He also said that he had long had the thought that one day he might persuade a distiller to put malt whisky into wooden bottles so that the whisky would continue to age after it had been bought. In a glass bottle it is the same when you take it out as it was when you put it in.

'What does 'proof mean?' I'd asked him.

'Three hundred years ago a spirit seller would prove that the liquid he was selling was alcohol by mixing it with gunpowder and igniting it. If it burned with a steady blue flame it was considered 100% proof that it was 50% alcohol.' He grinned, I remember. 'These days,' he'd continued, 'they do the testing with hydrometers but they still use the same daft scale. So if something is 75% alcohol they say its 150% proof. If it's 10% alcohol they say its 20% proof.'

All this I remembered as I sipped at my whisky and the tears rolled down my cheeks. Dr Brownlow had done so much for me. He had taught me almost everything of value that I knew.

'I don't want to go into hospital,' Dr Brownlow said suddenly.

I looked across at him. His eyes were open again. 'Bradshaw can look after me.'

'Bradshaw?' I said, surprised. It was difficult to imagine a man who wore a frock coat and white tie working as a nurse.

'He was a nurse in the army,' explained Dr Brownlow. 'Thirty years. He's very good.'

I was surprised. I hadn't known.

'I'll need some things,' Dr Brownlow said.

'Morphine.'

'Morphine. Lots of it.' He'd smiled. 'Don't worry. I won't have time to become an addict.'

I sipped at my whisky. It had been the first time a patient had told me what was wrong with him and what the prognosis was and I was still in a state of shock. As a doctor I was used to being the one handing out information. Ever since I'd first worked for him Dr Brownlow had been more of a father than an employer.

'There are quite a few things I need to work out,' Dr Brownlow had continued. He, of course, had had time to get used to his own shocking news. 'The one big certainty is that I want to be buried next to my wife.'

I nodded. When Dr Brownlow's wife had died several years earlier she had been buried in the gardens. There was a piece of consecrated ground that had been used as a burial ground when the house had had its own chapel. A gravestone, already bearing Dr Brownlow's name and birth date, had been prepared. All the stonemason would have to do was add the date of Dr Brownlow's death.

'Are you sure...,' I'd begun. My voice had cracked. I swallowed hard and looked away for a moment. I didn't know why but I didn't want to wipe the tears away from my eyes. 'Are you sure you don't want me to arrange for you to see someone else? A specialist?'

'No need,' Dr Brownlow had said softly. 'Really. There's nothing anyone can do.' He sipped at his whisky. 'I've had a good life,' he said. 'I'm not especially unhappy that it's over. Now I just want to go with as much dignity as I can muster.'

I nodded, accepting his judgement and honouring his decision.

'Will you come back and see me in a couple of days?' he asked.

'There are quite a few things I want to talk over with you.'

'Of course.'

I stood up. I was glad to be able to leave. I needed time to come to terms with what he'd told me.

'One other thing,' he said. 'I'd rather people in the village didn't know just yet. Bradshaw knows, of course. And you can tell Patsy. But...'

'I won't tell anyone else unless you ask me to,' I assured him. I bent down and put a hand on his shoulder. 'I'll do everything I can to help you,' I promised him. 'Everything.'

He put his hand on top of mine and looked up at me. 'I know you will,' he said. He smiled. 'Don't worry,' he said. 'We're all dying.

It's just something we all have to live with.' His smile broadened. 'Besides,' he added, 'I come from a long line of dead people.'

I squeezed his shoulder and tried to say something but the words wouldn't come out. I nodded and left.

Outside, as I walked back to my car I felt the tears pouring down my cheeks. I couldn't understand how the sun could keep shining. How could the birds keep singing? Didn't they know what was happening inside that house?

I put the car into gear and sped away, spraying gravel everywhere.

* * *

That evening, after dinner, I put on an old Barbour and a flat cap and went out into the garden.

'There's a huge pile of old clippings left over from the autumn,' I explained to Patsy. 'I'd better bum them.'

Getting rid of the clippings was only an excuse. I have always found lighting and managing a bonfire to be an excellent way to find some temporary respite from sadness and stress. Patsy knew this, of course. When I went outside it was raining steadily. It had started during dinner as a typical Devon drizzle, just more than mist but slightly less than drizzle, and had steadily built up into a downpour. By the time I got to the part of the garden we use for bonfires the rain was pouring down.

All the clippings and dried leaves and other bits of rubbish that I'd been storing were piled up ready to be burnt. Our gardener, Mr Parfitt, had, for weeks, been trundling the wheelbarrow, laden with garden detritus, to the site. But he'd been under strict instructions to leave the bonfire lighting to me. For him it would be just a chore, but it was, he knew, one of my favourite tasks in the garden.

I had taken several large cardboard boxes and a copy of the *Daily Telegraph* with me. Boxes are useful for keeping off the rain while the bonfire gets going. And the *Daily Telegraph* is the most inflammatory newspaper I know. Being a broadsheet helps, of course, but there's more to it than that. *The Daily Telegraph* seems to me to burn much better than other newspapers. Maybe it's the paper they use. Or something they put in the ink. Or maybe it's the words.

I put the boxes on their sides, placed screwed up pages of newspaper inside the boxes and then built piles of branches and twigs over and around the boxes. I picked out, and put on one side, the ash tree twigs and small branches because they make excellent kindling for fires in the house. The larger branches would provide the framework which would keep the sodden privet, bay, laurel and other cuttings away from the boxes while they caught fire.

A fire needs oxygen just as much as an animal does and the big mistake most bonfire builders make is to forget this and fail to leave enough space for the air to filter into the heart of the fire.

When the branches were hooped over the boxes, I piled the first few armfuls of clippings onto the top of the woody branches. I picked the greenest cuttings, the ones with the most leaves still attached, because these would help keep the rain off the underlying fire.

I bent down and lit the paper in each of the boxes. And then I stood up, took a pace or two backwards, and waited.

Within minutes the three boxes were ablaze. The bare, dry tree branches soon caught fire too. And then the smoke started. Plumes of white smoke from the drying and smouldering leaves and clippings. The laurel and bay crackled and threw off sparks as their oily, evergreen leaves caught fire. Some branches of rosemary added to the aroma. Coniferous branches crackled too. I fed an armful of leaves onto the top of the fire.

I stood there, watching the rising flames and the vast plume of smoke disappearing into the night. The rain was heavier. Suddenly I felt a hand slide into mine. I turned and looked at Patsy.

'You'll miss him won't you?'

'I will,' I whispered. The smoke was irritating my eyes. Tears were rolling down my cheeks. The two were not connected.

'Me too,' she said softly.

We stood there for a long time. We didn't speak again. Occasionally we leant against a nearby tree. From time to time we pushed twig ends into the fire to make sure that when the fire had burnt away there would be nothing left but a neat circle of ash.

When we went back up to the house it was still raining. I put the small branches of ash tree into the log shed and once inside the house we hung up our coats. I put the kettle on and Patsy took a couple of crumpets out of the bread bin and the toasting fork from its place beside the Aga. She opened the fire door to toast the crumpets. I could feel the heat across the other side of the kitchen.

'We must both reek of smoke,' I said. 'We need baths.'

'It's a lovely smell,' she said.

I took a bottle of whisky from the sideboard and put it on the kitchen table, ready to add a splash to the coffee Patsy was making.

Appropriately, I remembered, the whisky had been a Christmas present from Dr Brownlow.

There would be no more Christmas presents from him. I wondered how long he'd got.

I knew I would remember this day for the rest of my life.

* * *

That had been some time ago.

He'd lived longer than either he or I had expected. But now the end was approaching fast.

'Push me out onto the terrace,' he said. He was sitting in a wheelchair. It was only the second time I'd seen him use it.

'It's cold,' I warned him.

'I'm not a bloody orchid,' he said. 'There's a rug on the back of the sofa. Drape it around my knees. If I'm going to be an invalid I might as well look the part.'

I opened the French windows, took the brake off the wheelchair and pushed him outside. He grabbed the whisky bottle and two glasses as we passed the table. He didn't get the water jug. I parked him on the terrace where he had a good view of the gardens.

'That oak tree was there when I came here,' he said, nodding towards a huge oak about fifty yards from the house. He poured whisky into the glasses and handed one to me.

'A single oak tree is like a village,' Dr Brownlow said. 'One tree can play host to hundreds of different insects, flowers, fern and lichen. Did you know that? No other tree carries as many species as the oak tree.' He paused for breath. He had difficulty in breathing if he spoke too much. 'And because the leaf canopy offers protection from the elements without preventing light reaching the ground a whole host of flowers grow around its trunk - bluebell, wood sorrel, primroses.'

I admitted that I didn't know this.

'How many different mammals do you think live in or underneath an oak tree? Or benefit directly from its existence?'

'Squirrels?' I suggested rather lamely.

'Over thirty species,' he said. 'Badgers, deer, hedgehog and mice all eat acorns. Field mice climb up oak trees and steal eggs out of nests. So do weasels. Do you know how many birds make their nests in oak trees?'

I admitted that I didn't know that either.

'Nuthatch, tawny owl, jay, great spotted woodpecker, rook, pied flycatcher, tree creeper, blue tit and great tit. Nearly seventy species in all.' He paused. 'Even sparrowhawks live in oaks. They make their nests in old crows' nests. Sometimes they'll nest in an old squirrel drey. Did you know that a squirrel's nest is called a drey?'

I nodded.

'So, are you going to do it?'

'Do what?'

'Don't be obtuse. Open up a surgery again.'

I sighed. 'To be honest, I don't know whether they'll let me,' I said. 'The administrators are having a meeting.'

'They'll let you open up again,' said Dr Brownlow firmly.

'You seem very certain.'

'The villagers have decided they've been without a doctor long enough.'

I looked at him. 'But do you think the villagers can persuade the authorities to change their minds?'

'Oh, I think so.'

'Do you know something I don't know? Has Thumper told you something?'

Dr Brownlow turned to me and grinned. He ignored my questions. 'Will you open up your surgery again if they give you the opportunity?'

I nodded.

'Good.' he said. He raised his glass and held it out towards me. I raised mine and we clinked glasses and drank.

'I know you've got your books,' he said. 'It's different for you. But being a country GP was the only thing that gave my life meaning and purpose. Especially in the years since I've been alone.' He pointed at a squirrel running down the trunk of the oak. We watched it for a few moments. After Dr Brownlow's wife had died he had very much lived the life of a lonely bachelor. 'It made me feel that I was at the heart of the village.'

I didn't speak for a while. 'I know what you mean,' I said at last. 'I've missed it a lot.'

'It's meaning and purpose which give life to our lives. Without purpose life is just a compendium of routine, habit and drudgery. I always needed something to believe in, to work for, to make me feel contributing.'

The squirrel had disappeared.

'How do they do that?'

'Do what?'

'Disappear like that. Just disappear.'

'Magic.'

'I suppose so.'

We sat in silence for quite a while.

'If this isn't nice I don't know what is,' he said.

We sat for a little longer.

'It's important to notice the magic moments,' he said. 'We all rush around so much that we tend to miss them.' There was another long silence.

'We're all so busy racing through life, waiting for the bad news. Dealing with problems. Facing crises. The nice moments pass us by. We sort of enjoy them. But we don't savour them as we should.'

'I know what you mean,' I said. I sipped at the whisky. 'If I do start the practice up again, do you think I should let them pressure me into having an appointment system?'

'The dour men in suits will want you to have one,' he said. 'Appointment systems are all the rage now. The bureaucrats like them. It keeps everything neat.'

'I'm not keen,' I said. When I had taken over from Dr Brownlow I had followed his example and had refused to have an appointments system at all. It had worked very well. Patients had to wait but they always got seen within an hour or so of turning up. If there was a long queue, patients would tell the person they were in front of that they were just slipping out, perhaps to do a little shopping at Peter Marshall's. Or, if it was a fine day, they'd just go out and sit in the garden and read a magazine.

'Appointment systems probably suit a town practice,' he said. 'But you might be better without one here.' He sipped at his whisky.

'Up to you, of course.'

We neither of us spoke for a while.

'People in Bilbury don't all have the telephone,' he said. 'And half of those who do don't like using it.'

I nodded. He was right. When I'd been a GP many of the requests for visits had come on slips of paper passed over to the receptionist or slipped under the front door

'Actually, on thinking about it, I'm not sure appointment systems are right for doctors anywhere. Appointment systems are fine for lawyers and hairdressers. But patients can't be ill by appointment.' He stared at the oak tree. A squirrel scampered along a branch and then disappeared. It was impossible to see where this one had gone either.

'My son has an appointments system,' continued Dr Brownlow.

'Someone told me the other day that they rang up needing an appointment and were told they couldn't see a doctor for ten days.'

'I've heard that sort of thing,' I agreed.

'Bloody silly,' said Dr Brownlow. 'What are you supposed to do? Make an appointment ten days before you become ill or wait in agony for ten days when you have become ill?'

We sat, saying nothing for a while longer. Silences are difficult to endure with some people. I always found silences easy with Dr Brownlow.

'It's getting chilly,' I said at last, standing up. 'I'd better take you indoors.'

CHAPTER 5

Patsy was in Barnstaple attending her first antenatal class and so I called in at the Duck and Puddle to get myself some lunch. I found something of a crisis there.

'Frank has run out of pickled eggs,' said Patchy, as I walked in. 'We're thinking of making a formal complaint.'

'Who are you going to complain to?' demanded Frank.

'The Pickled Egg Marketing Board,' answered Patchy instantly. 'They'll be interested.'

'I couldn't get into town,' said Frank defensively. 'Peter Marshall doesn't sell the large jars of pickled eggs we need so I have to get them from the wholesaler. The car wouldn't start. The battery is flat.'

'Don't tell lies,' said Gilly. 'You'll only get found out.'

'The car wouldn't go!' insisted Frank.

'It's always the cover up that causes the most trouble,' said Gilly. She turned to Patchy. 'He hit a hedge. The car hasn't got a right front wheel.'

'Well, there's that as well,' admitted Frank. 'But the battery is flat too.'

'That's because you keep forgetting to get a new one,' said Gilly.

'You'd forget your head if it wasn't fixed on.' She turned, hurled the tea towel she was holding at Frank's head and stalked out of the bar. The tea towel hit Frank on the neck and stayed on his shoulder.

'What's wrong with Gilly?' asked Thumper. 'She seems a bit overwrought today. Not her usual breezy self'

'I forgot her birthday,' admitted Frank. 'Didn't even buy her a card.'

Thumper, Patchy and I sighed. An unhappy Gilly would make the Duck and Puddle unbearable.

'Apparently it was her 50th,' said Frank.

'Oh no,' groaned Patchy. 'You missed a milestone.'

'You've got to sort this out,' said Thumper.

'Cost you twice as much now,' said Patchy. Frank looked at him.

'Whatever you buy her now will have to be twice as expensive as it would have had to be if you'd bought it before her birthday,' explained Patchy.

'I didn't know she was that old,' said Frank.

'You didn't tell her that, did you?' said Patchy.

Frank paused. 'What was wrong with that?' he asked. 'It was a compliment.'

'It'll cost you three times as much,' said Patchy. He looked at Thumper who nodded.

'I haven't the foggiest idea what she wants,' said Frank glumly. There was a long silence.

'I wish I was married to the Queen,' said Frank eventually.

We all looked at him, puzzled. Frank had never previously shown any romantic interest in Her Majesty.

'Her birthday is printed in my diary,' he explained. 'I can't forget her birthday even if I want to. Prince Philip has got it easy.'

'She must have given you hints,' said Patchy. 'Women always give hints.'

Thumper nodded in agreement. 'Definitely,' he agreed.

'Patsy has been known to mention things,' I agreed. 'Subtle hints.'

'What do you mean?' asked Frank. 'What sort of hints?'

I thought for a moment. 'Oh, things like 'I saw a pair of green shoes in Barnstaple today. Size five. In that shop next to the tobacconist's. They were ridiculously priced. How can anyone justify spending that much on a pair of shoes?'

Frank looked at me blankly. 'What sort of hint is that?' he asked.

'That's telling you about something she doesn't want.'

We all looked at him. Patchy sighed. Thumper shook his head.

'How long have you been married?' I asked him.

Frank thought for a while. 'Can't remember,' he said at last. 'Long time though.'

'What's she talked about a lot recently?' asked Thumper.

'The bathroom sink is blocked,' said Frank. 'She's always on about that.' He brightened up. 'Maybe if I get a plumber in to sort it out? Or I could buy her a plunger. That would be cheaper.'

'You can't buy your wife a sink plunger for her birthday,' said Patchy.

'Not when it's after her birthday,' said Thumper. 'You might have got away with it if you'd bought it before her birthday. But not afterwards.'

From Thumper this was serious stuff. He had once bought Anne Thwaites, the mother of his child, a second-hand petrol driven chainsaw for her birthday. When she had shown slightly less enthusiasm than he had expected he'd pointed out that he would use it to cut logs for the fire to keep her warm.

'Her sister went to London a couple of months ago,' said Frank. 'Gilly went on about that for ages. Kept going on about it.'

'Take her to London for the weekend,' said Patchy firmly.

'London?' said Frank.

'London,' said Patchy. 'And take her round the shops and buy her something expensive. It doesn't matter what it is as long as it's expensive.'

'But we can't leave the pub!' said Frank.

'The brewery must have couples they send round to cover illness and holidays,' said Thumper.

Frank thought for a moment and then nodded.

'Patchy is right,' I said. 'Get a locum in to look after the pub and take Gilly to London for the weekend. Stay somewhere nice and take her shopping in Harrods.'

'You think that would settle her down?' asked Frank.

'Definitely,' said Thumper.

'We still haven't got any pickled eggs,' said Patchy. 'I'll have a packet of crisps as long as you've got the ones that have the salt wrapped up in a little blue bag inside them.'

'Why on earth do you want those?' demanded Thumper, as Frank disappeared under the counter.

'I like having control over my crisps,' replied Patchy. 'I don't want some unseen machine sprinkling salt on for me.'

There was a cry of delight from somewhere under the counter where Frank had been rummaging around cardboard boxes.

'Here you are!' he said, banging a large box of crisps on the bar counter. 'Crisps with little bags of salt inside.' He tore open the box, pulled out a packet of crisps and handed it to Patchy.

'Bit soft aren't they?' said Patchy, squeezing the packet rather critically.

'They're antique crisps,' said Thumper. 'Just up your street.'

'Very funny,' said Patchy, tearing the packet wide open. He rummaged around in the packet until he found the pinch of salt wrapped in blue paper.

'A mate of mine once found a five pound note wrapped up in one of those little blue twists,' said Thumper.

'I don't want a five pound note,' said Patchy, untwisting the paper. 'I want salt.' He sprinkled the salt on his crisps and then closed the bag and shook it.

CHAPTER 6

'Have you seen the local paper?' asked Patsy.

I hadn't. I had meant to pick up a copy at Peter Marshall's shop but I'd forgotten. We didn't have papers delivered to the house for two reasons. First, it was easy enough to get one from the village shop. Second, and by far the best reason, there were no newspaper deliveries in the village.

'Look at the letters in this week's paper,' said Patsy. She picked the paper up off the table and handed it to me. It was already opened at the correct page.

The lead letter, right across the top of the page, was headed 'Deteriorating Medical Care In Bilbury'.

Dear Sir,

As a long-standing Bilbury resident I am appalled at the quality if medical care provided by the general practitioner branch if the National Health Service. The other night I had the misfortune to trip over one if my Labradors in my own hallway. My good lady wife immediately telephoned our General Practitioner to inform him that his attendance would be required forthwith. Three and a quarter hours later a seedy looking fellow in a cheap suit arrived. He informed me that he was a partner of my usual GP. I was in a considerable amount if pain for all this time. If I had done myself serious injury I could have died.

This situation is quite outrageous and the appalling decision to close the Bilbury practice must be corrected immediately. The people of Bilbury are just as entitled to receive decent medical care as are the citizens of any other town or village in the land. The NHS minions who made this appalling decision must be held accountable for their blunder.

Yours sincerely
(Name and address withheld)

There were three other similar letters underneath it.

Dear Sir

Ever since Bilbury lost its own resident medical officer the quality of care in the village has steadily deteriorated. If a patient dies because of this state of affairs I trust that the officials responsible will be prepared to explain their decision to the bereaved family and friends.

Yours sincerely

(Name and address withheld)

Dear Sir

When my little boy was ill with earache I called the doctor. An hour and a half later the doctor still hadn't turned up and so I telephoned a doctor friend who lives on the coast of South Wales. He has a motor boat which he uses for fishing. He was at my home less than ninety minutes after I called. The doctor from Barnstaple arrived 75 minutes after he had gone. What would have happened in a real emergency? If the authorities are determined to deny Bilbury its own general practitioner then perhaps they would allow us to register with a practice in Wales rather than forcing us to register with one in Barnstaple.

If a patient dies because of this bureaucratic decision I hope that those responsible will be hauled into the witness box to defend themselves.

Yours sincerely

(Name and address withheld)

Dear Sir

I am 87-years-old and since I have no car off my own I am entirely reliant on public transport. There is now a bus service between Bilbury and Barnstaple just twice a week. A bus leaves Bilbury at 11.30 a.m. on Tuesdays and Fridays and arrives in Barnstaple at 12.49 p.m. The return bus from Barnstaple to Bilbury leaves the bus station at 1. 19 p.m. and arrives back in Bilbury at 2.39 p.m. This means that anyone wishing to visit the doctor and not having their own car has just 30 minutes to get to the surgery, see the doctor and get back to the bus station. The bus station is three quarters of a mile from the surgery.

The result is that the people of Bilbury now receive very second rate health care. When - rather than if - someone dies because of this short-sighted attitude I hope that the police will want to interview the administrators whose decision to close down the practice in Bilbury led directly to this sad state of affairs.

Yours sincerely
(Name and address withheld).

'Thumper and Patchy have been busy,' I said to Patsy, putting down the paper.

'So it would seem.'

'Of course, it's always possible that four real people wrote these letters.'

'Though it is convenient that they all chose to write them this week.'

'Quite.'

'What sort of effect do you think they'll have on the NHS?'

I didn't have to think about it for long. 'The final paragraph of each letter is very powerful,' I said. 'In my experience the one thing bureaucrats don't like is being expected to take responsibility for their actions.'

'So you think the NHS might let you open up your surgery again?'

I thought about it for a while. 'For the first time, I do think it's possible,' I said at last. 'Thumper and Patchy have done a pretty impressive job.'

CHAPTER 7

A week after the meeting in the Duck and Puddle I received a telephone call from the local NHS bureaucrat who was responsible for administering general practice in the area.

He told me that the medical practice in Barnstaple which had been looking after Bilbury had unexpectedly decided that they no longer felt able to provide medical care for the villagers. He said that this news had been received in the administrative offices with some dismay, that it had put them in rather a difficult position and that in order to avoid the delay that would ensue if they had to advertise the practice in the normal manner he wondered if I would consider reopening my practice and taking on responsibility for the medical care of the people of Bilbury.

'You have experience of the area,' he said. 'And we would be very happy if you felt able to resume your previous responsibilities.'

'The GPs in Barnstaple no longer want to provide medical cover for Bilbury?'

'That is correct.'

'So I'd be completely responsible for patients in Bilbury?'

'Yes, that is our proposal.'

'Day time surgeries and night time care? Everything? I'd be an independent general practitioner? No ties whatsoever with any other practice?'

'Indeed, yes, that is our proposal.'

'When would you want me to start?'

'As soon as possible. I understand from our records that you ran your surgery from your home. Would you be doing that again?'

'I think so. Yes.'

'The committee would like to have a meeting with you on Thursday morning to discuss this.'

'No meetings.'

I hate meetings, I hate bureaucrats and I hate committees. I long ago decided that the main job of a committee is to meet. People make decisions. Committees have meetings. And nowhere on the planet are there any more self-important, self-congratulating, prevaricating, uncaring people than those sitting on health service committees.

'The committee...'

'No meeting,' I said firmly. 'You know who I am. I know what the job is. You need a doctor for Bilbury. There is no need to have a meeting. If you want me to do the job I will do it.'

There was a long silence.

'I will need to speak to the chairman.'

'Please do.'

'I'll ring you back.'

'Fine.'

He rang back in just under a quarter of an hour.

'Given the circumstances, would it be possible for you to take over responsibility for Bilbury from this corning weekend?'

'That's rather short notice.'

'The practitioners in Barnstaple are adamant that they won't provide cover for patients in Bilbury.'

'And you have a legal responsibility to find a general practitioner prepared to take on the care of the villagers?'

'Er, yes, that's correct.'

I thought hard. Never again would I be in a position of such negotiating strength with the local bureaucrats.

'I'll hire a receptionist, but also I'll need the NHS to pay for a district nurse to work with me,' I told him. I knew this would be something the bureaucrats would try to avoid.

I'm sure we can arrange for a nurse from Barnstaple to visit Bilbury once a week,' said the administrator.

'Dr Brownlow always had a full-time district nurse working with him,' I said. 'I don't think it would be possible to look after the villagers properly without the services of a district nurse.'

There was a long pause. 'I'll have to consult on this,' said the administrator.

'Fine,' I said. 'You know where to reach me.' I hesitated. 'Naturally, although you'll be paying her wages I will want to choose and recruit the nurse myself'

'Oh I definitely don't think we can agree to that,' said the administrator. He sounded very firm. 'We have procedures to follow.'

'Bilbury is a very small village,' I told him. 'We need a nurse who lives locally and who fits in with the community.'

There was a silence.

'I'll telephone you later,' he said. He paused again. 'Will those be your only stipulations? You choose a nurse and we pay her wages?'

'If you agree to do that then I'll take over as Bilbury's GP from this coming Saturday.'

I went into the kitchen where Patsy was baking a fruit cake. When I told her that it seemed likely that I was about to become a GP again she said she had never had any doubts about it. I said that I was waiting for the bureaucrat to call me back to confirm it. She said it was a formality and that he would ring back before the cake went into the oven. She was right. This time the administrator rang me back eleven minutes later to tell me that the health service had agreed to my terms. He said a contract would be sent out to me by recorded delivery mail. Patsy put her arms around my neck and gave me a kiss. I kissed her back.

'When I've finished this cake I'd better give your old surgery a clean,' she said, breaking away from me. Suddenly she started laughing. I looked at her, puzzled. 'You've got a ring of flour around your collar,' she said. 'It looks as though you've had a halo and it's slipped.'

I said I hoped this wasn't an omen. I looked at my watch. 'I need to recruit a nurse and a receptionist,' I said.

'Who are you going to get?'

'I need a slightly pernickety, fastidious receptionist,' I said. 'And a good reliable district nurse.'

'Miss Johnson,' said Patsy instantly, naming the receptionist who had worked for me when I'd taken over Dr Brownlow's practice.

'Absolutely,' I agreed. 'She is the only real choice for receptionist.'

Miss Johnson was kind, loyal, strong and hard-working. If you got in her bad books she could be stern and a recalcitrant, unmoving opponent; a cross between the headmistress of a girls' school and an English bulldog. I couldn't imagine how difficult it would be to try and manage the practice without her.

Doreen Johnson had been Dr Brownlow's secretary and receptionist for longer than even he could remember. Tall, slim and white-haired she was a martyr to her feet and always wore a single row of pearls. She always had a pair of gold-rimmed spectacles perched on the end of her nose. A thin gold chain hung from the arms of the spectacles and was draped around the back of her neck.

She had an inexhaustible fund of knowledge and information about the workings of the National Health Service bureaucracy and the idiosyncrasies of the patients. She also knew where everyone lived, what they did for a living, how they voted and what they were thinking. She could answer every question about any villager which began with the words 'Do you know...?' By lunchtime each day (including Sundays and bank holidays) she knew what everyone had for breakfast.

I knew that Miss Johnson had retired and that I would have to try and persuade her to unretire.

The other person I wanted to recruit was Kay McBride, the former district nurse. I hadn't seen Kay McBride for ages. As Kay Wilson she had been married to the local policeman. That marriage had ended tragically when PC Wilson had knocked down and killed a boy in the village. Full of remorse and unable to live with the guilt PC Wilson had hung himself. A couple of years later the widow had married a local tractor engineer called Ernie McBride. He was 22 years her junior but the marriage had apparently proved a resounding success.

'Do you know where Kay is living?' I asked Patsy. I knew exactly where I could find Miss Johnson.

'She's still in Ilfracombe, as far as I know,' said Patsy. She frowned.

'She's not still killing cats, is she?'

When she had still been Mrs Wilson, Kay had persuaded the vet to put down her husband's two cats. He had been heartbroken. Their only crime had been their age. I shared Patsy's concern. The killing of the cats had worried me then and worried me still. But I needed a district nurse and I needed one quickly.

'Miss Johnson will probably know where she is,' I said. 'I'll go and see her first.'

CHAPTER 8

Ibumped into Thumper(almostliterally)onmywaytoseeMiss Johnson.Hisvanwasparkedonacomerinanarrowlane justwide enoughtotakeonecaratatime.Thereweretwoothercarsparked infront ofhim. Ididn't recogniseeitheroftheother vehiclesor theirdrivers.

'What's up?'IaskedThumper.

'There'sacowlyingdowninthelane.'Hesteppedontotheverge andpointed toher.Isteppedupbesidehim.Hewasright.Alarge brownandwhitecowwaslyingdownontheroad.She'dpositioned herselfinsuchawaythatshecouldmunchatthelushgrassgrowing intheverge.Sheseemedquitehappy.Shelookedatusandcarried onchewinginthatlazyyetdeterminedwaycowshave.

'Can't anyone move her?'

'She won't budge. I've tried shouting at her to move. She takes no notice.'

'Who does she belong to?'

'Dunno. Probably one of Sam Houghton's. When he moves his cows from field to field he usually just opens both gates and lets the cows meander down when the fancy takes them. The cows know where to go so he leaves them to it.'

'But this one seems to have gone on sit down strike.'

'Apparently so.'

We stood and waited for a while. The cow kept chewing in the way that cows do. She showed no sign of wanting to move. Thumper told me he was on the way to Cornflower Cottage.

'New people there,' he said. 'Have you met them?'

I shook my head.

'Phatt,' he said.

'All of them?' I asked, misunderstanding.

'No. That's their name. They're called Phatt.' He spelt it for me. 'I've been doing some work on the cottage for them. They're having a new kitchen and a new bathroom put in.' He screwed up in nose. 'Ghastly,' he said. He shuddered. 'They got me to put in a maroon bathroom suite. Maroon bath, maroon handbasin and maroon lavatory.' He shook his head sadly. 'I nearly refused,' he said. He grinned. 'But they're new. They're paying townie prices.' Thumper was one of the kindest men I knew. He was always doing favours for old people who had no money, and when he worked for friends he could rarely be persuaded to take more than the cost of the materials he'd bought. But he had no qualms about overcharging people whom he regarded as fair game. It was, I suppose, his way of playing Robin Hood.

'They've agreed to let me open up the practice,' I told Thumper.

He grinned. 'I thought they might.'

'How did you get them to agree?' I asked. 'What have you been up to?'

'There were a couple of letters in the local paper.'

'I saw them. That might have influenced the bureaucrats but I think there was something else.'

'You think so?'

'Yes.'

Thumper smiled, thought for a moment and then shook his head.

'I don't think you want to know.'

'Was it legal?'

'Entirely.'

'I didn't want to know beforehand,' I told him. 'But I do now.'

Thumper hesitated, sighed and then made up his mind. 'We had a sick rota,' he told me. 'Two dozen of us took it in turns to ring the doctors in Barnstaple and demand home visits. We called them out three or four times a night.'

I couldn't help laughing. 'I'm not surprised they gave in!'

Just then Samuel Houghton's tractor pulled up behind my car. Samuel clambered out and meandered over to where we were standing.

'Why the queue?' he asked.

Thumper pointed to the cow. 'One of yours?'

Samuel nodded. 'Sorry about this,' he said cheerfully. 'It's the one I bought at auction last Thursday. She's deaf and a bit bloody-minded.' He walked slowly over to the cow, bent down until his mouth was about six inches from her left ear and shouted 'Get up my dear!' in her ear.

The cow got up.

Samuel tapped her lightly on the backside. He leant close to her ear again. 'To your field!' he shouted.

The cow set off down the lane.

'Deaf,' explained Samuel again. He got back into his tractor and sat there waiting for the traffic jam to disappear.

Still chewing, the cow started walking down the lane, following the trail of hardening cow pats left by her companions.

* * *

After the Government had closed down my medical practice Miss Johnson had decided to retire. She was old enough to take a small private pension to which she had contributed for most of her life, and her own modest savings had received a welcome boost when she had received an unexpected windfall after the death of an elderly aunt.

'I could never leave Bilbury,' she had told me. 'And since I can't drive a tractor or milk a cow I don't think I'll find any other work here.'

And so Miss Johnson had declared her intention to cultivate roses, read sentimental, romantic novels and never answer the telephone again.

After knocking on the front door of her cottage, I opened it and walked in. I don't think there are more than half a dozen doorbells in Bilbury. When visiting one another most people living in the village just knock and walk in. This can, of course, lead to some embarrassing moments but since the village's inhabitants tend to think of themselves as members of one large family these embarrassments are regarded as trivial and of little consequence.

Miss Johnson was sitting in the tiny living room of her tiny cottage. If she had changed at all in the time since we had both retired from medical practice it was to look younger and healthier. She was wearing a plain blue skirt and a white blouse. She wore her pearls, of course, and the gold-rimmed spectacles. 'I made a seed cake for you,' she said. Miss Johnson's seed cake was renowned and incomparable.

'How did you know I was coming?'

She looked at me over her spectacles. 'I would have been very disappointed in you if you hadn't come to see me.'

I laughed. I couldn't help it. Miss Johnson had always been the best informed person in the village. She usually knew who was getting married or having a baby even before they did themselves.

'How did you know I was going back into business as a village GP?' I asked her.

She looked at me over her spectacles again.

'OK!' I said, holding up a hand. Miss Johnson had never liked telling me the identity of her sources. 'Just one question: will you come back and work with me?'

'Of course I will!' she said emphatically.

'You're not enjoying your retirement too much?'

She leant forward. 'To be perfectly honest,' she said, 'I'm bored rigid. The roses don't take more than twenty minutes a day at the most and if I read any more of these wretched novels I think I'll go potty.' She pointed to a row of paperback novels sitting on her bookshelf

'You miss the gossip?'

'Of course I do! When are we starting?'

'This Saturday.'

'This Saturday! Gosh. Thumper's little plan did work well.'

I smiled. 'It would seem so.'

'I'll pop round to the Grange tomorrow shall I? When are they sending the patients medical records over from Barnstaple?'

I looked at her, not quite sure how to tell her that I'd forgotten all about the medical records. But I didn't have to say anything. My silence told her the answer.

Miss Johnson sighed, looked over her spectacles at me and shook her head in mock despair. 'Never mind,' she said. 'I'll ring the bureaucrats later on and get them to send the records over in a taxi.'

'Will they do that?'

'They will if I tell them that if they don't and someone dies you'll see that they're blamed.'

'Ah, yes.' I said.

'Your little trick never fails,' she said. 'You taught me that one.'

A year or two earlier I had used this threat to get the local health service administrators to rush me the medical records for a patient who had just moved into the area. The administrators had never forgotten the threat - or the lesson.

I smiled. 'And that was about the only thing I did teach you!'

'I'll go and get the cake,' said Miss Johnson. 'Shall we have a glass of my elderberry wine to celebrate?'

'A small glass,' I said. 'I like your elderberry wine but it's got a kick like a bad-tempered mule. And then you can tell me how I can persuade Kay to come back to work as the practice nurse.'

'Oh, if you're quick I don't think you'll have too much difficulty,' said Miss Johnson, with a twinkle in her eye. 'When I last saw Kay she told me she was working as a barmaid in a pub in Barnstaple I can't think that's quite her cup of tea.'

'Why on earth is she working in a pub?'

'There weren't any other vacancies for district nurses and she didn't want to work in a hospital,' answered Miss Johnson. 'I don't think our Kay likes authority too much,' she said.

* * *

It took me twenty five minutes to get into Barnstaple. I would have got there quicker except for the tractor which held me up for a mile or so between Winford Bridge and Garman's Down. The driver was too busy trying not to let his overladen load of straw topple into the ditch to notice that there was a car stuck behind him.

In Barnstaple, I left the car in the car park behind Bear Street and hurried through the town to the pub where Miss Johnson had told me I could find Kay behind the bar.

It was a dark and rather dingy pub that advertised itself as having been serving beer and sandwiches since the Middle Ages. It didn't look as if it had received a lick of paint since opening day. I wondered if they were still selling the same sandwiches.

I spotted Kay straight away. She was polishing a glass with a rather grubby tea towel and trying to ignore a small, skinny bald customer who had his shirt sleeves rolled up to display two large tattoos - one on each forearm. She was wearing a very low cut white blouse which was obviously fashioned to displayed her more than ample cleavage; the neckline of the blouse was edged with white lace designed to draw attention to an apparently bottomless pink canyon.

The customer was sipping his pint of beer and staring into the cleavage as though trying to hypnotise it. Or maybe he was the one who was being hypnotised.

'Your landlord claims to have been serving sandwiches since the Middle Ages,' I murmured.

'That's right,' muttered Kay. 'We've been serving ale and sandwiches since 1546.'

'Sandwiches weren't invented until the 18th century,' I said. 'They were named after the Earl of Sandwich. He ordered that one be made for him after he'd spent 24 hours at a gambling table.'

Kay stopped polishing, put down the glass, and looked at me. She was, I could tell, ready to snarl at me. But slowly a huge smile appeared on her face. 'It's you!' she cried. 'What on earth are you doing in this dump?'

'I came to see you.' I looked at her. She seemed different. Then I realised what it was. 'You seem taller. You must be wearing very high heels.'

She shook her head. 'I'm standing on an upturned beer crate,' she told me. 'There are three of them round here.'

'Why on earth are you standing on an upturned beer crate? Isn't it uncomfortable and unstable?'

'It's so that I have to lean forward a lot.'

'Isn't that bad for your back?'

'I'm sure it is. But it's good for business. The more the customers get to see of my cleavage the more beer I sell.'

'Oh.' I said, blushing.

She shrugged. 'It was the only bloody job I could get.' She looked down at her blouse and tried in vain to cover the open chasm that was her cleavage. 'The boss insists that all the barmaids dress like this. He calls us Ye Olde Englishe Barmaids,' she said. 'And he only employs barmaids with Ye Bigge Knockers.' She laughed and shrugged. 'Ah well, I need the work,' she said. 'Things aren't good in the tractor business at the moment.' She put down the glass and tea towel. 'How are you? What's happening? What are you doing? How's Patsy?'

'I want ·you to come back to work,' I said. 'I'm opening up the practice again. I need a district nurse who knows how to tie a bandage, how to dress a wound, how to comfort a bereaved widow, how to find cottages which don't have names on and how to work all alone except for a slightly eccentric general practitioner who constantly needs the help and support of a loyal, kind and sympathetic district nurse.'

Kay stared at me. She opened her mouth to say something but nothing came out.

'Do you know anyone who might prove suitable?' I asked.

She crossed her arms across her chest and studied me as though contemplating making a bid. 'Not me,' she said eventually. She shook her head to emphasise her reply.

'I start tomorrow,' I said. 'I only found out about it yesterday. It's all a bit of a rush. I need you.'

Kay carried on staring.

'Another pint, lovey,' said the skinny man with the tattoos. He pushed his empty glass across the bar.

'You can't...,' she began. 'The health service will have to advertise the job. I can't...'

'They agreed to let me choose my own district nurse,' I said. 'So if you want the job it's yours.'

'I haven't done any nursing for...,' she paused and thought. 'I can't remember!' she said at last. 'Since they closed you down.'

'Nor have I. It'll come back. Like riding a bicycle.'

'Hey, big girl,' said the skinny man with the tattoos. 'I want another pint.' He sounded threatening. He tried to lean across the counter but either he was too small or the counter was too high.

'How much notice do you have to give?' I asked her.

Suddenly she started talking quickly. 'I get paid three times as much here as the health service will pay me,' she said. 'My husband was laid off. I'm the only breadwinner.' She seemed embarrassed. 'It's a dump but it's busy at evenings and at the weekends. And I get a lot of tips.' She looked down at her own well-exposed cleavage. 'I don't much like the uniform,' she said. 'And the customers still bleed all over me, and vomit on me occasionally too.' She shrugged. 'But it's a living and to be honest I need the money.' She tried, unsuccessfully, to pull the two sides of her blouse a little closer together. Then she tried to smile. That didn't work either. 'Far too revealing for a modest country girl like me,' she said unconvincingly.

'Where's my bloody beer?' demanded the man with the tattoos.

Kay bent down and picked up a fresh glass from underneath the counter. She filled it carefully, tilting the glass so that there was no head on the beer. Then she reached across the bar with the glass in her hand.

'Here's your beer, you horrible, leering, nasty little man,' she said, pouring the pint over his head. She watched with obvious delight as beer ran down the startled man's face and neck, soaking his shirt and dripping onto what remained of the carpet. 'I hope you enjoyed that,' she said.

Surprisingly, the man didn't seem to mind as much as I had expected. He just shook himself and wiped his head with his hand. Kay threw him the damp tea towel. He used it to wipe his face.

'Sorry,' she said. 'Hope you find someone for the job.'

As I left I couldn't help reflecting that a society which paid people more to serve beer than to nurse had somehow got its priorities distorted.

And yet, although I wanted to feel disappointed by my failure to recruit Kay McBride, for some reason I didn't.

I kept remembering the cats she'd had killed.

Perhaps Kay McBride was a little too tough. Maybe I'd find a more suitable nurse.

* * *

When I got home I found that someone had attached a smartly painted sign to the front gate at Bilbury Grange. The sign had my name and the words The Surgery written on it. Underneath were the words 'No wart too small, no rash too faint.' Someone had obviously put a lot of effort into it so I left the sign where it was.

'I've given your surgery a good clean,' said Patsy. 'And I know you've managed to persuade Miss Johnson to come out of retirement because a man from Barnstaple came round with a box full of National Health Service stationery - prescription pads, national insurance certificates, X-ray request forms and all sorts of things. He said Miss Johnson had rung them up and told them they had to send round a boxful of emergency supplies. The man said there will be a proper delivery early next week.'

'Thank heavens for Miss Johnson,' I murmured to Patsy. I'd completely forgotten that I would need prescription pads. 'If I write out a list of emergency drug supplies would you ring the chemist in Combe Martin and ask him to deliver them?'

'Of course.'

I went into the surgery, found a piece of notepaper and a pen and, sitting at the kitchen table, hurriedly began to write down a list of what I thought I'd need for emergency supplies. 'I'll make this a private prescription,' I said. 'Tell the chemist that you'll give him a prescription when he delivers what I need. And ask him if he'd be kind enough to send us a bill with the drugs.'

I wrote down a list of emergency drugs I thought I'd need to start with:

Morphine 10mg/ml for injection x 6 ampoules

Codeine 30 mg tablets x 30

Prochlorperazine 5mg tablets x 30

Amoxicillin 250mg capsules x 56

Erythromycin 250mg capsules x 28

Trimethoprim 200 mg tablets x 20

Aspirin 300mg soluble tablets x 60

Adrenaline 1 in 1,000, 10 x 0.5 ml ampoules

I wrote 'Private Prescription - For Stock' at the top of the piece of paper, signed my name at the bottom, added the date and then handed the sheet to Patsy.

'I'll need more later,' I said. 'But those will do to start with.'

'Do you think he'll have all these in stock?' she asked.

'If there's anything they haven't got ask them if they would be kind enough to get it in for tomorrow,' I told her. 'By the way, Kay won't be coming. She's working as a barmaid.'

'She turned you down?'

I nodded. 'Probably for the best,' I said.

'You'll find someone' said Patsy. I nodded. She picked up my list of drugs and headed for the telephone.

'I'd better go and sort out my surgery and my bag,' I said. 'I need to make sure that everything is still working.'

CHAPTER 9

WhenIhadretiredfromgeneralpracticeIhadleftmysurgeryexactly asithadbeen when I'd worked init.BilburyGrangewasquite bigenoughforustoleavethethreeroomsdevotedtothepractice untouched.Oneroomhadbeenmysurgery,onethewaitingroom andathirdhadbeentheofficewhereMissJohnson worked.

Patientsenteredandleftthewaitingroomthroughadooratthe sideofthehousesoitwasquiteeasytoregardthethreeroomsas anentirelyseparatepartofthehouse.

A country GP's surgery, back in the 1970s, was hardly a storehouse of high technology but there were some bits and pieces I knew I would need to find.

I sat down at my desk, picked up a notepad and a pencil and made a list:

1. Sphygmomanometer (For taking blood pressure readings.)
2. Patella hammer (For testing reflexes.)
3. Ophthalmoscope (For looking into patients' eyes.)
4. Auriscope (For looking into patients' ears.)
5. Torch (For looking down patients' throats, into their outer ears and into any other dark orifice that needed close examination.)
6. Peak Flow Meter (Tube for patients to blow into in order to check their lung function.)

I looked at the list. There was something missing. I chewed on the end of my pencil. I knew there was something missing but I couldn't think what it was. Then I remembered.

7. Stethoscope (For listening to chests and, most important of all, for looking like a doctor.)

I found the first six items on the list straight away. The ophthalmoscope, auriscope and torch all needed new batteries but that was no problem; they all took standard sized batteries of which we had a supply in a cupboard in the kitchen. I got the batteries, put them in and checked. Everything worked.

But I couldn't find my stethoscope anywhere.

It wasn't in my black bag. It wasn't on my desk. It wasn't in any of the drawers in my desk.

I went back into the house and found Patsy.

'The chemist has got everything in stock,' she told me. 'He said he'll bring it all over when he closes up for the night. He asked me to say how pleased he was that you were opening up the practice again. And he especially said to tell you that that's not just because he'll dispense a lot more prescriptions with patients seeing you and not going into Barnstaple!'

I laughed. The chemist would do well. I was pleased about that. He was a good fellow.

'Have you seen my tubes?' I asked Patsy.

'Your what?'

'My Tubes. My stethoscope. I can't find them - it - anywhere.'

'That long dangly thing that you use to eavesdrop on people's chests?'

'That's the one.'

'I didn't know it was called tubes.'

'It's really a stethoscope.'

'I know. But you called it your tubes.'

'That's what we used to call them at medical school.'

'How sweet and boyish!'

'Whatever I call it I can't find it.'

She frowned. 'Isn't it in your surgery?'

'No.'

'Your black bag?'

'No. Looked there too.'

'I don't have the faintest idea where it could be. I don't suppose it's in your study?'

We had converted a spare bedroom at the top of the house into a writing room. It was quiet and there was no telephone in there. It was where I wrote my books. 'Good idea,' I said. I had no idea why I would have put my stethoscope up there but it was as good a place to look as anywhere.

I raced up the stairs.

Three minutes later I raced back down again.

'It's not up there,' I told Patsy.

'Have you not got a spare?' she asked.

I shook my head. 'I've only ever had one stethoscope,' I told her. 'It's the one I bought when I was a medical student. I won't look like a doctor without it.'

We searched everywhere in the house. But we couldn't find it anywhere.

At ten that evening I slumped down in an easy chair quite exhausted and very miserable.

* * *

'I know where it is!' I cried out, sitting up in bed.

Patsy woke up, rubbed at her eyes and sat up.

The two cats stirred on the bed but didn't wake up. Ben, the dog, opened one eye, decided that there was nothing to get excited about and went back to sleep again.

'You know where what is?'

'My stethoscope.'

'Where is it?'

'I lent it to Mrs Thingy for that play the school did a couple of months ago.'

'That's right!' said Patsy. 'I remember. You did. What was the play.'

'I can't remember the play but there was a doctor in it. One of the children played a doctor. And so they borrowed my stethoscope.'

'Mrs Bridge!' said Patsy. 'Ivy Bridge. She works as an assistant at the school. Her husband works for the council in Barnstaple She does a lot of drama stuff in schools.'

I climbed out of bed.

'Where are you going?'

'I'm going to get my stethoscope.'

'You can't!' laughed Patsy.

'Why not? It's my stethoscope.'

'It's four o'clock in the morning!'

'What if she's lost it?'

'She won't have lost it.'

'She might have given it to a jumble sale.'

'She won't have done that.'

'She might have lent it to some other school. By now my stethoscope could be draped around the neck of some junior would-be-thespian prancing the boards in Bratton Fleming or South Molton or Woolacombe.'

'I'm sure your stethoscope will be OK,' said Patsy, as soothing as only a good wife or mother can be.

Reluctantly, very reluctantly, I agreed to wait until the next morning to collect my stethoscope.

But I didn't find the waiting easy.

* * *

'I'm sorry to bother you so early,' I said. 'But I've come for my stethoscope.'

Mrs Bridge pulled her dressing gown a little tighter around her, stared at me and blinked. 'Doctor? Is that you doctor?'

'Yes,' I said. 'I've come for my stethoscope. I'm afraid I need it back.'

She stared at me as if I was completely mad.

'I lent it to you for the school play.'

'Oh yes,' she said. 'What time is it?'

I looked at my watch. 'Fourteen minutes to seven.' She blinked. 'It's a little early isn't it?'

'It's an emergency,' I told her brightly. 'I'm starting a surgery at nine o'clock and I need my stethoscope.'

'What is it dear?' asked another voice. A large, round man appeared behind Mrs Bridge. He was wearing blue and red striped pyjamas and looked rather put out. He was wearing a hairnet to keep his hair flat.

'It's the doctor, dear,' said Mrs Bridge. 'I borrowed his stethoscope for a play the school put on.'

'Good morning, doctor,' said Mr Bridge.

'Good morning, Mr Bridge,' I replied.

'Didn't you give it back to him?' Mr Bridge asked his wife.

'Apparently not,' said Mrs Bridge.

'Do you have any idea where it might be?"

'I suppose Geoffrey must have taken it home.'

'Geoffrey? Who is Geoffrey?'

'He's the boy who played the doctor.'

'What doctor?'

'Dr Thomas Stockmann.'

'Who is Dr Stockmann?'

'He's an important character in *A Public Enemy*.'

We both looked at her.

'It's a play by Henrik Ibsen.'

'You had ten-year-olds playing Ibsen?' her husband asked, astonished.

'They enjoyed it immensely,' said Mrs Bridge defensively. 'Children need to be stretched.'

'Yes. Of course. So you think Geoffrey might have my stethoscope?'

'He could have.'

'What's his full name?'

'Geoffrey Slater.'

'Where does he live?'

She told me. I thanked her and left. As I got into my car I could hear Mr Bridge berating his wife. 'I remember that play now,' he was saying. 'It's really not a suitable play for young children to perform.'

I didn't hear Mrs Bridge's reply. I was on my way to Geoffrey Slater's home.

* * *

Geoffrey remembered where my stethoscope was. He'd last used it to decorate a snowman they'd built in their garden. My stethoscope was eventually unearthed amidst a pile of half broken toys and completely broken plant pots at the back of their garage.

It was looking rather the worse for wear. But stethoscopes are pretty basic instruments; there isn't much to go wrong. And mine had survived. It still worked.

I felt a great sense of relief as I drove back to Bilbury Grange with my stethoscope lying on the front passenger seat.

Now I could be a proper doctor again.

CHAPTER 10

Iexpectedmyfirstsurgerytobequiet.

'We'll just open the door, wait around for half an hour or so and then close the door,' I told Miss Johnson. To help while away the time I had picked up a paperback copy of a Graham Greene novel I was reading and stuffed it into my jacket pocket before I went into the surgery.

But things didn't turn out quite as I had expected and the paperback stayed where it was. I'd just settled down behind my desk when Miss Johnson floated in. She had a talent for seeming calm and unhurried whatever was going on around her and it was good to know that she would be working alongside me.

'There are eleven here so far,' she said.

'Eleven what?' I asked, genuinely puzzled.

'Patients,' she said softly.

'Eleven!'

'Seven of them were waiting by the back door when I arrived,' she said.

I was, it seemed, back in business.

* * *

I was quickly reminded of the strange things people worry about. Thanks to articles and columns on health matters in newspapers and magazines, and to constant exposure to medical programmes on television and radio, many people have acquired a smattering of medical knowledge.

In general this is a good thing. But it can lead to some very strange conclusions.

Within fifteen minutes I had been reminded of the odd things people believe.

After a long, preliminary and utterly irrelevant discussion of her feet (she wanted to know if they were flat, which they were not) Mollie Leafinold confided that her husband suffered from premature ejaculation and wanted to know if this meant that she would have a premature baby. Thus I was reminded that when a patient says 'by the way, while I'm here' it invariably means that they are about to reveal the real reason for their visit. Mollie wasn't really worried about her feet. But she was shy about mentioning her real fear and needed time to work up to it.

Eighteen-year-old Amelia Raite wanted to know if it was true that a girl couldn't get pregnant if she or the man she was with wore a cap. Having been away from medical practice for a while I foolishly assumed she knew a little about contraception and was talking either about the Dutch cap or the condom but after some confusing, and for both of us rather bewildering discussion, it turned out that she had somehow gained the impression that if a man wore a flat tweed cap on his head the girl he was making love to would be protected from pregnancy.

'I didn't see how it could be,' she admitted, before she left. 'But it was my friend told me that.'

I managed to persuade her to re-educate her friend in the hope that this might do something to prevent the rumour spreading any further round the village.

* * *

MynextpatientwasDeanTaunton.

Hecameintothesurgery inquiteatemper.Brandishingaletterfromhismot her   hewanted toknowhowhecouldsuethehospitalinYorkshirewhereshehad beentreated.

'They'vehadamixup,'heexplainedwhenIaskedhimwhyhe wantedtosuethehospital.

'Tellmeaboutit,'Itoldhim.

'They   sentmymotherhomewithRaynaud's   disease,'hesaid. 'So,whatIwanttoknowiswho'sgotherdisease?'

ItoldhimIdidn't quiteunderstand.

'IfmymumhasgotRaynaud's   diseasethenwho   hasgothers andhowdidtheygetmixedup?' demandedMrTauntonquite indignantly.

Ieventuallymanagedtoexplainthatmanymedicaldiseasesare givennamescommemorating   theirdiscoverers.'Your   mother's diseaseisnamedafterthedoctorwhofirstdiagnosedthecondition,' Iexplained.

'Sillybloodyname,'saidMrTaunton.

'Not   assillyasitcouldhavebeen,'Iexplained. HeaskedmewhatImeant.

I told him that there are some disorders which are named after more than one discoverer. 'There is, for example, a type of muscular atrophy known as Wohlfart-Kugelberg-Welander disease,' I told him.

* * *

In any other small village Nigel Perkins would be the oldest resident.

Mr Perkins celebrated his 87th birthday a few months ago but looks (and behaves) much younger than his years. He still plays darts in the pub team, still plays cricket (though usually, it is true, only when the captain cannot otherwise make up an eleven) and still fancies himself as something of a ladies' man.

Despite his age he has very few real physical complaints. His heart ticks away like a Swiss watch and the rest of him was also clearly made to last.

His main complaint when I saw him was of muscle cramps in his arms and legs.

'How long have you had them?' I asked.

'About a week.'

'Are they getting better or worse?'

'Worse, if anything.'

'You're not taking any medicines are you?'

'Oh no,' he said. He shook his head emphatically. 'Don't like taking drugs.'

I examined him but could find nothing wrong with him.

'You're a medical mystery,' I told him.

'Am I?' he asked, apparently delighted.

'I'll have a look at you in a couple of days,' I told him. 'See how you are then.'

'There's something else I've been meaning to ask you about for years,' he said. I waited. 'Why has my hair lost its memory? Why does the stuff that used to grow out of the top of my head now grows out of my nose and ears?'

I laughed. 'I have no idea,' I told him. 'But it comes with the territory, I'm afraid.'

'What territory?'

'The being 87 territory,' I told him.

He snorted. 'You doctors blame everything on old age,' he said. He bent down and took a parcel wrapped in newspaper out of his bag. 'Brought you and Patsy a lettuce, doctor,' he said, putting the package down onto my desk.

'Thank you,' I said. I reached out and touched the packet. 'We're very grateful.'

Nigel stood up and waved a hand, brushing aside the thanks.

'I'll see you in a couple of days,' I told him.

When he'd gone I took the lettuce through to Patsy in the kitchen.

* * *

'Rick' Shaw, a taxi driver who works in Barnstaple, and whom I knew well, came in to see me looking very worried. He told me that he had been for an insurance medical and had been told by the doctor who had done the examination that he was suffering from asthma. He had, as a result, been told by his insurers that they would charge him a higher premium.

'I thought people with asthma had difficulty in breathing!' he said.

'They usually do,' I agreed.

'Well I don't,' said Rick rather indignantly.

I examined him and agreed that I could find nothing wrong. I asked him to tell me about the examination.

'The doctor got me to blow into this tube,' he said. 'I didn't manage very well. I think that was why he said I'd got asthma.'

'Could be,' I agreed.

I picked up my own spirometer and asked him to blow into it.

'Looks fine,' I said, when he handed the instrument back to me. 'No signs of asthma. Why didn't you manage very well at the medical?'

Rick went red and was clearly embarrassed. I waited for him to tell me.

'The wife said I should wear a collar and a tie for the medical,' he said. 'It being with a private doctor.'

I nodded. 'I don't think I've ever seen you with a tie,' I told him.

'No,' he said. 'I don't wear them.'

'Collar a bit tight?' I suggested. He nodded.

'Button up your collar,' I said.

He buttoned up his collar.

'Now try again,' I said, handing him the spirometer.

This time he produced a very feeble blow. I grinned at him.

'You'd better unbutton your shirt before I diagnose asthma,' I told him.

I said I would write to the insurance company for him and ask them to repeat the medical.

'There willprobablybeanotherfeetopay,'Iwarnedhim.'But Iexpectitwillbecheaperthanpayingbiggerpremiums.' Hethankedmeandgotup.

'Andifyoumustwearatieeithergetashirtwithabiggercollar orleavethetopbutton unbuttoned,'Itoldhim.

Hegrinnedsheepishly.

* * *

Ire-learnt alotofthingsIhadforgotten inthatfirstmorning backatwork.

Ire-learnt, forexample,thatalthoughmanypatientswillaccept adoctor's adviceiftheygenuinelythinkitisgoodforthem, there aresomepatientswhoareveryselectiveabouttheadvicetheyare preparedtotake.

EddieBusbyisfivefooteightinchestallandweighsjustunder twentystones.Hedrinksfivepintsofbeereverynightandadmits tosmokingfortycigarettesaday(whichmeansthatheprobably getsthrougheighty).Ilongagolostcountofthenumberoftimes Isuggestedthatitmightbetohislong-term advantagetocuthis consumptionofboth.Hetookasmuchnoticeofthatadviceashe tookoftheadvicetolosealittleweight.

'Ineedanothersicknote,'hetoldme,collapsingintothechair ontheothersideofmydesk.Iheardthechaircreakandhopedit wouldn't givewayunderhisbulk.

'Whyaren'tyouatwork?'I askedhim.

'ThedoctorinBarnstaplesaidIshouldn'tworksohard,'hetold me.'HesaidIneededtotakethingsalittleeasier.'

ThissurprisedmeforIknewofveryfewpeopleontheplanet whotookthingseasierthanEddie.

'Whydidhesaythat?'I asked.

'He seemedtothink myjobwasmakingmeill,' saidEddie. 'Stress,' he added. 'Plus Iget tired and breathless ifIdo too much.'

'You needtolosesomeweight,cutdownonthedrinkingand giveupthecigarettes,'Itoldhim.

Helookedatmeasiflhadtoldhimtotakeupembroideryor hang-gliding.'I'm notwellenoughtodoanyofthat,' hesaid.'I needtorestandbuildupmystrength.'

'What's yourjob?'I askedhim.

'Unemployed,'heanswered immediately.

'Takeyourshirtoff,'Itoldhim.

'Why?'hedemanded.

'SothatIcanexamineyou.'

Reluctantly, heremovedhisshirtandthrewitontomydesk.

'Andyourvest.'

Hetookthevestoffandthrewitontopoftheshirt.

Ilistenedtohisheartandlungs,tookhisbloodpressureanddid someothersimpletests.

'Good   news!Ithinkyou'rewellenoughtogobacktowork,'   I toldhim,whenhehadremovedhisclothesfrommydesk.

Hedidn'tlookasthoughthiswasgoodnews.

'ThedoctorsaidIneededtotaketimeoffwork,' hesaid.

'And you did,' I said. 'It's done you a lot of good. You're in much better shape. But you're still smoking eighty a day.'

'Forty,' he said.

'Eighty.'

He looked at me and backed down. 'How did you know it was eighty?'

'Icantell.'

'From listening tomychest?'

Inodded.Anodseemedlessofaliethanactuallysaying'yes'.

Helooked glum. 'Igetmoremoney when I'm onthesick.Do you knowhow expensive cigarettesare?'

'Iknow.'Iwrotedowndetailsof   hisbloodpressureonhismedical notes. 'Of course,'Isaid,'ifyou were making arealeffort tolose weight, tocut down your drinking andto reduce the numberof cigarettes you smoke then you would probably need afew more weeksonthesick.'

Hebrightenedconsiderably.

'But I'll need toseeyou every week,' Itold him. 'I'll weigh you andI'lllisten toyour chest.I'llknow whetherornot you're making aneffort.'

'IfIlosesome   weight   andcutdown   thecigarettes   you'llkeep meonthesickabitlonger?'

Inodded.Itwasthebestincentive Icould think of

Hefrowned.

'It'sthebestdealyou'regoingtogettoday,' Itoldhim. Ipicked up the relevant form and took the cap offmy pen. 'What'sthe decision?'

'I'll try,' hesaid.

Ihanded him abooklet explaining how hecould loseweight, abookletexplaininghow tostop smoking and asick note for a week.

* * *

The next two patientscameintogether.

Nancy and Doreen Norfolk are sisters, known locally as the Norfolk broads, and they live together in a cottage their parents left them. Nancy works as a children's book illustrator and Doreen makes home-made chutneys and jams which she sells on a stall in the Pannier Market in Barnstaple. If I hadn't got their medical records in front of me I would have never guessed their ages. Both are in their early forties but they look at least a decade younger.

'We've got a little problem,' said Nancy.

'A very little problem really,' added Doreen.

'But not so little that it doesn't worry us,' Nancy reminded her.

'No,' agreed Doreen.

It took me nearly ten minutes to get them to tell me what the problem was. We got there via details of a new recipe for tomato chutney which Doreen insisted I gave to Patsy, a discussion of the disappearance of the red squirrel (Nancy was doing the illustrations for a children's storybook about two squirrels) and a fairly extensive discussion of the Des Moulin's whorl snail, a tiny creature the size of a matchheadwhichis nowsorarethatbuildingdevelopers somewhereinthesouthofEnglandhadbeentoldthattheirplans foranewhousingestatehadtobeabandonedbecausetheywould disruptthesnails'naturalhabitat.

'We couldgetholdofoneortwoofthesnailsandgetthem toliveinBilbury,'saidDoreen.'That way ifanydeveloperseversuggestbuildingherewecouldstopthem.'

IsaidIlikedherideabutthoughtthatgettingholdofthesnails mightbedifficult.

Eventually,theytoldmetheirproblem.

'We haveabrother,' saidNancy.'He's calledArnoldandhis wifeisFelicity. TheyliveinNorthampton.'

'He's achiropodistandshe'sadentalhygienist,'said Doreen.

'Sothey'rebothmedical,'saidNancy.

'The problemisthattheyhavetoldourcousinJeffreythatwe aren'tnormal,'saidDoreen.

'Wedon't havemuchtodowithourbrother,' saidNancy.

'Nor withcousinJeffrey,'saidDoreen.

'JeffreyworksfortheGovernment,' saidNancy,inreverential tones.Sheloweredhervoiceandspokeina whisper.'Inland Revenue,'shesaid,inthesamesortoftonethatshemighthave usedhadhebeenanemployeeofMI5.

'Ah,' Isaid,noddingasthough Iunderstood whereallthiswas leading.BeingacountryGPmeanshavingalotofpatience.

'JeffreytoldusthatArnoldtoldhimthatwearen'tnormal,'said Doreen.

'Hasthatupsetyou?'Iasked.

'Not somuchupset,perhaps,'saidNancy.'Butwe'rea little concerned.'

'Can theGovernment haveusarrestedfornotbeingnormal?'

'Idon't thinkso,'Itoldthem.'InfactI'mprettysurethatthey can't.'

'Oh that'sarelief,'saidNancy.

'Howwouldtheydecidewhat'snormal?'I asked.Ithoughtfor amoment. 'Idon't thinkIknowanyonewhoisnormal,'Isaid.'In factI'mnotevensureIknowwhatitmeans.Doyou?'

Thetwosisterslookedatoneanother.'Isupposeitmeansbeing acoupleandhavingchildren,'saidNancy.

'ThumperandAnneareacouple,' Isaid.'They'vegotababy. Would yousaytheywere'normal'?'

'Well, no,notreally,'said Doreen, withalittlenervousgiggle.

'Isupposenot.'

'Isyourbrothernormal?'

'Oh definitelynot,'saidNancy.'Hefliesmodelaeroplanesand doesMorrisdancinginthesummer.'

Doreen shookherhead.'Idon't thinkhe'snormal,'shesaid.

'Then whyworry?'Iaskedthem.

'DoesJeffreyseemnormaltoyou?Doyouknow anyone else likehim?'

'Oh no,' theyboth said.'He keepsbudgiesandtakesthem to shows.He'sgotacabinetfulloftrophies.Wedon't knowanyone elsewhodoesthat.'

'WorkingfortheInlandRevenueandbreedingbudgiesishardly normal,'Isaid.

'No,'sheagreed.Theybothlookedalothappier.

'Sodoyoufeelabitbetteraboutthings?'Iaskedthem.

'Oh definitely,'theybothsaid together.Theylookedatone another, smiledandgotup.

'I'll bringsomerhubarbandbeetrootjamround foryoutry,' saidDoreeninawhisper.'It'smy latestrecipe.'

'It'swonderful,'saidNancy.'You'llloveit.It'sgotaveryunusual tangtoit.'

'Ilookforwardtothat,'Itoldthem.

* * *

'Isthatit?'IaskedMissJohnson.

IthadbeenamuchbusiersurgerythanI'dexpected.

'I'm afraidnot,doctor,' saidMissJohnson. 'One ortwomore arrivedwhileyouwerewiththelastpatient.'

Iopenedthedoortothewaitingroom.Theroomwasabsolutely full.Youcouldn'thavecrammedmorepeopleintothe roomif you'd been trying to get a mention in the *Guinness Book of Records* for having the most patients in a waiting room. The moment I opened the door everyone started coughing.

Appalled I looked around. I didn't recognise anyone. Every patient in there looked old, decrepit and scruffy. Most wore beards. The rest had long hair or scarves over their faces.

I backed out of the waiting room and closed the door.

'Where did they all come from?' I asked Miss Johnson.

'They all claim to be visitors,' she told me.

'They all came in together?'

'More or less.'

I sighed. At this rate I wasn't going to finish the morning surgery before the evening surgery was due to start. Heaven knows when I would get the visits done. Suddenly, and for the first time, I was beginning to wonder if I'd done the right thing by going back into practice. I opened the door again. Everyone started coughing. The noise was deafening. Something didn't look or sound quite right but I wasn't sure what it was.

'Who's next?'Iasked.

'Me!'theyallcriedatonce.

I scratched my head and looked around again. Although I didn't recognise anyone they all seemed vaguely familiar. And then I spotted Patchy's shoes.

Patchy Fogg always wears the same pair of brown calf length boots. He wears them with jeans and he wears them with suits. He would, I felt sure, be wearing them on his wedding day. And the patient sitting just to the left of the potted plant in the comer of the room was wearing brown, calf length boots. I looked closer and harder. And then I got it. I pointed at him and started to say something.

As soon as they realised that I knew what was going on everyone in the room started to chuckle. Wigs and false beards and scarves were quickly removed. I turned round. Miss Johnson was smiling and blushing. 'Mr Robinson and Mr Fogg said you wouldn't mind, doctor.'

'Oh no,' I said, grinning. 'I don't mind. But I'll get my own back on Mr Robinson and Mr Fogg.'

CHAPTER 11

WhenIfinallyfinishedthemorningsurgeryMissJohnsontoldme thatIhadjustonehome visittomake.

'Idon'tthinkit'surgent, doctor,'shesaid.

Ilooked atmywatch. 'I think I'llgoandgetitdone now,'I said.

The visitwastoGloria, theextremely slenderwifeofthenew villagepoliceman.

The policeman'snamewasRussellRossthoughhewasalways knownasRuss. This wasboth confusing andconvenientfor everyonebecauseitmeant that no one ever knew whetherthey wereaddressinghimbyhisChristiannameorhissurname.Russhad takenoverwhenP.C.Wren,Bilbury'spreviousrepresentativeofthe Devon constabulary, moved ontobecome asergeant somewhere inthesouth east.

Aspecialunkindness of fatehadmeantthatRusscouldnot pronouncethe letter 'r'and sowhen he introducedhimself to people itsounded asif his name was Wuss Woss. This was not a name to inspire confidence. It is difficult to maintain respect when a policeman introduces himself with the words 'Good morning, I'm PC Wuss Woss'.

Russ's biggest problem had been with other policemen and he had requested a transfer to a village constabularybecausehefound workinginawell-staffedpolicestationtobesomething ofatrial.

Nooneinthevillageeverlaughedathim, butalthoughthesmiles mightnothavebeenvisible theywereneverthelessthere.

GloriaandRusshad movedintothevillagetwomonths previouslybuttheystillhadn'tfinishedunpacking.Everyroomin their tinyhome, theofficialpoliceman's residenceinthevillage, wasstillpiledhighwithcardboardboxes.

'Moving houseislikechildbirth,' saidMrsRoss,who hadtwo childrenbyapreviousrelationship.'Ifpeoplecouldrememberjust how painfulitistheywould neverdoittwice.'Sherippedopen anothercardboardboxwithherfingernails.'Whypeopleevermove isamysterytome.'Shedelvedintotheboxandpulledoutagarlic press,anightdress,ahalfusedbarofsoapwrappedinaface   flannel andabox ofstickingplasters.'And here'sanother mystery,' she continued.'Why   is   thatthepeoplewhomakestickingplasterscan neverquitemake   themflesh   coloured?'sheasked.'Don'ttheyknow whatcolour flesh really is? Does anyone actually know someone whose skin is the colour of sticking plasters?' She put the box of sticking plasters down in a colander.

'But those aren't real mysteries,' she went on. She picked up a handful of socks, that had been lying on the kitchen table. 'When I put the washing into the machine this morning I counted the socks. There were fourteen of them. Exactly fourteen. That's seven pairs. I counted them twice. But when I took the socks out there were thirteen. So, what happened to the other sock? My washing machine is a better magician than David Nixon.' She sighed and threw the socks into the colander with the sticking plasters. 'I'm sorry, doctor,' she said. 'I don't expect you've got time for my rants. But with Russ out all day and the children off at school I'm all by myself It's nice to be able to talk to another human being for a change.' She picked up a jumper and moved it. She didn't seem able to keep still.

'That's OK,' I said. 'What can I do for you?'

Shelookedatmeratherblankly.'Whatdoyoumean?'

'Youaskedmetovisit,'Iremindedher.

'Oh yes,'shesaid.'Justhangonaminute.'

Ihungonaminutewhileshedisappearedandmadeaconsiderable amountofnoiseupstairs.Eventuallyshe   camebackdown.Shehad changedand waswearingwhatlookedlikeabrandnewpairofjeans.

'Ineedyouradvice,'shesaid,   turninground.'Doesmybumlook biginthese?'BeforeIcouldreplyshe   addedsomethingelse.'Most peoplewanttoloseweight,'shesaid.'I'vealwayshadtheopposite problem.Ijustcan'tputonanyweight.ButRusslikesplumpwomen andsoI'verecentlybeenmakingarealeffort.'

'Soyouwantyourbumtolookbig?'Isaid,ratherhesitantly.

'Oh   yes,'saidMrsRoss.'Icouldn't   thinkofanyoneelsetoask whowouldtellmethetruth.'

'Well, it's quite big,' I told her. It wasn't easy ignoring the usual social conventions and telling a woman that her bum looked big.

'Oh do you think so?' She smiled.

'Quite big,' I confirmed.

She half turned and peered over her shoulder, trying to see her own bottom. 'I'm so thrilled,' she said.

'Have you always been underweight?' I asked her.

'No,' she said. 'Up until about four years ago I was like everyone else I know. But then I just started to lose weight. I thought I had cancer and I went to my doctor. He said that there was nothing wrong.'

'That was when you lived in London?' She nodded.

'Do you know if they tested your thyroid?'

She frowned. 'Oh, I don't think anyone said anything about that.'

'Let me feel your pulse,' I said.

She offered me her wrist. Her pulse was fast and a little irregular.

'Do you sweat easily?' I asked.

She laughed. 'Oh I sweat a lot!' she said. 'In the hot weather I have to change clothes three times a day.'

'Would you describe yourself as nervous?'

'Russ certainly would,' she said. 'He says I'm like a kitten.'

'Would you pop into the surgery tomorrow?' I said. 'I'll take a blood sample and get a simple test done.'

I didn't say anything but I thought it was quite likely that Gloria Ross had thyrotoxicosis.

* * *

When I left Gloria Ross I drove round to see Dr Brownlow. He insisted on shaking my hand. He smiled. 'I'm so pleased you're opening the practice up again,' he said. 'A village needs five things...'

'...a pub, a shop, a church, a school and a doctor!' I finished for him.

His smile broadened.

'That's what Gilly said at the meeting the other night,' I explained.

Dr Brownlow sighed deeply. 'I'm glad you're back,' he said. 'But they shouldn't have ever closed you down.' He paused and I could see a tear forming in one eye. He poured us both a whisky.

I didn't know what to say. So I said nothing.

We sat in silence for a while. The silences with Dr Brownlow were always comfortable. I never felt I had to speak just for the sake of breaking the stillness.

'I used to be in a hurry all the time when I was young,' said Dr Brownlow. 'But, curiously, now that I am old I feel I can wait. I've had a fair innings and I feel more at peace with myself- though not, I have to admit, with the world. I get cross about the things they're doing to the country. This Beeching thing- closing down half the country's railways- is the most stupid, short-sighted thing I've ever heard of With no railways the roads are going to become unbearable.'

I nodded. I agreed with him. It seemed short-sighted to me too.

'I've had a lot of time to think,' he said. 'Sitting here alone. I read a bit. I look out of the window. But I spend a lot of time thinking.'

I sipped at my whisky. Drinking alcohol in the daytime was becoming a bad habit.

'Have a biscuit,' said Dr Brownlow.

I helped myself to a ginger biscuit.

'How's the pain?'

'I need some more morphine I'm afraid.'

'How much have you been taking?'

I'd brought him a boxful of morphine ampoules and a bundle of syringes.

'Enough.'

'OK. I'll bring some more.' It didn't really matter how much morphine he took. We both knew he wasn't going to live long enough to become an addict. And what did it matter if he did?

'Did you get Miss Johnson to come out of retirement?' I nodded.

'Have you found yourself a nurse?'

'Not yet.'

'You need a district nurse in a village. Your patients can't get into hospital to have their dressings done. And if you have a district nurse you can keep more of your patients at home. Better for them to be at home. And, if only the bureaucrats had any sense they'd realise it saves them money.'

I nodded.

'I always dreamt of opening a cottage hospital,' he said. 'Bilbury could do with a cottage hospital. Just a small one.'

I said it sounded like a wonderful idea but that I doubted if the Government would ever pay for one.

'You could do worse than hire Bradshaw.'

I looked at him, more than slightly surprised.

'As a nurse.'

'As a nurse?' I repeated, sounding stupid.

'You can't have him until I've gone,' he said. 'But he's reliable and surprisingly gentle. He's kind, respectful and caring and he doesn't panic. What more can you ask for in a nurse?'

'I hadn't thought of Bradshaw,' I admitted.

·'Bit old?'

'Bit older than most nurses.'

'He's in good shape,' said Dr Brownlow. 'You hardly notice the Parkinson's Disease.'

I nodded thoughtfully. If I could wait a while Bradshaw would indeed probably make a good, if slightly unusual, district nurse.

'Of course, I've known prettier nurses,' said Dr Brownlow. 'His legs aren't terribly attractive and he has no bosom to speak of'

* * *

Icalled inattheDuckandPuddleonthewayhome.Thumper, andFrankwerehavingadiscussionaboutnewsignswhich Frank wasplanningtoputontothepub'stoiletdoors.

'Theselooknice,'saidFrank,handingmeacataloguetoexamine and pointing to a photograph of two plastic signs. One said 'Pointer' and the other had the word 'Setter' on it.

'Bit corny,' I said.

'Have you seen them before?' asked Frank.

'I think so,' I said.

'We could have these,' suggested Frank, turning the page and pointing to two signs which carried male and female silhouettes. The male silhouette was wearing a top hat and carrying a cane. The female silhouette was wearing a huge ball gown and a large bonnet.

'Very nice,' I said.

'We'll have those then,' said Frank.

'Are you having new lavatories put in?' I asked. The door to the ladies' lavatory led to a single cubicle. The door to the gents was an outside door which led directly into the field behind the pub.

Frank looked at me as though I was barking mad. 'No, I'm not!' he said firmly.

Before I could say anything more Patchy turned up. He was looking pretty grumpy.

'I've just driven back from Exeter,' he told us. 'Some idiot has put up a huge sign warning that they're blasting daily at the quarry.'

'Well, they do!' said Frank. 'They do blast daily.'

'But what's the point of a sign?' demanded Patchy. 'What are you supposed to do when you see it? All these damned signs. They drive me crazy. Why do I want to know that they're blasting daily?'

No one could think of an answer.

I turned to Frank. 'I'll have one of your hot toddies,' I told him.

Thumper and Patchy said they'd have the same.

'What do you put in them?' asked Patchy. 'I don't like to admit this but your hot toddies are the best I've tasted.'

'Trade secret,' said Frank, firmly.

'Oh go on,' Patchy wheedled. 'You know us. Tell us what you put in your hot toddies.'

'If I tell you that you'll make your own and I won't have any customers,' said Frank.

'Don't be daft,' said Thumper. 'We come here for the decor, the company.'

'And the lavatories,' I added.

'Definitely the lavatories,' said Patchy.

'It's a trade secret,' said Frank, firmly. He stomped off to make three hot toddies in the back room so that we couldn't see what he put in them.

'They're always putting up daft signs,' said Thumper. 'I saw one theotherdaysaying'Road LiableToSubsidence'.Whatareyou supposedtodowhenyouseethat?Ididn't know whether togo slowerincasetheroadcollapsedortodrivefastersothatI'dget throughtherequicker.'

Weallthoughtaboutthis.

'There's asignnearPottington thatwarnsofoverheadcables,' said Frank,fromthebackroom.

Thumper turnedoverabeermatandgotoutapen.Wedecided tomakealistofthetenmoststupidroadsigns.

Aftersomethoughtthisiswhatwecameupwith:

1. Lowflyingaircraft
2. Parttimesignals
3. Roadliable tosubsidence
4. Blastingdaily
5. Heavyplantcrossing

6. Mudonroad(Frankwantedtoknowwhytheydidn'tjustclear awaythemudinsteadofgoingtothetroubleandexpenseof puttingupasign)

7. Bewareof falling rocks(whydon't theyjustmovetheloose rocks)

8. Deerforseveralmiles

Our list making (which had now spread to a second beermat) ended when Patchy said he'd seen a notice on Lynmouth beach which said simply 'Do not throw stones at this notice.'

'I don't believe you!' said Frank.

'There is!' insisted Patchy. 'I told two blokes about it a few months ago. They didn't believe me so we all got into a car and drove there.'

'What did you do?'

'It was there. No other warning. No other admonition. Just a large white notice which stated boldly: 'Do not throw stones at this notice.'

'But what's the sign there for?' asked Gilly who had helped Frank carry the hot toddies into the bar.

Patchy shrugged. 'Dunno.'

'What did you do?' asked Frank.

'We all threw a stone at it and left,' said Patchy.

'I'll pop down to the beach next time I'm in Lynmouth and take a look,' said Thumper.

'Don't forget to throw a stone at it,' said Patchy.

'I won't,' said Thumper. 'I'll try anything once.'

'That's a silly saying,' said Frank.

'What is?' asked Patchy.

'I'll try anything once,' replied Frank. We all looked at him.

'Well it is,' he said. 'You would have to be mad to jump out of an aeroplane without a parachute.'

'Don't run before you can walk,' said Thumper. 'That's another silly thing people say. Why would you be able to run if you couldn't walk?'

We thought about it for a minute.

'Put your best foot forward,' I suggested.

'It's the best thing since sliced bread,' said Gilly. 'What's so brilliant about sliced bread?'

'He knows which side his bread is buttered,' offered Patchy.

'You'd have to be a complete moron not to know, wouldn't you?'

'Don't take it personally,' Frank suggested. 'How else should you take it? Whatever it is.'

'It will be in the last place you look,' said Thumper. 'If you've found it then you stop looking don't you?'

'She wants to have her cake and eat it,' said Gilly. 'What good would it be if you had cake and didn't eat it?'

As the discussion continued I looked around the pub, and thought back on my first day's work.

It occurred to me that working as a country GP is a uniquely satisfying way to earn a living. And it also occurred to me that it is a rather curious form of employment; a job perfectly suited to a loner, an individual.

How many people have the power of life and death over their customers? It is difficult to think of many jobs where the daily responsibilities are greater. And yet it is also difficult to think of many jobs where the opportunities for job satisfaction are greater.

It would, I thought, be a tragedy if the bureaucrats succeeded in taking over general practice as they were threatening to do and in the way that they had already taken over the hospitals. I wondered how general practice would look in a quarter of a century, at the turn of the millennium.

I looked around again and suddenly realised that I was almost certainly the only person in the pub to have seen more than half the other customers utterly naked.

It was a sobering thought.

CHAPTER 12

Bythetime   IgottoDrBrownlow'stherainwascomingdown   so
fastthatthewindscreenwipershadmoreorlessgiven   up.Iparked
thecarasclosetoDrBrownlow'shouseasIcouldandranthecouple
ofyardsthatremained.EvensoIwassoakedbythetimeBradshaw
hadletmein.Ishook myself,morelikeadogthanadoctor.

'Canyourememberwhenyoufirstdecidedtobecomeadoctor?'
DrBrownlowasked.Helooked tired and, if possible, thinner than ever.
He was wasting away at a frightening rate.

'I can.' I could remember it as if it were yesterday.

'Pour us both a drink. You look as if you need one.'

I poured out two whiskies. I added water to mine since I still had
to do an evening surgery, but not to the one I'd poured for Dr
Brownlow.

'I was eleven and visiting an elderly aunt with my parents,' I
continued. 'She was a live-in housekeeper who looked after a
bachelor. He lived in a beautiful thatched cottage. I remember the
garden. I'd never seen so many flowers. Roses. And a pond with
lilies. Going through the gate was like walking into a painting by
Monet. I don't know what her employer did for a living but he was
obviously quite rich. My aunt had made tea for us and while she was
showing us around the garden her employer appeared. I can't
remember his name. Actually, I can't remember her name either. He
wandered over to introduce himself and asked me the question
grown ups always used to ask children of the age I was at the time.
He asked me what I wanted to do when I grew up. I didn't have to
think about it. I was, I suspect, a rather strange child. I used to visit
the public library every week and bring home as many books as I
could carry on my bicycle. Half of them were medical books and the
other half were legal books. I had discovered that the library had a
vast collection of old trial reports. I can't imagine why. I used to
read them in the same way that other boys read comics containing
stories about Dan Dare. I told him that there were only two things I
wanted to be: a doctor or a lawyer. It never occurred to me then that

I might not be the one to choose what I did. I confessed that I wasn't sure which of these I wanted to be.'

Dr Brownlow, listening carefully, sipped at his whisky and said nothing.

'My aunt's employer nodded sagely at this precocious selection.

'Easy to choose,' he told me in a deep, rich baritone voice. I can still hear him. 'If you become a doctor you will spend your life helping people and making some of them happier than they were. If you become a lawyer you will spend your life making people miserable."

'So, not being a sadist, you chose medicine?'

'Absolutely.' I sipped at the whisky I'd poured myself 'Remarkable isn't it? Someone I met once and with whom I exchanged no more words than I've just told you changed my life more than anyone else I've ever met.' I sipped at my whisky. 'Now, it's your turn.'

'My parents were very poor,' began Dr Brownlow. 'My father once smashed his big toe with a hammer because we needed the compensation. But in some ways I had a very satisfying childhood. It was often hard but I learned the values of self-sufficiency. My father could mend his own boots or repair a leaky bucket with just a few tools he kept in his shed. He never hired anyone to do anything with a brush or a screwdriver. I never saw a workman in the house. My father could build a dry stone wall or a chimney, mend a bicycle or dig a well. He could mend everything we had. If the mangle broke he'd mend it. If the clock wasn't working he could mend that too. He could repair chairs and I once saw him put a new leg onto our kitchen table. When he'd finished you couldn't tell the difference between the leg he'd made and the three original legs. Poverty, to us then, was a misfortune, not a sin and we knew that real poverty had nothing to do with money but was more to do with quality of life. I lived in a village, much like Bilbury, and we pitied the people living in the cities, even though many of them might have had more money than we had. We didn't need the outside world or want anything it could offer us. We had our own water from a well in the garden and we grew our own vegetables on a small plot of land behind the house. My mother could spin and weave. She had an old spinning machine in the bedroom and she would collect bits of sheep's wool from the hedges and make us jumpers and scarves for Christmas and birthdays. The only person I envied was a boy whose parents kept corn and wheat in bins, salt beef in a barrel and a smoked ham in the chimney. They could have survived for months without any outside help. We were poor but we had home-made cider and several types of wine. I had an aunt who made elderflower wine and my grandmother made parsnip wine.'

'People speak of the industrial revolution as though it was something wonderful,' continued Dr Brownlow. 'But it put families into terraced houses and factories and chained them to grimy factory benches and took away people's pride and joy and independence and enthusiasm and replaced the missing joy and pride with boredom and dullness and insecurity and fear. They built schools it is true but they were only to prepare children for working long days in factories and to keep them out of the way so that mothers could work too. The industrial revolution was never a revolution of or for the people but a revolution for the rich. The Tolpuddle martyrs were right and more people should have listened to them. People sneer at the Luddites but they had a point.'

I enjoyed listening to Dr Brownlow. He was kind and wise: two things which don't often go together.

'I had a rich uncle. He was very kind to us. He and my aunt didn't have any children of their own. He gave my parents money so that we could stay on at school and try and get to university. He was a very generous man. He told my brother and I that as soon as one of us turned 17 he would buy a car. I remember him saying it. The way he said it made it sound as though he wasn't sure which one of us would get to 17 first. But I knew that since I was eighteen months older than my brother I stood a pretty decent chance of getting there first. True to his word my uncle bought me a car. He taught me to drive in the local cemetery. He said I would be unlikely to hurt anyone there. He did more than he promised; he did the same thing for my brother when he got to 17. We were the only boys we knew who had cars of our own.'

'I needed money to pay for petrol and during the holidays one summer he got me a job with a friend of his who was a doctor but who had a number of small businesses. I did errands, delivered things, drove him or his wife around occasionally. We talked and I ended up wanting to be a doctor too.'

His glass was empty. I got up and refilled it for him. He nodded his thanks.

'I'm glad I practised when I did,' he said thoughtfully. 'When I started out doctors wrote out prescriptions in Latin, patients were polite and respectful and had faith. We didn't have so many wonderful medicines but we didn't kill so many people either.' He sighed and looked at me. 'You'll see big changes in your lifetime.'

'What sort of changes?'

'The first is that by the turn of the century the bureaucrats will be running medicine,' said Dr Brownlow quietly. 'The result will be a constant state of war between the medical profession on one side and the politicians and the bureaucrats on the other. Bureaucrats have destroyed the doctor's authority because they want the power. The tragedy is that in taking away the authority they are also taking away the willingness to take responsibility. Doctors may fight but they won't win, of course. The biggest losers will be patients.'

'The end result will be that .GPs will stop providing 24 hour cover. In the end GPs will end up working the sort of hours civil servants work. And that will destroy medicine as you and I know it because patients need to see the same doctor every time when they are ill. If doctors work the average working week of 40 or so hours then that would mean someone who was dying might see four or five different doctors in a week. That would kill a lot of patients and it would be the death of medicine as you and I know it. When that happens continuity of care will be replaced by chaos.'

'Oh, I can't believe that will ever happen!' I said.

'I fear it will,' said Dr Brownlow. 'The next thing that will happen will be that the lawyers will get their claws into medicine too. People are becoming increasingly litigious. And that can only get worse not better. If Isaac Newton were alive today, and he sat under a tree and an apple fell on his head he wouldn't think 'Aha, gravity!' he'd think 'Aha, lawsuit!' and instead of having invented the theory of gravity he'd have gouged five guineas plus costs out of the owner of the orchard. I have a friend in America who's a doctor. He's retiring early because he's been sued four times in the last six years. He's a good doctor but he can't take any more. He's retiring to open a nursing home for the elderly though I think that could bring him just as many problems. Sadly, I think it will be the good doctors who suffer. The bad ones will simply set up companies and protect themselves. The good doctors won't be prepared and they'll be the ones who will be destroyed. There will come a time when people will believe that everything bad that happens to them is someone else's fault. Doctors will become terribly defensive.'

'Do you really believe that will happen?'

'I do. It won't affect everyone. But it doesn't have to affect everyone.'

We sat in stillness for a while.

'And the final thing that will change,' continued Dr Brownlow, 'will be that doctors will lose control of the information they use. Knowledge is being redistributed but it was always knowledge that gave doctors their power. Now patients have some of that power, and so doctors have lost some of theirs. Everything has changed. There are news reports about new treatments published in the newspapers before they appear in the medical journals. The result is that patients know about new discoveries before doctors do. Researchers promote their discoveries to politicians and to the press in order to get bigger grants. But ordinary people don't know how to differentiate between the good, the bad and the deadly. And the information they are fed is biased and controlled by people who aren't as disinterested as doctors would be. If people find a way to share information between computers, as they say they will, then things will just get worse. Patients will think they're better off but they won't be. They'll just be exploited more efficiently. And they'll think they don't need doctors.' He sighed. 'And I suspect that nurses will want to have degrees. Just caring won't be enough for them and they'll believe that only degrees will give them status and power and money. And once they have degrees they'll want to start prescribing drugs and performing surgery and the dividing line between doctors and nurses will get blurred because the politicians will realise that its cheaper to train and hire a nurse than it is to train and hire a doctor and so everything will get worse.'

I thought (and hoped) that he was being far too pessimistic but I didn't tell him.

'I'm glad I won't be here to see it all happen,' said Dr Brownlow

CHAPTER 13

Therewerefourteenpatientsintheeveningsurgerythatday.Three ofthem, Samuel Houghton,Harry Burroughsand Gilly Parsons, thelandladyfromtheDuckandPuddle,weresufferingfromstrange muscle cramps. Counting Nigel Perkins that made four. I had no idea what was going on butitwasclearlysomethingspecifictothe village.

'Whatdoyouthinkitcouldbe?'askedPatsywhenwe'dfinished dinner thatevening.

'I don't have the faintest,' I admitted. 'It could be something in the drinking water.'

'Samuel Houghton and Harry Burroughs both get their drinking water from private wells,' said Patsy who had lived in the village all her life.

'What about Nigel Perkins? Where does his drinking water come from?'

'He's on the mains. He gets town water.'

'So it can't be a problem caused by anything in the drinking water,' I said. I thought some more. 'But there must be some common factor.'

'Three of them are male,' Patsy pointed out.

'And one of them isn't,' I said. I sighed. This was proving to be quite a puzzle.

'So, what are you going to do?' asked Patsy.

'I'm going to call round and see them all tomorrow,' I said. 'I'll ask them some more questions. See if I can spot a link.'

'I bet it will be a drug they're all taking,' said Patsy. 'You always say that drug side effects are now a major cause of illness.'

'But none of them are taking anything!' I said. 'I did ask them all.'

It was a real puzzle.

CHAPTER 14

Patsywasbeginning tobloomandthematernity dressesshehad boughtintheveryearlydaysofherpregnancywerenowessential. Shelookedwonderful,andinsistedthatshefeltthatwaytoo.

In view of the fact that Bilbury is some distance from Barnstaple, and I was the only doctor in the village, we had discussed the possibility of Patsy staying with friends in Barnstaple during the last week or so of the pregnancy. In the end she decided not to.

'You've got to stay in Bilbury,' she said. 'And if I stay in Barnstaple who will look after you and answer the phone and take messages if you have to go out to see a patient?'

Having someone to answer the telephone is as essential to a country GP as a stethoscope. Since I had opened up my practice again we had relied on Mr and Mrs Parfitt, our gardener and his wife, the former Miss Hargreaves, to answer the telephone when we were out. Mr Parfitt, who had a grey curly beard, always wore a floppy tweed hat that was two sizes too small for him and looked a bit like a pixie, once worked in a bank in London but had given it all up to live a simple life in the country. Miss Hargreaves had been a spinster and a schoolteacher for many years before she and Mr Parfitt had fallen in love. Miss Hargreaves was an avid reader who kept all her books segregated by sex. She kept all the male authors in a bookcase in the living room and all the female authors in a bookcase in the bedroom. She was the only person in the village to call Thumper by his real name.

It sounds rather grand to say that we had a gardener. It wasn't quite like that.

The Parfitts had made a wonderful home for themselves in the flat above the stables at Bilbury Grange. Mr Parfitt looked after the Bilbury Grange garden and in return we let him and his wife have the flat free of any rent. We also paid him a small wage and let him have whatever food he wanted from the produce which was grown in the garden. Since Bilbury Grange had a large garden, which produced far more food than Patsy and I could possibly eat, this was a splendidly symbiotic relationship. We all benefited. And we all ate a healthy diet of fresh potatoes, carrots, broccoli, Brussels sprouts, peas, runner beans, broad beans, onions, garlic, cabbage, cauliflower, apples, pears, plums, redcurrants, strawberries, blackberries and blackcurrants. We also had more different herbs than I'd ever heard of.

Mr Parfitt also cut logs and collected twigs for our fireplaces and for the Aga and if there was any trouble with our water supply it was he who checked that the spring wasn't blocked and that the water pipes which brought water to the house weren't leaking.

It was with his help that we had made Bilbury Grange very self-sufficient.

Mrs Parfitt did a little cleaning and cooking for us (she made wonderful bread and a home-made wine that had quite a kick to it) and helped her husband in the garden. We had somehow found a tactful way to decline her help with the ironing after she had ironed my best trousers without first removing the banana which I had carelessly left in the pocket.

Selfishly, I was relieved and delighted by Patsy's decision. This was not because I wanted her to be at Bilbury Grange to look after me and answer the telephone but because I didn't want us to be parted for an hour more than was absolutely vital.

But, inevitably, the knowledge that we wouldn't have to separate, even temporarily, came at a price.

Patsy was being looked after by an obstetrician and a midwife at the hospital in Barnstaple and if all went according to plan, and the baby had the courtesy to give ample warning of his or her arrival, I would drive Patsy to the hospital, take her to the ward, and settle myself down, in the time honoured traditional way, with a cup of coffee and an eleven-year-old copy of*Reader'sDigest.*

Neither of us wanted me to be there at the birth itself (it had recently become extremely fashionable for fathers to sit in the delivery room and to watch the baby being born - a thought that made both Patsy and I shudder) but both of us wanted me to be nearby.

'I want you to walk in and find me sitting up in bed, in a clean nightie and with the baby in my arms,' said Patsy. 'I want my hair combed and my lipstick looking fresh.'

The plan was that before leaving Bilbury I would telephone Miss Johnson who would drive to Bilbury Grange and answer the telephone for me. She would then telephone me at the hospital if there were any emergencies. If necessary, Mrs Parfitt would also help out with answering the telephone.

That was the plan.

It sounded simple and foolproof

Patsy had an appointment at the hospital and left early that morning. Her sister Adrienne had offered to drive her there.

'All the best, sweetheart,' I said, through the open passenger door window of Adrienne's car.

'Everything will be fine,' she promised me. 'Good luck with your mystery! I hope you find the answer.'

I waved them goodbye and then went into the house to start my morning surgery.

I didn't have to wait until the end of the surgery, as I had expected, to start reconsidering the mystery of the strange muscle cramps.

The fourth patient that morning, Jennifer Orsey, had exactly the same problem.

Miss Orsey was quite a character.

Now well into her sixties she had been retired for two years but she was well-known in North Devon for the shop she had run in Barnstaple Called 'Orseys for Corsets', it had been the place all the well-dressed women ofDevon visited for their corsetry and indeed, their lingerie. Miss Orsey had once told me that she had customers from as far afield as London and Manchester.

The walls of her shop had been decorated with blown up black and white prints of a beautiful curvaceous young woman wearing nothing but corsets and stockings.

'She looks like you,' I'd once said, when accompanying Patsy into her shop. 'Is she a relation?'

Miss Orsey had smiled and shaken her head.

'It's you!' said Patsy, turning away from a display of silk slips and camisoles and looking at one of the photographs.

Miss Orsey had nodded. 'It is,' she admitted. 'I was regarded as quite a looker in those days. I couldn't afford to hire a model for the clothes so I did the modelling myself.'

Miss Orsey lived in a beautiful thatched cottage and was surrounded by an extraordinary mixture of furniture. Everything in the cottage was old, worn and used. Some of it was downright ugly. I'd once commented on her eclectic taste.

'Every piece of furniture in my house holds a memory and has a meaning for me,' she had explained. 'Try me,' she had said. 'Ask me about any piece of furniture in this room.'

'That one,' I said, pointing to a huge, oak bookcase.

'That's easy. It was my uncle's. He bought it at a house auction in Goodleigh. It used to belong to a Member of Parliament and six years after my uncle bought it he found all sorts of papers in a secret compartment. Old copies of Hansard and memos scrawled on House of Commons notepaper. My uncle knew I admired it and he left it to me in his Will.'

'The sofa,' I said, pointing to a rather tom and threadbare sofa in front of the fireplace.

'I bought that with my winnings after the 1949 Grand National,' she said. 'The cats have clawed it and scratched it and it needs recovering but I don't have the heart to change it. Every time I look at it I'm reminded of all my cats. Nine of them. Every single one loved that sofa.'

Each time I visited her at home she told me the story of another piece of her furniture.

With the addition of Miss Orsey, I now had five patients with the same symptoms. And I still couldn't put my finger on the problem. I was beginning to worry that I had been away from medicine for too long.

'How long have you had the cramps?' I asked her.

'Three or four days.'

'Any other symptoms?'

She shook her head. 'I've been a bit worried about it,' she said.

'My father had a blocked artery in his leg.'

'Intermittent claudication?'

'That's right. That's what they called it.'

'Does exercise make it worse?' She shook her head.

I checked her leg. Her pulse was good.

'It's not intermittent claudication,' I told her.

'Could it be a deep vein thrombosis?'

'That was my worry,' I told her. 'But a deep vein thrombosis is caused by a clot in the leg. And the leg is usually swollen.' I took a tape measure out of the drawer of my desk and compared the circumference of her painful calf with the circumference of her healthy calf. The painful calf wasn't swollen.

90

'I don't think it's a deep vein thrombosis,' I told her. She looked relieved. I looked at her medical records. 'You're not taking anything are you? No medication?'

'Just aspirin,' she answered.

'What for?'

'I've been getting a bit of arthritis in my left knee,' she said. 'You told me to take soluble aspirin for it.'

I looked through her medical records, went back a couple of years and found the note in my own handwriting.

'Have you been taking anything except aspirin?'

'No,' she said firmly.

'Nothing at all?'

'No.'

'And you take how many?'

'Two tablets three times a day. It says on the packet that you can take two tablets up to four times a day.'

I couldn't stop thinking about what Patsy had reminded me.

Side effects are a major cause of illness. And it isn't just the main constituent of a drug which can cause problems. Drug side effects can (and usually do) cause problems when you least expect them. None of us is immune. And both doctors and patients are usually far too slow to consider drug side effects when they are looking for a cause for new symptoms. We are all likely to forget or under-estimate the danger. I had even formulated my very own law, (and called it Coleman's Law) which stated that when a patient who is being treated by a doctor developed new symptoms then the new symptoms should, unless proved otherwise, be assumed to have been caused by the treatment for the first disease.

Somehow I knew that this problem had to be drug related. But the only drug I'd been able to link into this problem was aspirin. And although aspirin can cause quite a number of side effects it doesn't usually cause muscle cramps. It was inconceivable that it should suddenly start causing muscle cramps among five separate patients - all living in one small village.

And then, purely out of desperation, I asked if I could see the packet containing the aspirin Miss Orsey was taking. I don't know why I did this. She opened her handbag and took out a packet of aspirin. It wasn't a brand I'd ever seen before. There was a sticky label on it carrying the words Aspirin and the usual warnings and recommendations about dosage. I pulled at the comer of the label and peeled it off. I could now read the printing on the box. Or at least I could have done if it had been in English. The printing on the box was in French.

'Where did you get this?' I asked her.

'Peter Marshall's shop,' she replied. 'He's got a special offer on them. I don't know where he got them from.' She frowned. 'Are they all right, doctor?' She paused. 'I rather like them,' she said. 'They fizz when you put them in water. Loads of bubbles. And they taste quite pleasant. Not bitter in the way that aspirin usually is.'

'I don't know if they are all right,' I said. 'But I want you to stop taking them for the time being. I'll pop round and see you later and tell you more.' I stood up. 'There are one or two other patients all with similar symptoms to you. I want to see if they're also taking aspirin they bought from Peter Marshall.'

* * *

I couldn't wait for the surgery to end that morning. I was desperate to try and get at the bottom of the new medical mystery.

As soon as I'd seen the last patient, and signed a few letters Miss Johnson had typed for me, I rushed out and drove round to Nigel Perkin's home. Of the other patients with muscle cramps he lived closest.

'Show me the aspirin you've been taking!' I said, bursting into his kitchen.

He looked at me, frowning. 'How did you know I've been taking aspirin?'

'Where is it?'

'It's in the kitchen,' he told me. 'By the kettle,' he shouted after me, as I headed for the kitchen. 'It's only aspirin!' he shouted. 'It's not medicine.'

And there, by the kettle, was a packet of aspirin. A packet identical to the one Jennifer Orsey had shown me.

'Did you get this from Peter Marshall?'

'Yes. Is there something wrong with it?'

'I don't know,' I told him. 'But stop taking it until I get back to you, will you?'

From there I went to see Samuel Houghton, Harry Burrows and Gilly Parsons at the Duck and Puddle.

They were all taking aspirin from Peter Marshall's shop.

I'd found the link.

I felt as proud as Sherlock Holmes at the conclusion of a difficult case. Except that I still didn't know why the aspirin sold by Peter Marshall should be causing such a strange problem.

I carefully examined the packet which Harry Burrows had produced. It had been prepared and packaged in France and was undoubtedly something Peter had managed to import at a rather special price. But the pack wasn't out-of-date and the aspirin tablets themselves hadn't started to break down in the way tablets can when they are old.

But when I checked the packet I discovered that, in addition to the aspirin, the tablets contained sodium bicarbonate. The bicarbonate was there to help the tablets dissolve quickly. And there was enough sodium bicarbonate in the tablets to cause the alkalosis.

And the cramps.

'What's the problem?' asked Mr Burrows.

'It isn't really a problem,' I told him. 'These aspirin tablets are really best taken occasionally - when you've got a headache, for example. They contain sodium bicarbonate to make them fizz when you put them in water and so when you take more than three or four in a day you might develop cramps.'

'The aspirin is causing my cramps?'

I nodded.

'But I often take aspirin,' said Mr Burrows. 'I've never had this problem before.'

'I don't mind betting that you've never taken this brand of aspirin before!'

'No, that's true,' admitted Mr Burrows.

'Put these in a cupboard and use them for headaches and other occasional aches and pains,' I told him. 'But for your arthritis take ordinary plain old soluble aspirin. It'll be safer. It isn't the aspirin that has caused your cramps-it's something they've put in with the aspirin. You've taken so much sodium bicarbonate that it has caused a metabolic alkalosis - a fairly common cause of cramps.'

'So do I have to stop taking aspirin?'

'Just stop this brand,' I told him again. 'You can take ordinary soluble aspirin.'

I went round to the other patients and told them the same thing. They were as relieved as I was that the puzzle was solved.

And then I went to see Peter Marshall.

'There's nothing wrong with them, is there?' he asked, clearly worried.

'Nothing wrong with them at all,' I reassured him. 'But when you sell them to people make sure they know that they shouldn't take them too often. No more than two a day. If they need a bigger dose then they should take ordinary soluble aspirin.'

Peter held up a packet of ordinary aspirin.

'These?'

'Absolutely.'

'Don't worry,' he said. 'I won't be selling any more of the French stuff. They were quite popular, and I got them very cheap from the wholesaler, but I've run out now and I won't be ordering them again.'

'That's very public spirited of you!' I told him. This was a new side to Peter. A caring, more thoughtful side than the one most people knew.

'I don't want my customers developing cramps,' said Peter, rather spoiling his new caring image. 'If they've got cramp they can't get out and walk to my shop, can they?'

* * *

That evening I was having dinner when the front doorbell rang.

I was exhausted and tempted not to answer it. But a country GP doesn't have that luxury. With a sigh I got up from the table and answered the door.

It was Frank Parsons, the landlord from the Duck and Puddle.

'Come in, Frank!' I said.

'No thanks,' he said. 'I must get back. I just wanted to bring you this.' He handed me an envelope. I looked at it. 'What's this?'

'Just a small thank you for solving Gilly's problem,' said Frank, turning away and heading back for his car. Bilbury Grange isn't far from the Duck and Puddle but Frank isn't a great walker.

'You don't have to...' I started. 'This isn't money is it?'

Frank, halfway into his car, looked up. 'Don't be daft,' he said.

'I wouldn't give you money, would I?'

I smiled, as he drove out of the drive and headed back to the pub.

'Who was that?' asked Patsy, when I got back to the dining table.

'Frank,' I said. I held up the envelope. 'He brought this.'

'What is it?'

'Dunno. Frank said it's a thank you for sorting out Gilly's problem. She was one of the patients suffering from aspirin induced cramps.'

'Open it then.'

I opened the envelope and took out a scruffy piece of lilac notepaper which had been folded in two. I unfolded the paper.

Here is what was written on it:

Frank's Recipe for Spiced Hot Toddy (Serving For One)

1. Three table spoonfuls of the best whisky you can find
2. One teaspoonful of honey
3. A squeeze of lemon juice
4. Three cloves
5. A teaspoonful of cinnamon
6. Half a slice of fresh orange
7. A pinch of nutmeg
8. Top up with boiling water

Stir with a cinnamon stick and serve in a Russian tea glass.

'What on earth is it?' asked Patsy.

'It's Frank's recipe for hot toddy.'

'My Dad's been trying to get that recipe from him for twenty years,' said Patsy. 'That's the biggest 'thank you' Frank could give you.'

'I know,' I said. 'I'm honoured.'

I folded the paper once again, put it back in its envelope and slipped it into my jacket pocket.

Sometimes there are wonderful perks associated with being a country doctor.

CHAPTER 15

SpringburstintoBilburylikea   manonahorsewithanurgent
messagetodeliver.

On Tuesday night we went to bed and said goodnight to a grey,
cold world; the weary fag-end of an interminable, harsh winter
which had long overstayed its welcome.

On Wednesday morning we awoke to what seemed to be an
entirely different world. It was as though a benevolent and
understanding god had lifted up Bilbury Grange and spirited it away
to a land of sunshine and greenery. The greyness had gone and had
been replaced with promises of summer months to come.

Looking out into the garden I saw buds bursting into life and
birds singing light operetta. The rough lawn around the trees was
studded with daffodils. Wordsworth would have been in ecstasy.
Soon the birds would be building nests and the cherry blossom trees
would be sprinkling the garden with nature's pink confetti.

And with Easter, the daffodils and the sunshine came the promise
of the first visitors of the year to Bilbury Grange.

If you live somewhere pleasant then it is an unavoidable fact of
life that friends, relatives, half-forgotten classmates, vague
acquaintances and even people who don't like you very much, and
from whom you hardly ever hear, will always want to come and stay
with you.

Mortimer Gregory, a friend I'd known when we were both
medical students (and who, therefore, fell into the half-forgotten
classmates category) telephoned one evening to say that he and his
family were driving down to Cornwall to stay in a cottage his wife's
family had owned for years. I hadn't heard Mortimer's voice for
years and when he told me who was calling I had difficulty
reconciling the smooth sounding Mortimer Gregory who was on the
telephone with the rough-edged Mortimer Gregory with whom I'd
once shared a flat.

'Where are you? What are you doing? What's been happening to
you?' I demanded, firing off questions in the way people do when

they hear from someone they used to know well but haven't seen for years.

'I practice complimentary medicine,' he replied. 'Married. Two kids. Mortgage so big it makes my eyes water when I think about it.'

'You mean you're doing acupuncture and stuff like that?' I asked, surprised.

'Oh, good heavens, no!' laughed Mortimer. 'That's complementary medicine spelt with an 'e'. Load of rubbish. I mean I get up when patients come into my consulting room and I say 'Good morning Mrs Davenport, you're looking lovely today.' He laughed again. 'It makes them feel good about themselves and good about me. Basic principle of medicine for money.'

'You're in private practice?'

'Sort of. Officially I'm the youngest NHS consultant in the area but that doesn't take up much time. Just helps give me a bit of credibility and attract the patients. I've got consulting rooms in a posh part of town. They cost me a fortune. And a posh receptionist whose daddy owns half of Cheshire, and who looks a bit like the horse she rides every weekend, but who sounds really classy when she answers the phone.'

I murmured something suitably appreciative. He didn't ask about me and so I didn't tell him anything.

'Anyway, we thought it would be nice if we could drop in and say 'hello',' he said. 'We're driving down from the north so we'd welcome a bit of a break.'

'Would you like to stay the night?' I asked, already knowing the answer before I asked the question. Bilbury is hardly on the direct route from the north of England to Cornwall but I hadn't succeeded in persuading myself that Mortimer wanted to make the detour just to see me. Staying with us would be considerably cheaper than finding hotel accommodation for the night.

'Gosh, that would be very decent of you,' said Mortimer, feigning surprise and doing it rather badly.

* * *

'You'll love him,' I told Patsy. 'He's quite a character. He and I once rented a tiny two-bedroomed cottage in the north of Scotland. We were going to spend a week walking round the Scottish countryside. Deer stalking, that sort of thing.'

'But you don't shoot?' said Patsy, surprised.

'Oh no, we weren't going to shoot anything. Just see if we could spot a deer. You know I've always been a great fan of the book *John MacNab* by John Buchan?'

Patsy nodded. She had grown to share my love of all things Buchan. *John MacNab*, not as well-known as The Thirty Nine Steps but in my view by far Buchan's best book, is a magnificent story of a politician, a banker and a lawyer who add missing zest to their lives by stalking deer and salmon on huge and magnificent Scottish estates. The book is, perhaps, most notable for its marvellously evocative descriptions of the wild Scottish highlands.

'We got to the cottage late one night,' I told her, 'dumped our bags in the tiny hallway and went straight to bed. We'd been driving in Mortimer's old van for fourteen hours. His van was a terrible wreck. I remember the steering wheel used to come off. If he had anyone new in the van Mortimer would remove the steering wheel and hand it to the passenger asking them if they wanted to drive for a while. There was a hole in the floor and you could see the road rushing by underneath.'

'We were woken up about two hours after we'd arrived by someone coming into the cottage. It turned out that the person who owned it had made a mistake and had double booked the place. The result was that we found ourselves sharing the cottage with a couple from Basildon. They had two fast developing teenage daughters.

Since the cottage really was in the middle of nowhere, and there was absolutely nowhere else for any of us to move to, we decided to divide up the cottage. The family from Basildon had the upstairs and the living room and we had one room downstairs. We shared the bathroom and the kitchen. When they found out that we were medical students they built a barrier at the top of the stairs to protect their daughters. In fact although we were there for a week we didn't see either of the daughters at all after that first night.'

'Wise parents,' said Patsy.

I ignored the remark and continued. 'The father was a fisherman. He went out every day and every night he came back with a variety of fish. He always pretended he'd caught them himself But we were driving near a small bay one day when we spotted him buying a dozen mackerel from a travelling fishmonger selling out of the back of a scruffy Ford van. He didn't see us. When he came back that night he showed us the twelve mackerel he'd caught.'

'Did you tell him that you knew he'd bought them and not caught them?'

'Oh no! The guy was a complete pratt but we wouldn't have embarrassed him.'

'How many of them are coming?' asked Patsy when I'd finished telling her the story of my Scottish adventure with Mortimer.

'Just Mortimer, his wife and their two boys,' I said. 'And they'll only be here for one night.'

'That's fine,' said Patsy. 'I can get the two spare bedrooms at the back of the house ready for them.'

The one thing we weren't short of in Bilbury Grange was space and I found myself looking forward to Mortimer's visit.

CHAPTER 16

ThelastpersonIsawinthesurgerythenextmorning unwittingly reminded
methatineverypracticetherearesomepatientswho
are,forwantofabetterdescription,   usuallyreferredtoasindog
Latinasbeing 'dolor gluteus maximus'. Roughly translated this
egregiouspieceof   Latin   nonsensedenotespatientswhoare'apain
inthebackside'.

Lieutenant Colonel Harper was a pompous and humourless man
who suffered from what Patsy and I described as 'irritable person
syndrome'. He was, without a shadow of a doubt, a pain in the
backside.

His one redeeming feature was his loyalty to his wife. The
Colonel was a widower and still wore a black tie every day even
though his wife had been dead for nineteen years.

'She said she chose a military man because she wanted a husband
who could cook, sew and make the bed,' he used to say, occasionally
adding that she had also told him that she thought that military men
were better suited to marriage because they were accustomed to
taking orders.

He had a nose like a vulture's beak and an exaggerated limp
which he said was the result of an old rugby injury but which was, as
I alone knew, a consequence of a large bunion on his left foot. A
'recurrence of an old sporting injury' sounds rather romantic and is
always good for a few oohs and aahs of sympathy in the pub. A
bunion, on the other hand, is likely only to attract sniggers since it is
the sort of health problem usually associated with women who have,
through vanity, chosen to compress their feet into narrow, high-
heeled shoes. I think the Colonel might have feigned a war injury if
he'd known enough about wars to create a believable story. He had,
however, spent his entire military career at an army camp in northern
England and was, therefore, a military man without either a fund of
old war stories or an old wound and I suppose he felt he needed
something to give himself an aura of manly respectability. His
military career had been spent supervising the maintenance of

military vehicles. I don't think he'd ever travelled more than twenty miles away from the camp on army business.

I obviously didn't mind the nose and I didn't much mind his minor deceit with the bunion.

But what did sometimes get under my skin was the fact that the Colonel was one of those people whose problems are always worse, much worse, than anyone else's. Tell him that you had broken your leg and he would tell you that he had once broken two at once - both compound fractures. Tell him that you were feeling under the weather with the flu and he would insist on telling you lengthy stories about the many usually fatal illnesses he had succeeded in overcoming. Tell him that you had just got back from a trip abroad and you'd spent an hour and a half fighting your way through over-officious customs officials and he'd insist on topping your story with an account of how he'd once spent half a day trying to find a piece of missing army paperwork for a faulty tank.

He was, to be honest with you, an extraordinarily easy man to dislike. Even my wife Patsy, who was the most tolerant of women, had confessed that she found him rather difficult to stomach. If this made him sound like a fatty meat pie then the analogy was well founded because that's exactly what he looked like.

'I've got a brain tumour,' he told me, lurching into the surgery and collapsing into a chair.

'What makes you say that?' I asked.

'Dizzy,' he said. He reached out and grabbed hold of the edge of my desk. 'It feels like I'm on a ship.'

'Are you getting headaches?'

'No.'

'Any other symptoms?'

'No.'

'Just dizzy?'

'Isn't that enough?' he demanded. 'I keep falling over. People think I'm drunk.'

I examined him, peered into his ears and did some simple tests.

'You've got labyrinthitis,' I told him eventually. I wrote out a prescription. 'Fortunately, it's quite mild.'

'No brain tumour?'

'No sign at all of a brain tumour.'

'What's the prescription for?' he demanded. He didn't seem in the slightest bit relieved by my diagnosis.

'A course of antibiotics and some tablets that should help relieve the dizziness,' I told him. 'Have you got someone who can go to the chemists for you?'

'No. I'll go myself,' he said.

'How did you get here?' I asked.

'Drove myself in the Bentley. 1956 S1. Best car ever made.'

'A friend of mine at medical school had one of those,' I told him. 'Bought it at an auction. He lived in it for a week when he was thrown out of his flat.'

'Why was he thrown out of his flat?'

'He hadn't paid the rent. Said he couldn't afford to keep the Bentley on the road and pay rent.'

The Colonel snorted. I couldn't tell whether it was a snort of approval or disapproval. 'Beautiful cars. Mine has the two-speed windscreen wipers,' he said. 'First model to have them.'

'You shouldn't be driving anything,' I told him. 'I'll drive you home.' I picked up the prescription, tore it in half and threw it into the waste bin. Then I stood up, opened a cupboard behind me and took out two packets of tablets. I wrote out two labels, stuck the labels on the packets and handed them to him.

'What are these?' he demanded.

'Medicines. It'll save you going to the chemist,' I told him.

'What do I owe you?' I told him.

'Is that all?'

'I can charge you more if you like.'

He glowered at me, pulled out a handful of change, picked out the right money and put it on the desk.

Much to his disapproval I made him sit in the waiting room until I'd finished dealing with the messages Miss Johnson had accumulated during the surgery and then I put my bicycle into his car boot and drove him home. He lived in a large cottage set so far back from the road that I'd never noticed it before.

There was a horseshoe pinned up over the front door. He saw me looking at it as I escorted him from the car into the house.

'I'm told you don't have to believe in it for it to work,' he said rather gruffly. 'Can't do any harm anyway.'

'It would do you plenty of harm if it fell on your head,' I said. He smiled at that.

'Just rest for a few days,' I told him.

'There is one thing,' he said. 'Do you have a minute before you go?'

'Literally just a minute or so,' I told him. 'I must get back.'

'Do you need a pee?'

I was startled at this. 'I can hang on until I get back to the Grange.'

'Take my arm and walk with me, doctor,' he said.

Together we staggered around the side of the house and into a well-looked after back garden. There was a large, neatly mown lawn and several extensive rose beds. Something had been digging up the lawn.

'Moles?' I asked.

He shook his head. 'Badgers,' he said.

'Ah. I know who to recommend for moles but I'm afraid I don't know anything about getting rid of badgers.'

'I do,' said the Colonel. He let go of my arm, unzipped his trousers and started to urinate. 'Just pee where you're standing, doctor, if you don't mind.'

I stared at him, wondering if my diagnosis of labyrinthitis was right, after all.

'Badgers are wonderful creatures,' he said. 'Love em to bits. But they dig worms and burrowing bumblebees and cranefly larvae out of the lawn and they make a hell of a mess.'

'So I can see,' I agreed, looking around.

'The one thing that keeps them away is the smell of male pee,' he said. 'Has to be male pee. The female variety doesn't work.'

I was beginning to understand.

'So if you would just pee on the lawn for me it would help enormously,' said the Colonel.

Feeling rather self-conscious and hoping that none of his neighbours chose this moment to pop round to borrow a cupful of sugar, I did my bit to help keep the badgers off the Colonel's lawn.

CHAPTER 17

As I drove to my first home visit I found myself remembering my days at medical school.

I know people who spend their adult lives reminiscing about their days at school or university, and whose lives are defined by their scholarly and sporting achievements during those days of learning.

In contrast, I've never been terribly keen on holding onto those days. I had turned down an invitation to attend a medical school reunion without a moment's hesitation. But Mortimer's telephone call had, inevitably, brought back a host of half-forgotten memories.

The things I remembered in greatest detail were the odd, almost irrelevant, moments.

The haematology lecturer who was so genuinely absentminded that he regularly arrived at lectures an hour late and who, on one memorable occasion, wore two ties at the same time. We were mesmerised by this and I don't think any of us heard or remembered much of what he said. I don't think this mattered very much. I do remember that he spoke only about immensely rare blood diseases and never even mentioned disorders such as anaemia or leukaemia.

I remembered that our ophthalmology course (which lasted half a day) was inexplicably scheduled for the same time as our half day dental course. Since it was easy to avoid both by pretending to be at the other we all succumbed to temptation and took an unofficial half day holiday. Sitting in a cafe in the city someone pointed out that if we ever qualified as doctors we would be legally entitled to practice as dentists even though we had never spent one second studying dentistry. I never did find out if it is true that doctors can practise dentistry but several people have insisted that it is.

Five of us spent a whole year dissecting an old lady and learned the name and location of every vein, artery, nerve, muscle, bone and tendon in her body. Most of this I forgot within 48 hours of the examination I took. Today I doubt if I can remember 1% of the details I learned in anatomy. I never knew the old lady's name but in a macabre sort of way it is, I suppose, true to say that I knew her more intimately than I have ever known anyone.

I remembered the multiple choice examination we were given. Such devices were new at the time and the lecturers who had set the exam had devised a format which meant that many marks were deducted for wrong answers. It seemed to me that the best policy was to hand in an entirely empty sheet. I came top of 120 students with a final score of nought and incurred the wrath of the lecturers who had set the examination. They complained that I hadn't entered into the examination in the proper spirit. I replied that I didn't realise that there was a 'proper spirit' for taking examinations and that I had assumed that the sole aim was to obtain the highest possible mark. I claimed that I had shown initiative and eventually this was grudgingly accepted.

I remembered sharing a flat with Mortimer and three other medical students.

It was a huge flat and we couldn't afford heating. Mortimer claimed it was so cold that he could clean his teeth without moving the brush. The rent was cheap but the flat was several miles from the hospital and medical school and several miles out of town. One Saturday night Mortimer had missed the last bus home and so he walked into the local bus station, climbed into an empty bus and drove it home. No one tried to stop him. He left the bus parked outside our flat. ('What else could I have done with it?' he asked later.

'There wasn't any point in driving it back to the garage and buses are tricky things to hide.') When he was called to see the medical school dean he explained that the buses had stopped running and that he didn't have enough money for a taxi home. The dean had accepted this explanation and had, somehow, settled things with the police and the bus company.

I remembered my first house job. My consultant invited all his junior doctors to have dinner with him. A friend of mine who was invited took a bottle of wine. He couldn't afford anything decent and picked up the cheapest bottle the local off-licence had on offer. The consultant's wife opened the bottle and put it on the table. The consultant examined the label with some suspicion and then poured himself a sample. After spluttering and spitting the wine back into his glass he glowered at his wife. 'Where did you pick up this muck?' he demanded. 'Our guest brought it,' she replied without a pause. After a few embarrassing moments they poured the wine into a saucepan, added sugar, cloves, slices of orange and cinnamon and turned it into a very acceptable hot toddy.

I remembered working on a surgical ward.

Every Sunday evening a patient died in the same bed in the intensive care unit. No one knew why. Eventually, I made the diagnosis. It didn't require any medical knowledge. I happened to be in the unit one Sunday and I watched in horror as a cleaner entered the ward, pulled out the life support system plug, and put her floor polisher into the vacant socket. I dashed across and switched the plugs back. It turned out that she had been allowing her polisher to whirr away for a few minutes every Sunday. When she was finished she put the life support system plug back into the socket and left the intensive care unit unaware that she'd just killed someone.

Remembering all this I nearly missed my next turning. I slammed on the brakes, slowed down and turned left onto a deeply rutted track. I then headed south towards Tarrydown Woods where the first patient on my morning call sheet lived on a small farm. As I turned the car down the track so the skies went grey. Moments later the rain started.

Many of the metalled roads in Bilbury are only wide enough for single traffic and have grass growing through the tarmacadam in the middle, but we still call them 'roads' rather than 'tracks'. In Bilbury a 'track' is something that is really only suitable for a tractor. When the ruts are particularly deep it is useless to try and drive with the car wheels in the ruts. If you do that then the exhaust pipe, number plates and other bits and pieces near to the ground will be torn off the car, even at agonisingly slow speeds. The only safe way to drive down them is to put the nearside wheels on the ridge in the centre of the track and the offside wheels on the edge of the bank on the right hand side of the track. (You could put the offside wheels on the ridge and the nearside wheels on the other bank, but if you did that then you would be less likely to spot dangerous obstructions in the bank.) Hoping that no one had dumped anything too solid on the bank, and that any drainage ditches cut into the bank weren't too deep, I gingerly made my way down the track, eventually managing to park in a small courtyard, alongside an elderly and extremely battered old tractor. A rather sorry looking farmhouse lay on one side of the courtyard and barns and stables made up most of the other three sides. The usual bits and pieces of rusting farmyard detritus proved that this was a working farm. Even with his car doors and windows shut a townie would have known that the owner of the property kept pigs. By now the rain was coming down fast and the sky was black.

The patient I was visiting was called Lydeard Lawrence and I'd never met him before, though I'd heard about him. Even in Bilbury, Mr Lawrence (I don't think anyone ever called him Lydeard) was known to be both rather eccentric and rather reclusive. He had never been further than Barnstaple in his whole life. He had, so Patchy Fogg insisted, only ever made one visit there. That had been back in the 1950's and the shock of the hustle and bustle had convinced him that big city life was not for him. Thumper once told me that Mr Lawrence came from stem stock. His father had worked on a farm in Ilfracombe and had walked there from Bilbury every morning and had walked home again every evening. The round trip each day must have been over twenty five miles. When he hit his seventieth birthday Mr Lawrence senior took a job in Combe Martin because the journey was shorter.

Both father and son were, said Thumper, the sort of countrymen who would hand plough six acres and milk twenty four cows before breakfast, plant four bushels of seed between breakfast and lunch, walk a flock of sheep to market in the afternoon and milk the cows again in the evening. At the end of the day they would regard themselves as having had a day off.

Someone, I wasn't sure who, had telephoned the house while I was having my breakfast, spoken to Patsy and asked her to arrange for me to call in and see Mr Lawrence. It was amazing how quickly word had got around that Bilbury had its own doctor again.

I don't know whether it was because the dogs hadn't heard me arrive, or because they were craftily waiting for me to get away from the safety of my vehicle before they showed themselves but I was stranded ten or twelve feet from the car when the two Alsatians appeared. They bore little resemblance to the sort of dogs of that breed which can be seen walking along the pavements of our towns and cities. These were the scariest looking dogs I'd ever seen. Their coats were shaggy and unkempt and their eyes wild. Their teeth seemed more like fangs.

I've always been nervous about dogs and I've been bitten enough times to feel satisfied that my nervousness is a useful form of self-preservation rather than a phobia of some kind. Dog owners usually make things worse by saying things like 'he only bites if he can tell you're nervous' or, worse still, 'don't worry, he doesn't bite'.

The first of these remarks simply adds to my anxiety and, therefore, the risk of my being bitten. The second remark (which may well be a lie, of course) means, at best, that the dog hasn't yet bitten anyone. Whenever I hear this I am always conscious of the fact that all dogs who bite have never bitten anyone before they do so for the first time.

Over the years I've been given masses of advice from well-meaning dog owners. Some say that a dog won't bite if you keep quite still. Some suggest walking away as quickly as you can without actually running. A few claim that you should crouch down, make yourself look like a big dog and then bark and growl. All this conflicting advice means that I never know what to do except cower, whimper and panic.

'Who's there?' called someone from deep inside a barn to my right. The question was followed by a loud grunt.

'The doctor!' I called back. 'Could you call your dogs, please?'

'Adolf!' yelled the voice. 'Hermann!' There was then another grunt.

The two dogs, which had looked to me as if they were trying to decide which bit of my flesh to eat first, pricked their ears and turned in the direction of the voice. From the fact that the delay in their response matched the delay between the two names I thought it safe to assume that the two dogs were called Adolf and Hermann. Knowing their names didn't make me feel any better.

The voice called again, this time adding 'Come here you buggers!' Every few words were punctuated by grunts.

The two dogs turned and trotted into the barn.

'Follow the dogs!' called the voice. Reluctantly, I did as I was told.

It was dark inside the barn and after walking through the open doorway I stood still for a few moments, allowing my pupils to enlarge and my vision to develop a little. Gradually I could see that the barn was divided up by wooden planked walls into a number of stalls. Some of these were filled with stacks of hay and straw. I could see no sign of any living creature.

'Over here!' called the voice. There was, inevitably it now seemed, another grunt.

Gingerly, I walked towards the sound. The floor of the barn was covered with straw which needed changing. The straw was so wet that every footstep made an unpleasant squelching sound. My wellington boots were, of course, still in the car boot. Eventually, I reached the wooden partition from behind which the sound seemed to have come. I peered over the partition.

On the other side of the wooden planking lay about a dozen piglets in a large nest made out of bales of straw. Lying alongside them was a human figure dressed in an old blue boiler suit. In addition to the boiler suit he wore wellington boots and a very battered brown trilby hat. Adolf and Hermann were sitting at attention just a couple of feet away from his head. The man was holding glass feeding bottles in each hand and had a third bottle tucked between his thighs. Three of the piglets were sucking greedily at the teats. Every ten or fifteen seconds the man made a loud grunting sound. It was one of the strangest sights I'd ever seen.

'Mr Lawrence?' I asked.

'That's me.'

'Are you all right?'

'The sow up and died just after giving birth,' explained Mr Lawrence. 'The little ones will only take the milk if they think I'm their mother.' He pulled a half empty bottle from one piglet and offered it to another who took it greedily.

'And the grunts are to help convince them that you're their mother?'

Mr Lawrence didn't answer but just grunted.

I stood and watched this extraordinary scene for ten or fifteen minutes. Eventually, Mr Lawrence dropped the now empty bottles onto the hay and rolled over onto his back. One of the piglets jumped up onto his chest. Mr Lawrence brushed it off as if it were a troublesome kitten.

'Give us a hand will you,' he said.

I clambered over the wooden fence, keeping a careful eye on the two dogs, bent down and helped Mr Lawrence to his feet. Or, rather, helped him half way to his feet. This took some time and was accompanied by a good many oohs and aarrhs and ouches. When he was eventually standing he was bent double, with his top half horizontal to the floor.

'I can't straighten up,' he complained.

'How long have you been like this?' I asked.

'Four or five days.'

'How long have you been feeding the piglets?'

'Same time.'

'I think there might be a link,' I told him.

He turned his head (it wasn't as easy as it should have been) and glared at me. 'You being funny?'

'No, no!' I said quickly.

'Take my arm,' he said. 'We'll go into the house.'

I moved forward to take his arm. The two dogs growled menacingly and edged closer to me. One of them (I couldn't tell whether it was Adolf or Hermann) bared his yellowing teeth to show me what I could expect if I hurt his master.

The four of us then edged slowly out of the barn, across a muddy courtyard and into a small farmhouse. As we moved into the kitchen the farmer kicked the door to behind us, shutting the dogs out. They barked and growled on the other side of the door. The kitchen was quite large and was furnished with a huge old Welsh dresser, a large pine table and four pine chairs. There was a large white sink under the only window. The sink was served by a single, presumably cold, tap. The glass in the small window was so dirty that it was difficult to see anything.

'Where's the light switch?' I asked, after having helped Mr Lawrence into one of the chairs.

He turned, with some difficulty, and looked at me. 'What do you want light for?'

'It's a bit dark in here,' I explained. 'I can't see to examine you properly.'

'I don't have the mains,' said Mr Lawrence. 'You need to pedal.' He nodded towards an elderly bicycle which was fixed into a strange contraption which kept the rear wheels off the ground.

I looked at the bicycle, wondering why my riding an exercise bicycle would help produce some light.

'The bicycle powers the light bulb,' explained Mr Lawrence. 'Climb on the saddle and pedal away.'

I put my bag down on the table, climbed onto the bicycle and started pedalling. It wasn't easy to get the bicycle going but slowly a glow appeared as a light bulb hanging down from the kitchen ceiling acquired some colour. The frame on which the back wheel was balancing wobbled alarmingly.

'Is this your only source of electricity?' I asked him, beginning to feel warm.

'It is,' he replied. 'And it's free and it doesn't break down when the wind blows.' He looked at me. 'And it keeps me warm too.'

And so I sat on the bicycle and pedalled while Mr Lawrence eased off his shirt and pointed to the places where the pain was at its worst. It wasn't quite the way I'd been taught to practise medicine but it was the best I could manage. A physical examination was, of course, impossible because the moment I stopped pedalling the light would go out and while I was pedalling I couldn't examine him. I gave him a small bottle of anti-inflammatory painkillers which I had in my bag and told him to take two tablets every four hours. He said he would and I thought he would. The tablets were huge and dark red and looked extremely potent. I scribbled out a prescription for more of the tablets. I also told him not to lie down in cold, wet straw beside the piglets. I was less convinced that he would obey that suggestion.

'Have you got someone who can get your pills?' I asked him.

'My sister calls in to tidy up,' said Mr Lawrence. 'She'll get them.'

When I'd finished I climbed off the bicycle and helped him put his clothes on. I promised that I'd go back and see how he was getting on.

* * *

By the time I left Mr Lawrence's cottage it was nearly half past one and I decided to go back to Bilbury Grange to grab some lunch before completing the remainder of the day's calls. It was still pouring with rain and the track back up the main road had become a small river.

When I finally got back home it was after two o'clock. It had taken me nearly an hour to do a journey which normally took less than fifteen minutes.

A Volvo estate car was parked in the driveway, almost blocking the entrance. If whoever had left it had done so intending to cause the greatest possible inconvenience they had been entirely successful.

It didn't for a moment occur to me that the car might belong to Mortimer. The last time I'd seen him he had been driving a souped up Austin Healey. He'd drilled holes in the exhaust pipe so that it sounded like a racing car.

I just managed to cram my Morris Minor into the driveway. By the time I'd made my way to the house I was soaked. Cold, wet and hungry I was not in the best of moods.

Naturally, the rain stopped and the sun came out again the minute I walked into the house.

CHAPTER 18

'Your friends arehere,'saidPatsy.Icouldtellfromhersmilethat shewasstrugglingalittle.We hadmetinthekitchen.Mortimer andhisfamilywerenowheretobeseen.

'Are you OK?' I asked, quietly.

'Oh yes,' she said. But I knew she wasn't. I could hear what sounded like the smashing of china. We looked at one another. 'I left them in the living room,' said Patsy. Her voice seemed thin and strained but there wasn't time to talk more. She led the way and I followed.

I hardly recognised Mortimer.

He had changed enormously from the rather scruffy, long-haired medical student I remembered.

The Mortimer I'd known had worn horn-rimmed spectacles, garish shirts with long collars, huge 'kipper' ties, cowboy boots with huge heels and green corduroy trousers held up with a leather belt which fastened with a huge silver clasp designed to look like a skull. His hair had always fallen over his eyes and he had, I remembered, always had a rather lopsided, sheepish grin.

The new, well-polished and presumably much improved version of Mortimer wore no spectacles (they had, I discovered later, been replaced by contact lenses), a pair of beige slacks, a cream shirt and a pair of highly polished brown brogues. He had a pale yellow cashmere sweater draped around his shoulders, with the arms knotted loosely at the front in the French style. His hair, which looked to be thinning, was expensively cut and neatly combed. He looked like an advertisement for something unreasonably expensive.

There were three people with him.

The woman I assumed to be his wife was tall, extremely thin and blonde. She wore a dark green hip hugging skirt, a lighter green blouse and green high-heeled shoes. She had a string of pearls around her neck and wore pearl earrings. She was standing and clutching a small, green leather handbag.

The two boys, obviously Mortimer's sons, were fighting and had tipped over a small wooden table. The tray, tea cups, saucers, plates and cake which Patsy had put on the table were spread over the carpet. The table had a broken leg. Neither the boys nor their parents seemed concerned by this.

'Good to see you!' said Mortimer, holding out a hand. I took it and received a limp, rather half-hearted handshake. 'We've met your wife, Patsy.'

'Sorry I wasn't here when you arrived,' I apologised.

'My wife,' said Mortimer, waving a hand in the appropriate direction. He didn't ask where I'd been or what I'd been doing.

'Lovely to meet you. The last time I saw Mortimer,' I told her, 'he'd just started going out with a large nurse called Clarice.'

I was about to add that Clarice had been hideously bad-tempered, so huge that she must have weighed fifteen stone in her underwear and had a laugh like a drain emptying. I would have completed this pointless and hazardous monologue by adding that I could never work out why Mortimer went out with her and that it was a relief that he didn't marry her.

But I never actually said any of this because everyone's attention was on the two boys who had rolled into a small, antique oak table which Patsy's parents had given us as a wedding present. Realising that the table was about to tip over I reached over them and lifted it up. By then I had temporarily forgotten what I had been about to say.

'I'm Clarice.' said Mortimer's wife, introducing herself.

I felt myself reddening. 'Amazing coincidence,' I said, putting the table down. It was heavier than it looked. Both the table and I had had a narrow escape.

'I went on a diet and lost a lot of weight,' she said. She allowed herself a rather ghostly imitation of a smile. I shook hands with her. Or, rather, she allowed the tips of her fingers to touch mine.

'The boy on top is my son Spotty,' said Mortimer, ignoring my gaffe and nodding towards the two boys writhing on the floor. 'His real name is Dick but he had measles when he was five so naturally we called him Spotted Dick. The name Spotty has just sort of stuck. And the one underneath with his foot up against your television set is Rupert. The boys both suffer from hyperactivity,' he said, as though in explanation. 'Nothing much can be done about it, of course.'

'Hello Spotty,' I said. 'Hello Rupert.' The boy on top looked me up and down as though deciding whether or not to answer. He obviously decided against the idea for he said nothing. The youngest boy seemed to reach the same conclusion without any discernible effort.

'You'd better stop that for now,' said Mortimer. The boys ignored him.

'Stop it,' snarled Clarice. I turned, astonished. It was strange to hear such a powerful and venomous voice come out of such a thin and delicate looking woman. The boys stopped fighting and clambered to their feet.

'My dad's car is posher than your car,' said Spotty. 'I expect he earns more than you do.'

'He almost certainly does,' I agreed.

'We saw you park your car,' said Rupert. 'It looks as if it's covered in mud.'

'Actually most of it is slurry,' I confessed. 'It smells terrible. But when we go to Barnstaple or Exeter it's easy to find. We just sniff and head towards the smell.'

'Yuk,' said Spotty, screwing up his nose.

'I thought you were supposed to be a doctor?' said Rupert.

'Er, I am,' I told him.

'My Dad's a doctor and he's got a Volvo Estate. If you're a doctor why are you driving a rubbishy old Morris Minor?'

'Maybe it's what he wants to drive,' suggested Mortimer.

'Not all doctors earn as much money as Daddy does,' said Clarice.

* * *

I had hoped that Mortimer and I could reminisce about our student days together.

'Do you remember when we had a pal who was secretary of a Hall of Residence?' I asked him. 'At the end of one summer term he decided that he ought to empty the bar. He said he thought that the opened bottles of spirits would go off if we left them where they were. He got a few of us to go and help him. He was adamant that alcohol deteriorates dangerously if left unattended. The six of us emptied the entire booze cupboard. I wonder what on earth happened to those other three guys?'

'Richard is a consultant surgeon in Glasgow, Anthony is a consultant anaesthetist in the RAF and Peter is a consultant radiologist. I've rather lost touch with him. The chap who was secretary of the Hall of Residence was struck off two years ago for some sort of prescription fraud.'

'Do you remember we once shared a room when we were doing our maternity work. You woke up in the middle of the night screaming? You'd had a nightmare. I remember you said you'd been told that you needed a brain transplant and that the only organ available belonged to Prince Philip.'

'I don't remember that,' said Mortimer, after glancing in his wife's direction.

'Then there was that time we went on a coach trip to a mental hospital. You sat next to the emergency window and noticed that it said 'In emergency break glass with hammer'.' I reminded him. 'No one on the coach had a hammer and you made the driver stop at every shop we passed until you managed to buy a hammer.'

'I think that must have been someone else,' insisted Mortimer.

'No, it was you!' I insisted. 'And you must remember that posh, middle aged woman you admitted when you were working on the hospital's private wing?'

Mortimer frowned and shook his head.

'You asked her if she had hot flushes.' Mortimer shook his head again.

'She said 'Oh no, we use cold water like ordinary people'.'

'I think you must be exaggerating,' said Mortimer.

'Then there was the time that three of us were working in a general hospital in Selly Oak. The other bloke was a real nerdy type. Bruce I think his name was. When he went to bed at night he always laid all his clothes out very nearly so that in an emergency he could be dressed in seconds. He used to position his shoes very precisely so that he could slide his feet into them the moment he got out of bed. He told us he kept his socks on, I remember.'

Mortimer shook his head. 'I don't remember any of this,' he said.

'Oh you must!' I insisted. 'Bert Whatsisname went into his room one night and glued Bruce's shoes in position - the whole hospital had awful green linoleum on the floor - so that when he leapt out of bed and put his feet into his shoes his body kept moving but his feet didn't. He smashed his head into the door. Bert was the duty surgeon and he put six stitches into Bruce's forehead. I had a card from Bert a year or two ago. He was working as a proctologist in Sunderland.'

Mortimer didn't seem to remember many of the things I remembered. The few he recalled seemed to have happened quite differently to the way I remembered them. I began to wonder if we'd ever known one another at all.

I was enormously relieved when the surgery doorbell went. 'A patient,' I apologised. 'I shouldn't be long.'

'How on earth do you know it's a patient?' asked Mortimer.

'The door to the surgery, the door patients use, has a different bell,' I explained. 'It bing bongs. The bell on the front door goes more ding ding.'

'Oh I think I'd have them the other way round,' said Clarice. 'I think I'd prefer the ding ding for patients.'

I headed for the surgery.

'Do you mind if I come with you?' asked Mortimer. 'Be interesting to take a look at how a country GP operates.'

I hesitated before nodding. I really didn't fancy the idea of him breathing over my shoulder.

'I'm sorry to bother you doctor.' It was Tom Kipple. He works as a farm labourer. 'I've cut myself. The wife tried putting a plaster on it.' He shrugged and grinned. He held out his arm. It was wrapped in a blood soaked towel. I explained to Tom that Mortimer was another doctor and asked him if he minded if he stayed. He said he didn't.

'How on earth did you do this?' I asked. Tom had a long, savage looking gash in his forearm. At its deepest it was half an inch deep. I could see bone.'

'Clearing a hedge,' he said. 'Bit of old tractor.'

'Rusty?'

He nodded.

'Did Sally bring you?' Sally was his wife. Another nod.

'Where is she?'

'Sitting out in the car waiting for me.'

'Why didn't she come in?'

'Shy. She saw the Volvo and guessed you must have visitors.'

'Is she OK there?'

He nodded. 'Happier in the car,' he said. 'She'll drive me home afterwards.'

'When did you last have a tetanus injection?'

He thought for a moment. 'Four, five years ago,' he said. 'I cut myself mending the tractor. Hand and thigh. Thirty two stitches altogether. You done 'em for me. Neat job. I had a full course of jabs after.'

'Good. I'll give you a booster jab when I've cleaned this up,' I told him.

He nodded.

'Aren't you calling an ambulance?' asked Mortimer, clearly appalled. 'This man needs hospital attention.'

'He needs sewing up,' I said. 'It'll take an hour for an ambulance to get here and another hour for the ambulance to get him to the hospital. It's a bouncy, twisty, unpleasant road in a car, let alone in an ambulance. Then he'll have to wait for someone to see him. When they've finished with him he'll have to find his own way back here unless his wife follows the ambulance and if she does that she'll need to find a babysitter first. If his wife can't find a babysitter he'll be there all night if he hasn't bled to death or died of boredom.'

'He should still be seen in a hospital,' said Mortimer, rather less sure of himself

'Do you want me to send you to the hospital?' I asked Tom.

'No thank you, doctor. I'd rather you did it for me.' He paused and looked at me. 'Much rather you did it than some doctor I don't know.' He grinned broadly. Most of his front teeth were missing. He had a denture but I'd never seen him wear it. He kept it in a drawer in the bedroom for special occasions. 'Sam Houghton put eight stitches in his own leg last year,' he told me. 'Cut himself on barbed wire. Own silly fault.'

'Why on earth did he do that?' asked Mortimer. 'Sew himself up?'

'We didn't have a doctor in the village then,' explained Tom. 'It was in the middle of harvesting. He didn't have the time to waste.'

'But what did he use to sew himself up?'

'Same stuff as he uses for the cows, of course,' said Tom. Mortimer said nothing.

'Do you want me to give you an anaesthetic?' I asked him.

He shook his head.

'He needs something,' said Mortimer. 'Valium?'

'Nothing thank you,' said Tom. He spoke to me. I cut off the remains of his shirt, cleaned up his arm and carefully removed all the dirt from the wound.

'You're taking a lot of time over cleaning that wound,' muttered Mortimer.

'Tom works on a farm,' I reminded him. 'Billions of tetanus spores. If I leave any dirt in the wound the spores will grow even though he's immunised. I once saw a farm labourer who'd been to the hospital after he broke his leg. Compound fracture. The doctors set the bones but failed to clean them out properly. He nearly died of tetanus. In the end they had to re-break his leg and clean out the bone.' As I talked I cleaned, working as fast as I could to minimise the blood loss.

'There you are,' I said at last. 'Now we can sew you up.'

'Good heavens,' murmured Mortimer quietly.

I sewed up the wound as neatly as I could and then gave him a tetanus injection.' Don't suppose Sally will want the shirt or the towel back?' I said when I'd finished.

'Don't think so, doctor,' said Tom, grinning.

I tossed the shirt and towel into my rubbish bin. 'I'll get you an old coat to go home in,' I told him. I popped out for a moment, found an old sports jacket hanging in the hall and took it back to him.

'I'll bring it back round in the morning,' he promised. I went outside with him, said hello and goodnight to his wife and then went back into the house. Sophie the cat followed me in. She had clearly been rolling in something exceedingly unpleasant. Her fur was matted and she smelt disgusting. Naturally, she leapt straight up onto my shoulders and started to rub herself against the back of my head. Gently, I plucked her off, cleaned her off as best as I could with a towel and then deposited her in her basket. She purred contentedly and started to clean off the remains of whatever it had been. I was glad I didn't know. I wiped my neck and the back of my head with a handkerchief

'Do you get this sort of thing a lot?' asked Clarice, when I returned. Mortimer had found his way back to the dining room while I'd been dealing with Sophie.

'What sort of thing?'

'Patients troubling you in the evenings?'

'It happens.'

'How many nights a week are you on call?'

'All of them.'

'Yuk. You smell horrid,' said Rupert suddenly.

'It was the cat's fault,' I said.

'Every night?' continued Clarice, ignoring her son. 'Monday, Tuesday, Wednesday, Thursday...all of them?'

'There are no other doctors around here,' I said. 'No one close enough to organise a rota with.'

'And weekends?' I nodded.

'Oh how absolutely awful!' said Clarice.

'It's what being a village doctor means,' I said.

'Why don't you charge extra for sewing people up?' asked Mortimer. 'You don't have to do it.'

I looked at him, horrified.

'We'd better eat,' said Patsy, diplomatically changing the subject quickly. 'Or dinner will be ruined.'

* *

*

'That was very nice,' said Clarice, pushing away her plate. She'd hardly touched anything. 'But where on earth do you manage to buy such wonderful vegetables? You're miles out in the middle of nowhere!'

'We don't buy our vegetables,' replied Patsy. 'We grow them.'

Clarice looked astonished. 'Oh darling Patsy how wonderful that is! You mean to say that you actually put seeds into the ground and then harvest your very own cabbages and potatoes?'

'Something like that,' agreed Patsy, standing up and starting to clear away the plates. I stood to help her.

'How marvellous. You're like those self-sufficient people we see on the television sometimes,' said Mortimer. 'What a great way to save money.'

I started to say that we didn't grow our own vegetables to save money but because we wanted better vegetables, but Mortimer wasn't interested.

'Here's a little tip for you,' he said, holding up a hand to silence me. 'It'll save you a few pence when you next go travelling. A patient of mine told me about it but we prefer eating at hotels. You wrap some salmon fillets or pieces of chicken in aluminium foil and wedge them around the car engine. When you stop for lunch they will be cooked.' He paused and thought for a moment. 'I suppose you could use sausages just as well,' he said. 'They'd be cheaper. My patient chappie reckons 200 miles at a steady 60 mph should do it nicely.'

'We don't eat meat,' I said. 'We're vegetarian.'

'Don't eat meat!' said Clarice. 'Oh how awful for you!' She reached out and patted Patsy on the arm. 'Poor dear,' she said.

'You'll have to get that husband of yours to get a job in a town where the pay is better.'

Patsy started to say something but Clarice wasn't finished. 'It's awfully sweet, living in the country, but I could never live somewhere like this,' she said, wiping her lips with her napkin.

'Oh!' said Patsy. 'Why not?'

'Far too far from the heart of things,' replied Clarice. 'And no shops! My dear, I think you are wonderful, being able to live so far from decent shops.'

'There's a department store in Barnstaple,' said Patsy.

Clarice laughed. 'Well, yes, I'm sure there is,' she said.

'And we've got most of the big High Street stores too,' Patsy said defensively.

'Boots, Smiths, Marks and Spencer, Woolworths?'

'Yes,' said Patsy.

'Not quite what I was meaning by shops,' said Clarice. She put all the emphasis on the word 'shops'.

'Shopping is Clarice's main hobby,' said Mortimer rather proudly. 'She's terribly good at spending money.'

'My sister Adrienne spends a lot of time in shops,' said Patsy. 'She loves charity shops. She's got this theory that she can help the world by spending money. She buys a dress in a charity shop and then immediately gives it to another charity shop.'

Clarice screwed up her nose and looked confused. 'I've seen charity shops,' she said. 'But I'm not sure I understand how that might work.'

'It's simple,' I said. 'Imagine she pays the first charity shop £1 for a dress and she then gives that dress to a second charity shop which sells it to someone else for £1. The total charity shop profit is £2. But she has only spent £1. So, somehow, she has managed to turn £1 of her money into £2 of charity shop money.'

'If Adrienne was Chancellor we'd all have jam on both sides of our cake,' said Patsy.

Clarice, who looked utterly confused, looked at Mortimer for help. He frowned and scratched and then shook his head. 'Sounds as if there must be a flaw but I'm damned if I can spot it,' he said eventually.

'I'm quite terrible,' said Clarice. 'When I went into town to have lunch with a friend last Tuesday I saw these lovely shoes in a shop window. I just had to buy them. But when I'd got them I realised that I didn't have anything to wear that went with them. So then I found a dress that went with them absolutely perfectly. Then, of course, I had to get a handbag to go with the dress. That lunch ended up costing me £80!'

'Probably more than you spend on clothes in a year, eh Patsy?' said Mortimer.

Patsy, who was wearing her best dress, flushed slightly with embarrassment. I went red too - though mine was partly through guilt (I couldn't remember when Patsy had last had a new dress) and partly through anger.

'Mind you, they probably save themselves a fortune by growing their own food,' said Mortimer to his wife. He had an annoying habit of talking about us as though we weren't there. 'A GP living in a village like this won't be making much money.' He turned to me. 'Do you have any private patients?'

I shook my head.

Mortimer turned back to his wife. 'There you are,' he said, satisfied that his point was proven.

'Apple pie for everyone?' asked Patsy, who now had an armful of plates and was heading for the kitchen. 'With custard!' she added, managing to force a smile.

'Is it home-made?' enquired Mortimer.

'It is,' said Patsy proudly. Her apple pies were magnificent and much admired, even within a village where every woman was an excellent cook.

'Oh,' said Mortimer, clearly disappointed. 'I rather like the ones they sell in Sainsbury's.' He paused. 'Well never mind,' he said magnanimously. 'I expect yours will be fine.'

'I don't want any,' said Rupert. 'I don't like home-made things. They're cheap and nasty. I like chips and burgers best and puddings out of boxes. That's what my mummy gives me. I want ice cream now.'

With some difficulty I resisted the temptation to smash the dishes I was holding over the child's head. I wondered how he would look with a carrot rammed in each ear and cabbage leaves draped over his skull.

Patsy had gone pale. 'We haven't got any ice cream,' she said quietly. 'I'm afraid I forgot to get any.'

'I want ice cream,' said Rupert

'I'm so sorry,' said Patsy. 'What an awful hostess I am.'

'Don't be silly, Patsy!' I said. 'You're a wonderful hostess.' No one else made any effort to agree with me.

'You should never put yourself down, my dear,' said Clarice. 'You will never have any difficulty in finding people who are perfectly prepared to do that for you. And other people will do it so much better than you ever could. Ironing, cutting the lawn, car maintenance and putting yourself down - those are just some of the things best left to others.'

'I want ice cream,' said Rupert, turning up the volume this time. He actually banged his fork handle on the table. I'd never seen anyone, not even a child, do that before.

'Oh dear,' said Clarice, looking around. 'I don't suppose we could get some from somewhere could we?'

'They live in the middle of nowhere,' said Mortimer. 'Where are they going to find ice cream at this time of night?'

'It's only eight o'clock,' said Clarice.

'Peter will be shut but I'll give him a ring and ask him to open up,' I said. To be honest I expected Mortimer or Clarice to tell me not to bother.

'Oh that would be so kind,' said Clarice. She thought for a moment and frowned. 'Who is Peter?' she asked.

'Peter Marshall,' I replied. 'He runs the local shop. He sells everything.'

Clarice laughed. Her laugh was beginning to annoy me. It was more a sneer than a laugh born of amusement. 'Everything?' she said. She closed her eyes and shook her head. 'I rather suspect not.'

Patsy headed out for the kitchen. I followed, with an almost empty serving dish in each hand.

'I'm so sorry,' I said to Patsy, when we were out of earshot.

'I don't think they're quite used to country life,' she said. 'I've let you down, haven't I?' There were tears forming in her eyes. She put the plates she was carrying down by the sink. I put the serving dishes down beside them and put my arms around her. 'Listen to me!' I said. 'They're the rudest, nastiest family I've ever met in my life. I don't know what happened to Mortimer but he's become a completely different person.'

Patsy pulled away and looked at me.

'People change,' I said. 'And Mortimer has changed.' I sighed. 'Thank heavens they're only staying one night. I don't think I could stand them for any longer. I nearly killed those obnoxious kids four times this evening.'

'Oh dear,' said Patsy. 'That reminds me. There was something I meant to tell you earlier.'

I looked at her and grinned. 'Don't tell me,' I said. 'Clarice is having such a good time that her sister is coming to stay next week and is bringing her four kids and obnoxious husband.'

Patsy shook her head.

I was beginning to feel cold. I knew from her face that the news wasn't good. 'What is it?' I asked Patsy.

'Clarice had a telephone call from her father while you were out,' she said. 'Mortimer gave his secretary this number in case of emergencies.'

'What did her father want?'

'Apparently there is a problem with the family cottage in Cornwall.'

Now I knew it was bad.

'There's a problem of some sort with the drains. Clarice's father says they can't stay there.'

'Can't stay there?' My stomach shrank and I shivered. I knew what was coming next.

'What else could I say?' asked Patsy plaintively.

'How long?'

'The week.'

'A whole week?' She nodded.

'They're staying here a whole week?'

Patsy nodded again. I put my arms around her. We held one another tightly.

Our moment of peace was interrupted by a yell from the dining room. 'If you can get the ice cream Rupert would prefer chocolate,' shouted Clarice in a voice that would have carried across a steelworks. 'Not strawberry. He's allergic to strawberry. Peach is fine. Not coffee and not mint unless it's the one that comes with the bits of chocolate in it. Raspberry is acceptable as a last resort but definitely not vanilla unless it's extra creamy.'

'I'll think of something,' I said quietly. 'Or Thumper will. We're not having those people here for a whole week.'

I telephoned Peter from the phone in the kitchen. He said he had ice cream in the freezer and that, although he'd locked up, the shop would be open by the time I got there. I didn't ask him what flavours he'd got in stock. Instead I asked him what were the three oddest items he had for sale in the shop. He thought for a few moments and then told me.

'What on earth was that about?' demanded Patsy.

'You'll see in a few minutes,' I promised her. I led the way back to the dining room but before we could get there the door bell went again. It was a bing bong so I knew it was a patient.

'Don't worry,' said Patsy. 'I'll tell them you've got a patient.'

Dealing with the caller took only a couple of minutes.

'What was that one?' asked Clarice.

'Chap who lives in the village,' I said. I didn't name him. 'He works in Exeter and can't get here during the daytime. He needed a prescription. And he wanted me to look at his piles.'

'That's outrageous!' said Mortimer. 'He should take time off work if he wants to see you.'

'It would mean losing a whole day if he did that,' I explained.

'It only took me a couple of minutes. Peter is opening up his shop so that Rupert can have some ice cream,' I said.

'What make is it?' demanded Rupert.

'The best available,' I told him. 'Peter describes it as the ice cream no one can lick.'

Only Patsy laughed.

'Not strawberry,' said Rupert. 'I can't stand strawberry.'

'I heard you were allergic to it,' I said.

'I don't like it,' he said.

'It brings him out in a sort of rash,' said Clarice. She hesitated, embarrassed perhaps. 'Maybe not a full blown allergy. But it makes him upset and when he's upset he goes red.'

'Right,' I said. 'No strawberry then.'

'What flavours have they got?' demanded Rupert.

'I forgot to ask,' I confessed. 'But I expect Peter will have something you like. His shop sells pretty much everything.'

'I bet it doesn't sell everything,' said Rupert instantly.

'We try to teach him not to exaggerate,' said Mortimer.

I thought, but didn't say, that it might be better if they taught their loathsome child some manners.

'Peter sells all sorts of things,' I said. I picked up the notepad which always lies beside the telephone in the dining room. 'I'll get the ice cream and I'll test him out on a couple of other things.' I sucked on the pencil and pretended to think hard. 'I'll ask him if he's got a jar of pickled eggs, a street map of Llandudno and a carburettor for a 1956 S1 Bentley,' I said. I grinned at Clarice. 'I bet you even Harrods would have a job finding you all of those.'

'That's stupid!' sneered Spotty. 'He can't possibly have all of those stupid things in one shop.'

When I returned fifteen minutes later I had two large brown paper bags with me. One contained a tub of chocolate ice cream (the only variety Peter had in stock). The other contained a jar of pickled eggs, a street map of Llandudno and a carburettor for a 1956 S1 Bentley.

Rupert, Clarice and Mortimer ate the ice cream. I had a very large slice of Patsy's home-made apple pie. No one said thank you for the ice cream. But they were all extremely impressed at the success of my small shopping trip and, to my surprise, none of our visitors realised how easily I'd tricked them.

'Do you know where the nearest garage is?' asked Mortimer, while Clarice was putting Rupert to bed.

'There's Tolstoy's,' I told him.

'Tolstoy's?' He seemed puzzled.

'There's a garage in the village called Tolstoy's,' I told him.

'Why is it called Tolstoy's?'

'It's run by two chaps called Henry Waugh and Reginald Peace.'

'I don't get it.'

'War and Peace. Tolstoy.'

'Ah. Oh yes.'

'Do you need petrol?'

'Bit more than that,' said Mortimer. 'I've been having a bit of a problem with the Volvo.'

'What sort of problem?'

'The wipers on the headlamps won't switch off'

'You've got wipers on your headlamps?'

'Oh yes,' said Mortimer. 'The headlamps are equipped with washer nozzles too. When the headlamp glass gets muddy I can clean it.'

I thought for a moment that he was having me on. But then I realised that the 'new' Mortimer probably didn't waste too much time joking. 'And they won't switch off?'

'No. They just keep wiping away.'

'I can see that would be a bit of a nuisance,' I lied. I thought about it for a moment and something occurred to me. 'How did you find out?' I asked him.

'There's a complex system of warning lights on the dashboard,' he told me. 'The system gives me instant information when something isn't working properly.'

'Right,' I said. 'Of course.'

'You don't have that sort of system on your car?'

'No,' I said. 'The Morris Minor isn't equipped with those. But I do have two of those little orange indicator arms that pop out when I intend to turn left or right.'

'The soft top is manual I suppose?'

'Oh yes. But it's fairly easy to operate when you've had a bit· of practice. I can get the roof up or down in less than twenty minutes.'

'Pal of mine has a sports car,' said Mortimer. 'His roof takes less than a minute to appear or disappear. At the press of a button on the dashboard.'

'Brilliant.' I said.

'You probably remember him,' said Mortimer. 'Roderick Furst.'

'Roderick Furst,' I repeated. 'Was he one of our crowd?' Mortimer nodded.

'Not Hugo?'

'That's the chap,' said Mortimer.

'Oh, I remember Hugo!' I said. 'He was a real card. We used to go to that pub together. The Barrel of Laughs.'

'I remember occasional visits to a pub,' said Mortimer cautiously. 'But I seem to remember that it was called The King George.'

'Oh, that might have been the name on the sign,' I agreed. 'But we called it The Barrel of Laughs because the landlord was a huge fat chap who never smiled at anything. Miserable sod with absolutely no sense of humour.'

Mortimer looked down and muttered something about not going there often enough to remember the barman.

'Why is he calling himself Roderick?' I asked.

'Hugo was just a nickname,' said Mortimer.

'Was it?'

'Yes.'

'Oh. What a pity. I always thought his parents had a great sense of humour.'

'He thought his real name, Roderick, gave him more gravitas.'

'P.G.Wodehouse had a potty doctor called Roderick in the Jeeves and Wooster books,' I said. 'Roderick Spode.'

'I've never read Wodehouse,' said Mortimer.

'Right Ho,' I said, knowing that he wouldn't recognise Bertie Wooster's famous phrase. It's undoubtedly unfair and prejudiced but I've always found it difficult to trust men who've never read P.G.Wodehouse.

'Hugo was so scruffy that when he stood around in the town centre people would give him money,' I told Patsy. 'I remember once he made eight shillings and nine pence while waiting for his mother at New Street Station.'

'If you meet him I wouldn't remind him of that these days,' said Mortimer rather stiffly.

'He was the only person to be thrown out of the rugby club for drinking and womanising,' I said.

'I don't remember that.'

'He always had cold hands. The patients used to call him Coldfinger.'

Mortimer, who didn't seem to enjoy my jolly reminiscing, shook his head to show he didn't remember that either.

'What did you say he's doing now?'

'He's a plastic surgeon. Very successful. He's got a villa in Portugal and two Labradors called Nip and Tuck.'

'He's a surgeon?' This wasn't so much a question as an expression of my disbelief

'Oh yes. I think he always wanted to be a surgeon.'

'Golly,' I said, genuinely astonished at this news. 'I remember once assisting with him at an operation. It was something complicated and the registrar had Hugo holding a huge textbook so that he could see what he had to do next. The book was very heavy and Hugo, who always used to get nervous, had very sweaty fingers. He turned over two pages at once and the patient nearly got the first half of one operation and the second half of another.'

Mortimer claimed he didn't know of that either.

'Are they any good?' he asked.

'Who?'

'These people at this garage of yours.'

'Oh yes,' I told him. 'Brilliant. When I had my first car someone told me that I should have it serviced regularly. I took it in and asked for a service. They couldn't understand what I wanted them to do and why I'd taken them a car which was still working.'

I thought this was quite charming and quaint. Mortimer clearly didn't. To amuse him I told him about the time I had borrowed a car from them and had discovered too late that it didn't have any brakes.

'I eventually stopped it by driving into a fishpond,' I told him.

He stared at me, disbelievingly.

'Actually, that's a bit of an exaggeration,' I admitted. 'Only the first two wheels actually went into the pond. But it was embarrassing. I had to knock on the door and ask Mavis Biddlecome if I could have my car back. Then I had to get Harry Burrows to tow the damned thing out with his tractor. Mavis was a bit miffed. I killed three of her goldfish.

'I would have left it for the garage to collect,' said Mortimer.

'I needed the car for the rest of my visits.'

'You surely didn't drive it with no brakes?'

'Oh, it was OK. I didn't go above thirty and slowed it down with the gears. Mostly. It wasn't terribly dangerous. The lanes around here have got grassy banks on each side.'

Mortimer grunted. 'How do I get there?' he asked. 'To this Tolstoy's of yours.'

'Turn left out of our gate and then right just before you get to the pink cottage which needs rethatching. Go straight down that lane which wiggles around a bit and go through the farmyard. Don't take any notice of the dogs. They make a lot of noise but they won't hurt you - and certainly not if you stay in the car and keep the windows shut. Go up the hill for a quarter of a mile and turn left. The signpost fell down a year ago and the council still hasn't put it back up but it's still there in the hedge. If you can see the church you've gone too far past the next turning so go on to the red farmhouse, turn round and go back, but slower this time, and turn a sort of half left just before you get to the Jubilee Watering Trough.' I looked at Mortimer, saw the glazed look in his eyes and realised that I was giving directions like a countryman. 'I don't know why the Jubilee Watering Trough is there,' I admitted. 'It's a silly place for it.'

'Could you draw me a map?'

'I'll show you the way in the morning,' I promised.

'Thanks,' Mortimer said, obviously relieved.

There was a silence. It felt uncomfortable. I put up with it for a couple of minutes and then gave in.

'So, how is life treating you?' I asked. I hadn't yet realised that Mortimer had become the sort of person who tells you how he is when you ask.

He responded to this fairly simple question by telling me how much he earned, how much their house had cost and how much he paid for the boys to attend private school. (The bill for the school fees was considerably more than I was earning, or could ever expect to earn in Bilbury.) He told me with great pride that he now employed a man to come round on Sunday mornings. 'He washes the car and mows the lawn.'

'Better than doing it the other way round,' I suggested. He looked at me, clearly puzzled.

'Washing the lawn and mowing the car.'

He remained puzzled. 'Mind you,' he said, continuing on as though I hadn't spoken. 'The stresses I have to cope with are pretty awesome.'

He went on to tell us about the problems he was having with the administrators at the hospital where he worked. 'I insist that I'm entitled to a dedicated parking space,' he said. 'But the senior administrator who is in charge of parking spaces is proving to be immensely stubborn. I've had six or seven meetings with him about it in the last two weeks alone.' He puffed up his chest a little. 'Still,' he said, 'I've no doubt I will win through in the end. I usually do.'

'And you must, darling,' said Clarice, who had reappeared. The two boys were, she said, reading comics in bed.

Mortimer then told us about the row he had had with the people who had installed the power shower in their second bathroom (he'd eventually made them take it out and replace it with something even more powerful) and the arguments he'd had with the man whom he paid to cut their grass.

'The ignorant fool cuts the grass reasonably well,' said Mortimer. 'But he spills grass cuttings all over our driveway when he puts them into the back of his trailer. I've had numerous rows with him about it. Last week I cancelled half a dozen patients so that I could stay at home and confront him. Clarice had spoken to him but some things do require a man's touch.'

I murmured sympathetic noises and resisted the temptation to suggest that it might be less trouble if he cut the grass himself

'I don't suppose you have many problems, living out in the country,' he said.

'Well, we do have one or two,' I said. I started to tell him about the storm that had destroyed several houses in Bilbury, making several villagers homeless, and isolating the village.

'Don't talk to me about storms!' Mortimer said, interrupting me before I could go any further with my tale of woe. 'We had a darned hurricane last winter. Lost three tiles. We were lucky no one was sitting outside in the garden at the time. They'd have been killed.'

I thought about asking him why anyone would have been sitting in the garden during a storm, but didn't. His comment had reminded me of someone but I couldn't remember whom.

'I had a terrible time finding a roofer to come out and do the repairs,' he continued. 'In the end it took three days before anyone turned up and it cost me £80 to have the repairs done. It took another three months to get the money out of the insurance company.'

I started to tell him about the battle the village had fought against developers who had wanted to build a massive new housing estate in the area but he interrupted me.

'Oh, you haven't seen anything,' he said, waving a hand around dismissively. 'I could tell you stories about developers and builders and planning people that would make your blood go cold.' He leant forward a little. 'Last summer one of our neighbours suddenly decided to build an extension above his garage. What they usually call a granny flat except it was for the au pair rather than the granny. We fought him tooth and nail, of course. We would have been able to see part of the extension from our bathroom window. Hideous thing. But the planning people wouldn't listen. In the end I had to have a word with a pal of mine in the Freemasons.' He looked at me and winked. 'Don't suppose you're a member?'

I shook my head. I had remembered whom he reminded me o(The Colonel. Both had a habit of trumping everyone else's misfortunes with misfortunes of their own.

'Didn't think you would be. Never mind. They don't ask many people. Anyway, my pal knows someone in planning. They sorted it out. Made them reduce the size of the extension.' He grinned and nodded and made a fist with his right hand. 'That's power for you!' he said.

I tried once or twice more to tell about things that had happened in Bilbury but every time I started to tell him something he interrupted, claiming that something similar had happened to him but had, of course, been considerably worse, considerably more dramatic and considerably more dangerous.

Finally, I gave up and he came to a halt. I peeped at my watch. It was half past one. Mortimer had been talking about himself for hours.

'OK,' he said, leaning back into the sofa cushions. 'That's enough about me. Let's talk about you. Tell me what you've been doing with yourself. How did you come to be living in a strange little forsaken backwater like this?'

I sat silently for a moment. I was fed up with his patronising twaddle and I was too tired to talk or to listen. I just wanted to go to bed. But, as host, I felt unable to go up to bed until Mortimer did so. I opened my mouth once or twice but nothing came out.

'I don't suppose you've got much to report, have you?' he said.

'Quiet life in a little dead end place like this.' He leant back and grinned. 'Always thought you'd end up a bit of a drop out,' he said. 'If you haven't got what it takes then it's probably the best option.'

I started to protest and to defend myself and Bilbury.

'By the way,' he said. 'You haven't locked up yet.'

'We never bother,' I told him.

Mortimer seemed appalled. 'Don't you worry about burglars?'

'Not round here,' I said, smiling. 'Not in Bilbury.'

Mortimer pulled a face and then looked around, as though assessing our belongings. 'Not much worth stealing, I suppose,' he said.

I didn't say anything.

'So, what do you think about what's happened to me, eh?' Mortimer asked. 'I don't expect you thought I'd be the successful one out of our group? Top of the range Volvo. Kids at expensive private school. Wife who has her hair done at least once a week - sometimes twice if we're going out to dinner.'

I muttered the sort of pleasantries and sounds of admiration which I knew he wanted to hear. Satisfied with this Mortimer grunted again, got up, said 'Goodnight', nodded and disappeared. It took me a moment or two to realise that he had gone to bed. For a while I sat where I was staring at the fire.

* * *

When I woke up I'd got cramp in my arm, where I'd been lying on it, and the room was cold.

The log fire had burnt itself out but I put up the fireguard anyway and then went upstairs. Ben, who'd spent the last few hours dozing on the hearth rug, padded up after me.

Patsy was sitting up in bed reading a novel by Georgette Heyer. The two cats were asleep by her side.

'You didn't have to wait up,' I told her.

'I don't like to go to sleep until you come to bed,' she said. 'Did you have a nice chat with Mortimer?'

'He has become truly very boring,' I told her. 'And either I'm remembering a lot of things that never happened or he's forgotten a lot of things which did.' I started to undress. 'What do you think of Clarice?'

'Did you see the number of suitcases they brought with them?' said Patsy, carefully avoiding my question.

'We could move house with less luggage.'

'Four of the cases were full of Clarice's clothes,' said Patsy. 'I helped her unpack. She brought six swimming costumes with her.'

'Six?'

'A red one, a green one, a pink one, two yellow ones and a black and white one. I asked her why she didn't have a blue one.'

'What did she say?'

'She said she would never wear a blue swimming costume in England because the water is so cold that people might think she was bathing nude.'

'So no blue bathing costume.'

'No. And she brought three evening dresses with her.'

'What on earth did she do that for?'

'She said you never know when you're going to be invited to a formal dinner. Apparently Mortimer brought his dinner jacket, cummerbund and bow tie.'

I sighed.

'Come to bed,' said Patsy.

I threw off my clothes and climbed into bed. Ben circled my clothes, like a group of Indians circling settlers' wagons, then settled down to go to sleep on top of my trousers.

'You really shouldn't let Ben sleep on your clothes,' said Patsy quietly. I looked at Ben. She sensed me looking and raised an eyelid.

'She seems comfy,' I said. 'And if she doesn't sleep on my clothes she'll sleep on the bed and keep us both awake.'

Patsy looked at him. 'Yes,' she said. 'Better to leave her where she is.'

She put her bookmark into her book, put the book on her bedside table and turned off the light.

CHAPTER 19

IgotupearlythefollowingmorningbecauseIhadacoupleof   things
Iwanted todo. Ihadwoken upinthenight having dreamt upa planwhich
might, Ithought,helpusreduce thelength oftimeour visitorswanted
tostaywithus.

They had been with us for only one night and although I had,
before their arrival, looked forward to seeing them they had already
long outstayed their welcome.

First, I called on Mr Parfitt, our gardener. When I explained what
I wanted him to do he was, at first, surprised and puzzled. But when
I explained why I wanted him to do it he immediately understood.
'I'll give it a good stir,' he promised. 'That should liven things up a
bit.'

Next I got into the car and drove round to see Patsy's father. I
suppose I could have telephoned but I was terrified that someone
might hear me and what I had to say was not something I wanted
overheard. Mr Kennett immediately agreed to do what I wanted. He
thought it was an excellent idea. 'Don't forget to tell Patsy to leave
all the windows open!' he called after me.

My two calls made I then drove back to the house, parked the
Morris Minor roughly where it had been and, after taking Ben for a
quick walk round the garden, went into the house for breakfast.

'Where have you been?' Patsy asked.

'Just taking Ben for a walk.'

'You've been a long time.'

'She seemed to want a longer walk than usual today,' I told her. I
didn't want to explain what I'd been planning. I thought it might be
better if it came as something of a surprise. Just then Mortimer
stumbled downstairs and wandered into the kitchen. It was, I
noticed, half past eight. He told me that he, Clarice and their two
sons had decided to stay on a little longer. He didn't mention the fact
that there were problems with the cottage they'd been expecting to
stay in.

'It'll give us all chance to catch up a bit,' he said. 'We've got some slides of our holiday in Disneyland in one of the suitcases. We always cart the slides around with us in case we meet people who'd like to see them. Most people can't afford to go to Disneyland so it's a bit of a treat for them to be able to see what it's like. See what they're missing.'

'I'm afraid we haven't got a projector,' I told him.

'Oh don't worry,' he said. 'We've got our own with us. All we'll need is a piece of white wall. Or Patsy can lend us a sheet which we'll nail up in your living room.'

'Right,' I said, though to be honest I had no intention of letting him nail sheets up anywhere.

'Splendid!' said Mortimer. 'And where do I put my shoes?'

'Er, I'm not sure, I understand,' I said.

'To be cleaned,' explained Mortimer. 'I got mud on my brogues. They need a clean. And I expect the boys need their shoes cleaning too.'

I stared at him in bewilderment. Was he really expecting me to clean his shoes?

'We did all leave our shoes outside our bedroom doors,' said Mortimer.

I had noticed this. I'd assumed they were being thoughtful and not taking mud into the bedrooms. It hadn't occurred to me that they had left their shoes outside their rooms so that I could clean them.

'Perhaps if we just leave them by the back door?' suggested Mortimer, interpreting my silence as simple indecision. 'Any decent polish will do on mine but I do like them buffed up with a soft cloth afterwards. Clarice will give you specific instructions about hers.'

'Fine,' I said weakly.

'What would you like for breakfast?' Patsy asked.

'Oh just the usual,' replied Mortimer. 'Bacon, eggs, sausage, fried bread, tons of coffee and a few slices of toast.'

'Gosh!' I said. 'Do you eat all that every morning?'

'Good heavens, no! At home I just grab a slice of toast and a coffee. But when I'm away I always have the full English.'

'What about Clarice and the boys?' asked Patsy.

'They'll have the same,' said Mortimer.

'Shall I cook theirs now?'

'Oh no. They'll all wander down when the fancy takes them,' said Mortimer. 'Be better to cook separately when they come down.' It didn't seem to occur to him that this would mean Patsy cooking breakfast four times.

'I'll pop to Peter's and pick up the bacon and sausage,' I told Patsy.

'Don't you have them in the house?' asked Mortimer.

'Afraid not,' I said. 'We usually just have toast and coffee. Besides, we're vegetarian.'

'Oh,' said Mortimer, surprised. 'I'm sorry to put you to so much trouble.' He hesitated and I thought he was going to tell me that he would, after all, settle for toast and coffee. But he didn't. 'Better make sure you stock up,' he said. 'This country air will probably give the boys quite an appetite. And if you load up for the week it'll save you going out to the shop every morning.'

'Thanks for the thought,' I said.

'By the way, you've got a ghost,' said Mortimer.

I looked at him, puzzled. 'Have we?'

'The upstairs loo flushed last night but there was no one in there.'

'Oh that would have been Emily,' I explained.

Now it was Mortimer's turn to look puzzled.

'Emily is one of our cats,' I said. 'She's taught herself to use the loo. It means she doesn't have to go outside in the mud when the weather's bad.'

'But it flushed

Oh yes,' I told him. 'She learned to use the flush too.' Mortimer stared at me disbelievingly though everything I'd told him about Emily was entirely true. I looked at my watch, grabbed a sip of the coffee Patsy had made, kissed her and set off for Peter's shop. If I rushed I would just get back in time to start the morning surgery.

As luck would have it there were three other customers ahead of me. For Peter's shop that constitutes something of a rush. All were tourists passing through the village. And as always there was entertainment to be had.

The first customer purchased three peaches which Peter was advertising as being on special offer. There was a handwritten sign fixed to the tray: Peaches: three for the price of two.

'I'll have three of those peaches,' said the customer.

Peter picked up three peaches, threw one into a rubbish bucket he kept by his counter, and put the other two into a brown paper bag. He handed the bag to the customer and held his hand out for payment.

'Excuse me! There are only two peaches in the bag!' protested the customer.

'One of them was bad,' said Peter. 'I threw it away for you.' The man was so startled by this that he accepted the paper bag and paid Peter. When he walked away he looked stunned. You could tell that he was still trying to work out what had happened.

The second customer, a large American who was obviously camping or caravanning somewhere in the locality, had purchased tins of beans, soup and fruit, a box of cornflakes and a supply of candles. Peter used a sheet of brown paper and a piece of string to wrap the man's purchases up in a small parcel.

'Don't you have a plastic bag?' asked the customer.

Peter stared at him as if he'd asked for a pound of best quality uranium. 'I do not!' he said firmly. Peter doesn't like Americans at the best of times. This one was wearing plaid shorts, a lime green, short sleeved shirt and a baseball cap and this was not, therefore, the best of times.

'How am I supposed to carry this?' demanded the American, picking up the parcel.

'You could put it under your arm,' suggested Peter, not irrationally.

'I want to carry it,' said the customer. He spoke slowly and loudly, as though speaking to the village idiot. 'There is no handle!'

Peter took the parcel from the American, unfastened the string and retied it. This time he created a small additional loop of string.

'There you are,' he said, speaking softly and carefully, as though talking to a small, rather backward child. 'Put your finger through the loop in the string and carry the parcel on your finger.'

'It's too heavy to carry on one finger!' snorted the customer.

'Then carry it under your arm, like a normal person would!' roared Peter.

Startled, the American waddled away as fast as his fat legs would carry him.

The third customer wanted two pasties. Peter put two pasties into a paper bag and handed him the bag.

'These feel stale,' said the customer, feeling the pastry through the bag.

'They're not stale,' insisted Peter. 'They're just firmly baked.'

'I don't know where these people think I'd get fresh pasties from at this time of the week,' said Peter crossly when the customer had gone.

'Some people just expect too much,' I agreed. I told him what I wanted.

'I thought you and Patsy were vegetarian? Changed your minds at last, have you?' He smirked and wagged a finger. 'I told you that you would.'

'Visitors,' I explained.

He handed me three paper bags, one containing bacon, one containing sausages and one containing eggs.

'Don't you have any egg cartons?' I asked.

'They're fresh eggs,' said Peter. 'They don't get laid in egg cartons, you know.'

'Sorry!' I said.

'I suppose you want it on the slate?'

'Yes please!' I called, as I got back into the car.

I got back to Bilbury Grange just in time to hand the bags containing the eggs, bacon and sausages to Patsy before it was time to start the morning surgery.

Thanks to our visitors I was starving hungry.

'I'll give Miss Johnson some biscuits to bring you between patients,' whispered Patsy.

'Chocolate digestive?'

'OK.'

I felt better.

* * *

At eleven o'clock I finished the surgery and popped back into the kitchen to see how Patsy was getting on with our visitors. They were still sitting around the kitchen table eating toast. Patsy was looking exhausted.

'I'm afraid the boys only came down ten minutes ago,' said Mortimer. 'Your wife's been tied to the Aga all morning.'

'I don't know how you manage with that old thing,' said Clarice. 'Mortimer bought me a wonderful new oven last year.'

'Eye level grill, built in fan, six hotplates, oven big enough for two turkeys,' said Mortimer proudly. 'Cost an arm and a leg as you can imagine.'

I helped Patsy move some of the dirty crocks from the table.

'What do you do with the dirty crocks?' asked Mortimer.

I looked at him, surprised. 'We wash them,' I replied. 'You don't throw yours away do you?'

'No, no,' he laughed. 'I mean, where is the dishwasher.'

'You're looking at him,' I said. 'Well, actually, Patsy and I take it in turns.'

'You haven't got a dishwasher?'

'No.'

'Good heavens!' he cried, as though I'd just told him we didn't have electricity in the house. 'You do believe in roughing it don't you?'

'We've never really thought them worthwhile,' I said. 'You have to load up all the dishes then, when the machine has finished, you have to take them all out again. It seems quicker to wash them, dry them and put them away in the cupboard.'

Mortimer put his dirty plate on the draining board and then laid a hand on my arm. 'You have to get yourself a dishwasher,' he said. 'Buy Patsy one for her birthday. She'll be thrilled.'

'I'm not entirely sure Patsy will be thrilled at getting a dishwasher for her birthday,' I said.

Mortimer ignored me. 'Get one of the new models that dry the crocks afterwards. We've got the top of the range model that takes a twelve piece dinner service.'

'We haven't got a twelve piece dinner service,' I said. I was about to mention that I didn't think we knew ten people we'd want to invite to dinner but I didn't.

'Then get one of the compact models,' he said. 'They're very reasonably priced. Even you could afford one.' He spoke with enthusiasm; the same sort of enthusiasm with which I remembered him once talking about sports cars.

'Splendid,' I said. I found it difficult to believe that I was listening to Mortimer talk to me about the relative merits of different brands of dishwasher. It seemed rather sad.

* * *

Half an hour later we left. I was going out on my visits and

140

Mortimer was going to follow me to Tolstoy's.

I took Mortimer round to the Bilbury garage.

Henry was busy fastening a loose exhaust pipe on a Ford Popular. He was doing this with a length of orange baler twine. ('The orange stuff is much better than the blue for cars,' he once told me. 'It's much the same sort of colour as rust and so it blends in and you can't see it.') Reginald was kicking the tyres holding up an old Ford Consul.

'What are you doing?' I asked him.

'Visitor brought this in,' replied Reginald. 'Said it wobbled.'

I nodded as though I understood these things. Mortimer frowned. 'So what are you doing?'

'Making sure the wheels are all in the right places.'

'Good idea,' I agreed. 'One on each corner is usually best.'

'Definitely,' said Reginald kicking another wheel. 'I call it an Optical Wheel Alignment Check.'

I waited until he had kicked the fourth tyre and then introduced him to Mortimer who explained his problem.

'Little wipers on the headlamps?' said Reginald.

'That's right.'

'And they won't stop wiping?'

'That's it.'

'Let's have a look.'

Mortimer took Reginald outside to look at his errant headlamp wipers. He turned on the engine so that Reginald could study the problem.

'Amazing,' murmured Reginald. 'I've never seen anything like it in my life.' He went back into the garage to fetch Henry and then the two of them stood and watched in absolute awe.

'Can you sort it out?' asked Mortimer.

'No problem,' said Reginald.

'No problem at all,' Henry assured him.

'How long will it take?'

'You can pick it up at two,' said Reginald.

'Will it really take that long?' demanded Mortimer.

'Afraid so,' said Reginald. He sucked air in through the gap in his front teeth. 'Could be a complicated job.'

Mortimer sighed and turned to me. 'Bit like rural Spain,' he said. 'What's the local word for manana?'

Reginald looked at me. Mortimer, who seemed to have noticed a mark, was rubbing at the paintwork on the rear offside passenger door. I shrugged and raised my eyebrows.

'I don't rightly think,' said Reginald, 'that we have a word which rightly conveys quite that sense of urgency.'

Mortimer turned and looked at him. He was clearly puzzled.

'Do you want a lift back to the house?' I asked Mortimer.

'No, I'll be fine,' he replied. He looked up at the sky. 'It's a warm day. I'll walk.' He set off back towards Bilbury Grange.

'Will you find your way?' I called after him.

'Oh yes,' he replied. 'I remembered the route. Photographic memory.'

'Friend of yours?' asked Henry, nodding towards the disappearing Mortimer.

'Used to be.' I replied.

'Used to be?' said Henry, checking.

'Used to be,' I confirmed.

'Seems a bit of a plonker to me,' said Reginald, who was not renowned for his patience or his tact.

'I'm afraid so,' I agreed.

Henry wandered off down the lane. 'I'm going down to the Duck and Puddle,' he called over his shoulder. 'I need a drink after that. While I'm there I'll see if I can find another one of these cars with wipers on the headlights.'

'He's a bugger for learning,' explained Reginald. 'We had one of them Audi things in the other day. Someone passing through. We couldn't work out how to open the bonnet. Henry drove around Devon until he saw someone driving something similar. He flagged them down and got them to tell him how to open the bonnet.'

'Shows initiative.'

'We didn't want to have to ask the owner,' explained Reginald.

'Damages the customer's trust.'

'I can see that it might. Did he find someone with the right car?'

'In Lynmouth,' said Reginald. 'In the car park near the river.'

'Good,' I nodded.

'But when we opened the bonnet we just shut it again.'

'Too complicated?'

'Too much engine in there,' said Reginald. 'Scary.' He shuddered. 'The chap had one of those metal RAC badges fastened to his bumper so we rang them up. A nice chap came out on his motorbike.'

'And he sorted it out?'

'Brilliant,' said Reginald. 'Henry and I are thinking of joining.'

* * *

Later I drove back to Lydeard Lawrence's cottage to see how he was getting on. He was in the kitchen filling his three feeding bottles with milk when I arrived. His back, he said, was much better.

'It's your birthday today,' I told him.

'It is,' he agreed. 'How did you know that?'

'I noticed your date of birth on your medical records,' I told him. I pulled the cardboard envelope containing all his medical history out of my jacket pocket and pointed to the relevant box on the outside of the envelope. His birth date was written there in faded blue ink.

'You're a hundred years old.'

'I am.'

'Aren't you celebrating?'

'What is there to celebrate?'

'You could have had a telegram from the Queen.'

'What would I do with one of those?'

'You could put it on the mantelpiece. You should show it to people.'

'Who?'

'Relatives? Friends? Visitors?'

'Haven't got any, don't want any and never have any.'

'Right,' I said. 'No point in having a telegram then.'

'One thing I can tell you,' he said.

'What's that?'

'The first hundred years are the hardest,' he said.

I looked at him to see if he was joking. He wasn't, of course.

'I reckon the next hundred will be a doddle.' I smiled.

'You probably don't think I've got much longer to live.'

I thought for a moment and then started to disagree but he spoke again before I could say anything. 'I'm probably not going to live much longer am I?' he demanded, staring at me defiantly.

Faced with this more definite question I agreed with him. 'Probably not.'

This seemed to irritate him. 'You think I'm on my last legs?'

143

'No, no,' I said hurriedly, back pedalling as fast as I could. 'I didn't mean that.'

'I'm as fit as a flea,' he said. He dropped to the floor and started doing press ups. 'I can still do sixty at a time,' he said. 'Proper ones too. Legs and body straight, chest to floor, arms fully extended.' He carried on doing press ups. It was an astonishing sight.

* * *

I called in at Tolstoy's on my way back to Bilbury Grange. Mortimer's Volvo had gone.

'Did my friend collect his car?' I asked Henry, who was making a car aerial out of a metal coat hanger.

'Half an hour ago,' said Henry.

'Did you manage to sort it out for him?'

'Certainly did. He was as pleased as Punch. Happy as a sand boy.' Henry winked at me. 'I don't think he thought we could do it.'

'He probably didn't,' I told him. 'Your laid-back attitude probably worried him.'

'We sorted it out for him,' said Henry. 'Charged him £10.'

'That seems fair enough,' I agreed. 'Did you find out what the problem was?'

'Nope.'

'How did you solve the problem then?'

'We cut the wires didn't we,' said Henry. He made a snipping motion with his right hand.

'You cut the wires?'

'Yeah. That stopped the bloody little wipers dead in their tracks. No electricity. No wiping.'

'But won't he notice? There's a little panel of lights on the dashboard that tells him when things aren't working properly. If it's been raining and he tries to clean his headlamps the warning light will come on.'

'Ah, we're not stupid,' said Henry. He tapped the side of his nose with a greasy finger. 'We thought of that. We took the little bulbs out of the warning lights.'

I thought about it. It really was unlikely that Mortimer would find out that his headlamp wipers weren't working and almost impossible that he would find out before he left Bilbury.

'Fantastic,' I said to Henry. 'I knew I could rely on you.' Henry winked at me.

'Did you put twenty pence on the dashboard?' He winked again.

'Brilliant,' I said.

'Tip?'

'A quid.'

'Brilliant.'

'Always works,' said Henry.

* * *

'That garage of yours may look a bit rough but they're real professionals,' said Mortimer when I saw him that afternoon. It had taken him three hours to find his way back to Bilbury Grange. He claimed he'd gone the scenic route but I didn't believe him. 'And honest too. Not only did they do a brilliant job on the headlamp wipers but when I picked the car up I found twenty pence in change in an envelope on the dashboard. There was a note with it saying that they'd found the coins underneath the mat when they were working on the car. I tell you it made me feel really warm inside.'

'Splendid,' I said. 'I'm so glad you were pleased.'

'You should have given them the twenty pence as a tip,' said Clarice.

'I did better than that,' said Mortimer proudly. 'I gave the chappie a pound note as a reward for his honesty.'

Patsy smiled at me.

I had to fight hard to suppress a giggle.

'I don't like to mention this,' said Clarice. 'But have either of you noticed a rather funny smell?'

Patsy and I looked at one another.

I shook my head. 'Nothing unusual,' I said.

Patsy blushed a little. 'I think there might have been some spraying in the fields near to us. I'm sorry about it. It's not usually this pungent.'

'You mean a farmer has been spraying something?' asked Clarice.

'They spray manure on the fields,' I explained.

'Manure!' said Clarice.

'Liquid manure,' I said. 'It'll probably go on all week now. They spray tons and tons of it. It helps make the grass grow greener.'

'I could...' began Patsy.

'I'm afraid we can't ask the farmer to stop it,' I said. 'It's just something they do.' I paused. 'I'm afraid they wouldn't listen to us anyway.' I shrugged rather sadly and impotently.

'Oh I'm sure I...' said Patsy. I looked at her and winked. She didn't finish the sentence.

'It happens so often that we did think of renaming our house Pooh Corner,' I said, with what I hoped was a smile.

'Well, it's made Spotty feel rather nauseous,' said Clarice indignantly. 'Me too for that matter.'

'Oh, I am sorry,' I said. I smiled sympathetically. 'We're so used to it now that we hardly notice it any more.' 'It stinks upstairs in our bedroom,' said Rupert. 'Its disgusting. I can't sleep up there.'

'I'm afraid that when they do the spraying it always rather stinks the house out,' I said as apologetically as I could.

'Can't you do anything about it?' demanded Mortimer. 'Explain you've got visitors staying?'

'Tell them Daddy is a doctor and he'll have them all locked up!' suggested Spotty.

'I'm sure there must be a law against it,' said Clarice.

'I think you'll find that farmers can pretty much do what they like,' I said. 'You'll probably get used to it after a while.' I paused. 'Though I admit we do find that the smell tends to linger in our clothes and hair for weeks.'

'I don't want to go back to school smelling of cow poo!' said Rupert, red-faced and full of indignation.

'It stays in the hair?' said Clarice. She touched the back of her head protectively.

'I'm afraid so,' I told her. 'But not for ever,' I added, in what I hoped was a reassuring sort of way.

Clarice looked at Mortimer.

'I want to go home,' said Spotty.

'Me too,' said Rupert.

Mortimer looked at me. 'I'm sorry about this old chap,' he said. 'But...' he shrugged. 'Clarice and I did talk about it before you came back. You country folk may be able to cope with this sort of thing but I'm afraid we aren't as used to it as you are.'

'Oh no!' I said. 'You're going to leave?'

'Afraid so,' said Mortimer.

'I'll go and pack,' said Clarice, heading for the stairs.

'Can we come with you to the golf club when we get back?' Rupert asked his father. 'We can play the fruit machines while you play golf'

'Yes, OK,' said Mortimer, glancing nervously towards the stairs. I got the impression that Clarice didn't approve of the boys playing the fruit machines. He lowered his voice and confirmed my suspicion. 'But don't tell your mother you play the fruit machines.'

The boys both looked pleased.

'Now, we'd better go and help your Mum pack,' said Mortimer. 'I want to get my suits into the cases before I need to send them all to the dry cleaners.' He turned to me. 'Do you think I'll need to have them all dry-cleaned to get the smell out of them?'

'I wouldn't have thought so,' I said. I turned to Patsy who was looking rather bewildered. 'What do you think?'

'Oh no,' she said. 'I'm sure they'll be fine.'

It took the four of them less than fifteen minutes to pack and to cram all their suitcases into the back of their estate car.

'Thank you so much for a wonderful stay,' said Clarice. She gave Patsy one of those light kisses on the cheek that models give one another and then she did the same to me. She was clearly desperate to get into the car and out of range of the smell of manure.

'Sorry we have to disappear so quickly,' said Mortimer. He smiled weakly. 'Hope you understand.'

'Absolutely,' I agreed, nodding.

'Maybe another time?'

'Look forward to it,' I said, knowing that we would never see them again.

Clarice and Mortimer got into the car. Mortimer was driving. He wound down his window.

'Say 'thank you,' hissed Clarice to the two boys in the back of the car.

'Thank you!' they chorused, without any discernible enthusiasm.

'I left the Morris out on the road,' I told him. 'So that you could get out of the drive.'

As we waved goodbye I turned to Patsy. 'If you put the kettle on I'll tell you how Tolstoy's managed to sort out Mortimer's headlamp wipers for him.'

Suddenly Patsy stopped and looked at me. 'You knew they were leaving before they did!'

I looked back at her, trying to look innocent. 'Why do you say that?'

'You left your car on the road so that they could get out of the drive more easily.'

'Well, I thought they might want to go off for a bit of a drive.'

Patsy frowned and looked at me. 'There's something going on,' she said.

As we headed for the kitchen Mr Parfitt appeared. 'Shall I put the lid back on now, doctor?' he called. 'Don't want any of the animals falling in, do we?'

'Yes please, Mr Parfitt,' I told him. 'And about that other thing, are you sure...?' he asked hesitantly.

'I'm sure,' I said.

'Seems an awful waste,' he said.

'I know it is,' I said. I grinned. 'That's the point.'

He hurried off down the garden path.

'The lid off what?' asked Patsy.

'Off the septic tank.'

Patsy stopped and looked at me. 'You told Mr Parfitt to take the lid off our septic tank?'

I shrugged and tried to look innocent. 'Just to give it an airing,' I told her. 'Septic tanks need an airing every now and then.'

'I suppose you got him to give it a good stirring as well?'

'Well, a bit of a stir. Just to liven things up a bit.'

'And what else was he asking you?' asked Patsy.

'He thinks it's a bit of a waste,' I said.

'It's a lot of waste,' said Patsy. She stood for a moment then folded her arms. 'He wants to put our septic tank contents on our vegetables?'

'I've told him 'No'.'

Patsy shuddered.

Mr Parfitt, our gardener, had developed a firm affection for manure in all its various forms and was a keen inventor of new forms of homemade liquid manure. The success of our raspberries was all the evidence he needed of the quality of his manure. He had two varieties of liquid manure with which to boost our crop production. One variety, allegedly rich in iron, had been prepared by putting armfuls of nettles into a tin bath full of water and leaving them to rot. The other variety, the type which Mr Parfitt preferred because he said it was particularly rich in nitrogen, was prepared by putting dirty wool. clippings into a water butt and leaving them there for a few months. Each summer when Patsy's father shaved our sheep he had sold the main fleeces to the wool merchants on our behalf but he left the grubbier bits of fleece behind - the bits taken from the non-eating ends of our four sheep. Mr Parfitt had discovered its value as a source of liquid manure.'And was it you who got my father to spray the fields on either side of the house?' said Patsy.

'I think I did mention that if he wanted to do any spraying now would be a really good time for us,' I admitted.

Patsy stared at me.

'You're not cross are you?'

She stared at me. I honestly thought she was going to be cross. 'Absolutely brilliant,' she said at last. She kissed me. 'You can have a double helping of treacle tart. And take a piece to poor old Mr Parfitt when he's put the lid back on the septic tank.'

'OK,' I said.

'And just make sure he puts the lid back on firmly,' she said. 'If I find he's been using anything from our septic tank to improve our fruit or vegetables I will buy all our greengrocery requirements from Peter Marshall.

CHAPTER 20

'ImetAdrienneinBarnstaple,'saidPatsythemomentIgothome. 'You'll neverguesswhat'shappening?'

Adrienne is Patsy's sister. Although a couple of years older than Patsy, Adrienne still lived at home on her parents' farm in Bilbury.

'So tell me!'

'No, no. You've got to guess!'

'But you've just told me that I'll never guess.'

'So, try!'

'She's joining the Navy and going to see the world.'

'Don't be silly.'

'She's bought a gypsy caravan and a horse and is going to set off round Britain.'

'No. That's more likely. But that's not it.'

'I don't have the faintest.'

'Try once more.'

'She's going to train to be an astronaut.' Patsy laughed. 'She's getting married!'

'Married! To whom?'

'Guess.'

'No! I can't go through all that again. Tell me!'

'To Patchy!'

'Patchy Fogg?'

'Yes.'

I was delighted at this news. But I was so shocked that I had to sit down for a minute. Offhand I couldn't think of two people less likely to make a couple. But many successful partnerships are created when unlikely individuals come together and of one thing I was certain: neither Patchy nor Adrienne were weak-willed enough to have been bullied into a marriage they weren't absolutely certain about.

* * *

Adrienne was an enthusiastic practitioner of alternative medicine and had nearly killed her and Patsy's father by mistakenly (and dangerously) prescribing hawthorn for him. I believed then, and still believe now, that if I hadn't stopped the hawthorn their father would have died.

Adrienne had never admitted that her herbalism might have dangerous consequences but she had moved into other areas of alternative medicine. At various times she had dabbled in reflexology, iridology, acupuncture and several other branches of alternative medicine. She was fascinated by all aspects of medicine. (I remember us once having a curious conversation about influenza. 'Is influenza catching?' she asked. 'Yes,' I agreed. 'It spreads by passing from one person to another?' I agreed. 'So,' she asked, 'how did the first person in the world to get the flu catch it? From whom did they catch it if no one else had ever had the flu?' She had been quite delighted when I had been unable to answer her question.)

She also had a number of curious medical theories of her own.

She claimed, for example, that as men get older they go bald because their hair gets trapped inside their skulls. She explained the phenomenon by arguing that the male skull gets thicker with age while the brain expands as it accumulates information. Eventually, the expanding brain blocks off the small holes through which the hair normally grows. This leaves the hair trapped inside the skull. She said the proof of this was the escaping hair that can be seen growing out of male ears. Her solution was to try to reduce the size of her patients' brains by teaching them to forget stuff and cleanse their brains of unwanted information. As far as I know she had never had any success but this hadn't diluted her enthusiasm for her theory.

* * *

I'd first met Patchy Fogg, the groom to be, when Patsy and I were buying old furniture for Bilbury Grange.

Patchy was an antique dealer and we'd met at an auction when, in order to push up the price he finally obtained, he had persuaded me to bid for a davenport that he was selling.

At the time Patchy didn't live in Bilbury but he was well-known in the village. His ponytail was tied back with a small red ribbon and he always wore what looked like the same dirty jeans and a grubby T-shirt. He and Thumper Robinson were great pals (the two of them played regularly in the spectacularly unsuccessful Bilbury football team) and were always thinking of new ways to help liberate tourists (especially American tourists) from money they didn't really need.

151

Patchy once sold an early Victorian television cabinet to a bumptious and self-confident American who had made millions as a stock market analyst. He even claimed that Queen Victoria herself had once owned the cabinet.

Pretending that the stuff he was selling had once been owned by someone famous (and invariably dead) was one of Patchy's favourite and most profitable ploys.

'Aren't you worried he'll go to the police?' I asked Patchy when I'd heard about the sale of the antique television cabinet.

Patchy, clearly unworried, shrugged. 'He'd have to admit he was stupid enough to buy a Victorian television cabinet,' he said with his usual lopsided smile. Selling genuine antique television cabinets was one of Patchy's most bizarre but most lucrative specialities.

Patchy described himself as a dealer in very nearly genuine antiques and had, over the years, taught me more than I probably needed to know about the antique trade. To be honest neither Patsy nor I really approved of many of the things he got up to. But the antiques trade is full of loveable but slightly dodgy characters and even though he was definitely slightly dodgy Patchy was also definitely loveable. We consoled ourselves with the thought that most of the people he cheated were already cheating someone else.

At an auction in South Molton I once found him staining an antique lace table cloth by pouring red dye onto the lace from a small glass bottle.

'What on earth are you doing?' I asked him, appalled.

'It'll wash out,' he murmured. 'Just a vegetable dye.'

'But why do that?' I asked him, naively.

'It'll put other people off and keep the price down,' he explained. 'I'll wash out the dye and sell it on for what it's really worth.'

A few minutes later I saw Patchy chatting to a big dealer from Exeter.

'What was that all about?' I asked him.

'He was interested in the lace tablecloth but didn't want to bid on it because it's got a nasty wine stain on it,' said Patchy. 'He was worried about whether the stain would come out cleanly.' He winked at me. 'I told him not to bother bidding because I had a perfect cloth, the same size, that I could let him have tomorrow.'

And so Patchy bought the lace cloth cheaply, washed it in his bath that night, dried it and sold it to the dealer in Exeter for several times what he'd paid for it.

On another occasion, at an auction in Lynton, I saw Patchy accidentally-on-purpose break a small piece of glass in the front of a magnificent bookcase.

'What on earth did you do that for?' I demanded. 'It's a beautiful piece of furniture.'

'But flawed now,' said Patchy, skilfully using a small screwdriver to remove a handle from one of the doors.

'And you just happen to have a piece of old glass that you can use to replace the piece you've just broken?'

'Something like that,' grinned Patchy, slipping the handle into his pocket. He then strolled away and hovered over a beautiful set of twelve Georgian silver fruit knives. 'Look at these beautiful knives!' he said, picking up one and showing me the handle. When he moved away the knife went with him, leaving just eleven remaining.

'That's stealing!' I told him. 'If they catch you...'

'I'm not stealing anything,' he replied, sliding the knife into a tray containing several dozen items of miscellaneous cutlery oddments. The knife disappeared underneath a layer of nondescript and unattractive electroplated forks and tarnished spoons.

Naturally, it was Patchy who was the successful bidder on the eleven Georgian silver fruit knives and it was Patchy who, to everyone's surprise, bothered to bid on the unwanted tray of kitchen cutlery.

Patchy didn't only cheat when he was buying. He was an equal opportunities cheat. I once visited him at home and found him dropping handfuls of shiny horse brasses into a bowl full of vinegar and brand new screws into a jar full of very salty water.

'It ages them nicely,' he explained.

And it was Patchy who taught me some of the more honourable tricks of the antiques trade.

At an auction in Barnstaple I spotted a first edition of a book by Graham Greene stuck in a row of old book club editions about gardening and cooking. The only book I wanted was the Greene. It still had a clean and bright dust jacket.

'Do you think the auctioneer would just sell me the Greene?' I asked.

Patchy looked at me pityingly. 'Don't draw attention to the first edition,' he told me. 'Just bid on the row of books and pay what you think the Greene is worth.'

I did as I was told and got the collection for a fraction of the value of the Graham Greene first edition.

'Pick up the book you want,' said Patchy.

I picked up the Greene and slipped it into my overcoat pocket. 'Now what do I do with all these books?' I asked. There were at least forty old books in which I had absolutely no interest.

Patchy took me across the room to the underbidder - the person who had bid £1 less than I had for the row of books.

'My chum only wanted one book from that last lot,' Patchy said. 'Do you want the rest for £1 less than you were bidding?'

'Great!' said the underbidder enthusiastically.

And so I got the book I wanted for a total outlay of £2.

* * *

Patchy's two main redeeming features were that he loved animals and had a heart of gold. I had first hand experience of this shortly after he and I first met.

Alfred Burton, a farmer who lived half way between Bilbury and Combe Martin, had gone bankrupt and his land, house and farm machinery were all being sold off at auction. Alfred had moved into a cottage in Combe Martin with his eighty-five-year-old mother and he wasn't too upset by what had happened. 'I used to work from five in the morning until ten or eleven at night,' he told me when I asked how he was. 'Nowadays I get up when I feel like it and the day is mine to do with as I like. Some days I go down to the coast and do a little sea fishing. Occasionally, I just walk in the woods.' He'd even discovered the joys of reading and could often be seen walking around the village with a book in his hand. I'd given him a battered old paperback copy of a novel by P.G.Wodehouse and he'd become a huge fan of Jeeves and Wooster.

Not having much money to spend on books (even second hand ones) he'd joined the local branch of the public library and every Thursday afternoon he took out half a dozen books when the travelling library bus stopped at Bilbury.

'The cottage is in my Mum's name,' he told me. 'If she lives another few years I'll be free of the bankruptcy and I can inherit the cottage without the bailiffs taking it from me.'

His one big sadness was that the bankruptcy people had decided that his dog was a saleable asset belonging to his farm. They'd confiscated the dog and put it into kennels so that it could be sold alongside the thirty cows, the milking machinery, the twenty-five-year-old Massey Ferguson tractor, a hundred and sixty bales of straw and all the rest of his worldly goods.

And so, on the auction catalogue there was a line which read: Lot 151: 'One working sheep dog (five-years-old). Name of Lady.'

Alfred was at the auction but only because he knew it was his last chance to see Lady. Good working sheep dogs fetch quite a high price and Alfred knew that there was no way he could afford to buy Lady back.

A bailiff led Lady into the barn where the auction was being held on lead fashioned out of a piece of string. Lady wasn't used to being on a lead- I don't think Alfred had ever put one on her - and she fretted. When the bailiff brought her into the barn she looked around the familiar sights and sniffed at the air. This was her territory. I don't know whether she smelt or saw Alfred but suddenly she made a leap in his direction. The bailiff couldn't hold onto his end of the string and moments later Lady and Alfred were temporarily reunited. When the bailiff, accompanied now by one of his colleagues, dragged Lady away from Alfred the barn fell totally silent. There were some hard men in that room but no one said a word. With tears running down his cheeks Alfred turned away and walked out of the barn. Held by the bailiff, Lady whimpered and watched him go. It was one of the most painful things I ever saw.

There wasn't much of interest to Patchy or to me at the auction. Most of Alfred's furniture was riddled with woodworm and neither of us was in the market for milk churns, butter making machinery or rusty farm equipment.

Patchy bought three old-fashioned three-legged milking stools (which he would later claim had once belonged to- and been used by Marie Antoinette - and sell to a London dealer for nearly one hundred times what he paid for them) but I didn't buy anything.

Lot 151 came up just before the lunch break and Patchy and I had already decided that we wouldn't bother staying for the afternoon session.

'I'm going to bid for the dog,' I whispered, as the auctioneer announced the lot.

'No,' hissed Patchy. 'Leave it to me. I've dealt with it.'

Like many professional dealers Patchy didn't make a big fuss when he made a bid and I didn't see him move or make any sign when he bid for the dog. Indeed, I wasn't even sure he'd been successful when the auctioneer suddenly brought down his gavel and announced a thirty minute lunch break. The whole thing had been over in a second or two.

'Did you get it?' I asked, but Patchy was off, heading for the desk where bidders paid for their purchases and got the slips of paper which entitled them to pick up their goods. I followed, several yards behind him, struggling through the crowd of people heading out of the barn and towards the van parked outside where a husband and wife team from Ilfracombe were selling coffee and hot dogs.

'Carry these,' he said, moments later, thrusting two milking stools at me. He carried the third stool in his left hand. And in his right hand he had the piece of string to which Lady was attached.

'Come on, Lady,' he said. 'Let's take you where you belong.'

We overtook Alfred a quarter of a mile before he got to his mother's cottage. Patchy stopped his old Volvo but neither he nor I had chance to get out of the car before Lady. The moment Patchy opened his door Lady squeezed past him and out into Alfred's arms.

Alfred didn't speak. He wrapped his arms around Lady's neck and his eyes, when he looked up at us, said everything that needed to be said.

'See you around Alfred,' said Patchy.

'Thank you,' mouthed Alfred silently, unfastening the string from around Lady's neck.

'Pleasure,' said Patchy, meaning it. Patchy headed back to Bilbury Grange.

'Let me pay half of what you paid for Lady,' I said.

'OK,' said Patchy, more quickly than I had expected.

'How much do I owe you?' I asked, reaching for my wallet.

'A halfpenny,' replied Patchy.

'Don't be daft. How much do I owe you?'

'A halfpenny,' repeated Patchy.

'How much did you pay for Lady?'

'A penny. Your maths isn't very good is it?'

'But...'

156

'No one bid against me,' said Patchy. 'I bid a penny and got the dog.'

I looked at him.

'I had a word with a few people,' he said. 'Everyone agreed to keep their hands in their pockets. The auctioneer's a good bloke. He didn't mind.'

I left my wallet where it was and fumbled in my pocket.

Eventually I found a halfpenny. I handed it to Patchy. He took it, nodded, and put it in his pocket.

It was the best halfpenny I ever spent.

* * *

'So, when is the wedding?' I asked Patsy.

'Two weeks on Saturday.'

'They're not hanging around, are they!' I paused. 'Is there, er, any particular reason for the hurry?'

Patsy laughed. 'No, we're the only ones who are about to become parents. They're both pretty impetuous people though. And having decided that they want to get married they thought they might as well get on with it.'

'Where are they getting married?'

'Bilbury Church.'

Suddenly, I caught sight of the clock. 'I've got more visits to do,' I said. 'If I don't get them done soon I'll still be doing visits after dinner tonight.'

'Will you be going past the shop?'

'I can do,' I said. 'Do you need something?'

Patsy looked slightly embarrassed. 'Could you get me a pot of Marmite and some ginger biscuits?'

I looked at her and smiled.

'I just fancy some Marmite on a ginger biscuit,' she said.

* * *

'I've had your results back,' I told Gloria Ross. 'You've got thyrotoxicosis. It explains why you've had a job putting on weight.'

She looked worried. 'Is that bad?'

'Not really,' I told her. 'Your thyrotoxicosis is quite mild. I want you to see a specialist so that we can make sure that we get your treatment right. But it shouldn't be difficult.'

'Will I need an operation?'

I shook my head. 'I don't think so. We can almost certainly control it with some tablets,' I told her.

'Will the tablets help me put on weight?'

'Yes.'

'Does this mean my bum will get bigger?' she wanted to know.

I told her that she could count on it.

She beamed with delight and said she couldn't wait to start the treatment.

It wasn't quite the response I usually got from patients. I don't think I'd ever before had a patient who had been thrilled that the treatment she needed would give her a bigger bottom.

* * *

I headed for home and picked up the items Patsy wanted on my way.

'Ginger biscuits and one pot of Marmite,' I said, putting one of Peter's brown paper bags down on the kitchen table.

'Oh wonderful,' said Patsy, grabbing the bag. 'I was hoping you wouldn't forget.' She opened the Marmite and the packet of biscuits and took a knife out of the cutlery drawer.

I then watched, transfixed, as she spread Marmite on one of ginger biscuits.

'You're not going to eat that?'

She didn't answer immediately but, instead, put the biscuit into her mouth and took a huge bite.

I stared.

'Khgj ty kdil wkhekt kehd kjgl qtkh ptkl ktlrk bklepwjg rtwkl kbjtlg kmnfght lktqpb kghys,' she said.

I didn't understand a word of what she said, but I knew exactly what she meant.

'This is what people mean when they talk about pregnant women having strange eating urges.'

Patsy beamed and swallowed. 'Oh that was wonderful,' she said. 'I'll just have one more and then I'll make dinner.'

* * *

We had finished dinner and we were sitting in the garden, on an old battered bench near to the lake. We each had a glass of fruit juice in our hands. The bottle was leaning against the trunk of a willow tree. Patsy had stopped drinking alcohol during her pregnancy and when I was with her I didn't drink either.

We both love sitting by our small lake. That year we even had a pair of swans nesting by it. We both love swans. As Patsy once put it, swans remind us of a wedding party full of brides. We had spent many happy hours watching 'our' two swans glide, apparently effortlessly across the lake, surrounded by a cygnet ring - a circle of young swans.

'We haven't talked about what we're going to call the baby,' said Patsy.

'It rather depends what sex it is.'

'It's going to be a boy.'

'How do you know that?' I asked. We had agreed not to let the doctors tell us the sex of our baby.

Patsy shrugged and smiled. 'I just know,' she said.

'Then assuming it to be a boy what do you want to call him?'

There was a flash of blue as a kingfisher swooped low over the water.

'Did you see that?' I asked, in a whisper.

'Yes,' she answered. There was a long pause. We both sipped our drinks. 'We could name him after you.'

I shuddered. 'Thanks,' I said. 'But I don't think I want that. He'd be known as Junior and it will look as if we're trying to start a dynasty.'

'I don't want to name him after my Dad,' said Patsy. Neither of us spoke for a while. Two moorhens swam silently among the bulrushes at the edge of the lake.

'No.' I said quietly at last. 'Perhaps not.' Patsy's father has two Christian names. The first is Gilbert. The second is Arnold.

'But we've got to call him something,' said Patsy. I agreed with her.

'There's one person I would like to name him after,' I said.

'Me too,' admitted Patsy.

'You first.'

'I wondered if we could perhaps name him after Dr Brownlow,' I suggested. 'He brought us together. I admire him a lot. He's always been good to us. If it hadn't been for him we would never have met and I wouldn't be living in Bilbury.' I paused. 'And I don't know anyone I respect more.'

Patsy nodded her agreement. 'He was my choice,' she said. 'I'd like that.'

We sat there for a while, holding hands.

'There's just one thing,' said Patsy.

'What's that?'

'I don't know Dr Brownlow's Christian name. Do you?'

I thought about this for a while. 'No,' l said at last. 'Maybe we should find out,' said Patsy.

'Certainly before the christening,' I agreed. 'I'll ask him.'

'I expect he'll know,' said Patsy.

'I expect so.'

'That's settled then.'

We sat in silence and watched the moorhens.

I picked up the bottle and shared its remaining contents between us. 'You could drink wine,' said Patsy. 'I wouldn't mind.'

'This is good,' I said, lifting the glass of juice and sipping it. We sat in silence for a while.

Patsy shivered.

'Cold?'

She nodded.

'Let's go indoors. I'll make a log fire and we'll create pictures out of the flames.'

Both of us love few things more than a nice log fire. All the joys of a bonfire but held indoors out of the cold and the rain.

Unfortunately, our log fire wasn't quite the success I'd hoped it would be. Minutes after I'd lit the fire the room was filled with smoke.

'I'm fed up with this,' I said wearily. Ever since we'd been at Bilbury Grange there had been problems with the fire. 'Maybe there is a blockage,' I said. 'Perhaps there is a nest.'

'Those people from Barnstaple wanted to fit a fan,' Patsy reminded me.

'They also wanted a small fortune,' I reminded her.

'I'll call the chimney sweep tomorrow,' said Patsy. 'Maybe he can do something to help.'

We gave up on the log fire and went to bed instead. It had been a long and eventful day. I took with me the novel I was reading. But I was fast asleep before I could even open the book.

CHAPTER 21

PatsywasawayinBarnstaplehelpinghersisterAdriennechoosea
weddingdresssoIwentroundtotheDuckandPuddleformylunch.
ThemomentIwalkedinthroughthedoorIsensedthatsomething
wasdifferent.Thebarsmeltofacuriousmixtureoffurniturepolish
andcooking.Butthecookingsmellwasn'tthearomaproducedby
piesbeingheatedupintheoven.Thiswasthesortofsmellyou
getinarestaurant.

'Good   morning,sir!'criedastrangevoicethemoment   Iwalked   in
through   thedoor.   Iturned   andlookedaround.   Asmall,thin
strangerwithasmallthinmoustachewasstandingbehindthebar.   Hewore
acheckedsportscoatwithawoollenshirtandaneatly
knottedmilitarytiewhichIdidn'trecognise.Hehadateatowelin
onehandandapintglassintheother.Inoticedthathiscufflinks
carriedanemblemwhichseemedtomatchtheoneonhistie.

'Good morning!' I replied. 'Where's Frank?'

'Mr and Mrs Parsons are on leave this weekend.'

'Ah, yes,' I said. 'I remember now.' Frank had taken Gilly to London for the weekend as a belated birthday present.

'I'm Sidney Weedon,' said the barman, 'but people usually call me Lionel. My wife, Mrs Weedon, will attend to any culinary needs you might have.'

I stared at him. I didn't mean to be rude but I was rather startled.

As a regular customer in the Duck and Puddle I wasn't used to this level of service.

The stand-in publican leant forward across the bar. 'Anything you might need to eat,' he explained.

'Yes,' I said. 'Of course.'

'What can I get you to drink, sir?' he asked.

I asked for a pint of Guinness. While he poured the drink, taking great care with the head, I looked around for the jar of pickled eggs which Frank usually kept on the bar counter. 'Where are the eggs?' I asked.

'We had to move them I'm afraid, sir,' he replied. 'Current health and safety regulations forbid the sale of such items unless the container is fitted with a sealed cap.'

'There is a lid somewhere,' I told him, looking around in the hope that I might spot it. 'I remember we were using it as a Frisbee a few days ago.'

Sidney, known as Lionel, lowered his voice. 'I'm afraid that according to the bar records the eggs were a little past their recommended date for sale,' he told me. I paid him, exchanged a few words about the weather we were having for the time of year and sauntered over to the far corner of the bar where Patchy and Thumper were watching horse racing on Frank's flickering black and white television set.

'Has anyone won anything?' I asked, sitting down next to Thumper. The chair had been polished and felt slightly sticky.

'We're just thinking up daft names for horses,' said Thumper.

'Thumper wants to have a really useless horse called The Winner,' said Patchy.

I looked at him and frowned. 'Why?'

'Because it will be fun when the chap who does the commentating has to say: 'And The Winner came last."

I nodded. 'I can see that would be mildly confusing,' I agreed.

'I want one called The Pantomime Horse,' said Patchy.

'...and The Pantomime Horse is corning up on the outside!' said Thumper, mimicking the sound of a horse race commentator.

'How about The One At The Back,' I suggested.

'The winner is The One At The Back,' said Thumper. He thought about it. 'I like that,' he nodded. 'Very good.'

'Heavily Doped,' suggested Patchy. 'And the horse who came in third was 'Heavily Doped'.'

Thumper and I both agreed that we liked that too.

I lowered my voice. 'Have you met the curious little bloke behind the bar?' I asked. The television flickered and slipped. Patchy stood up and slammed the side of the television with an open palm. The television stopped flickering and the picture reappeared. Patchy muttered something about the television set probably having been the set John Logie Baird had built when he'd invented television.

'Lionel known as Sidney?' said Thumper.

'I think it's Sidney known as Lionel,' I said.

'Whatever,' said Thumper.

'He's confiscated the pickled eggs and there's a smell of cooking coming out of the kitchen,' I said.

'I know,' said Patchy. 'I find it all rather worrying. I'm glad Frank and Gilly are only away for the weekend.'

'Have you eaten?' I asked.

'We were waiting for you,' said Patchy. 'We thought you'd be in since your good lady wife has gone off helping my bride-to-be to spend some money.'

'Don't misunderstand. We weren't waiting out of any sense of politeness,' said Thumper quickly. 'We wanted you here in case we get food poisoning.'

'Sensible,' I nodded. I half turned and called over to the barman. 'What are you doing for lunch?'

'I'll ask Mrs Weedon to bring you the menu,' he told me.

'A Big Brown Labrador,' suddenly suggested Thumper.

'And A Big Brown Labrador has thrown its jockey at the fourth fence,' said Patchy, nodding approval. 'I like that. Not as good as 'Heavily Doped' though.'

Mrs Weedon must have been on starting blocks in the kitchen. She appeared almost instantly. 'I've brought you the menus,' she said.

We all stared at her. Our staring had nothing to do with the fact that she must have weighed thirty stones and had a moustache bigger than her husband's but was entirely a result of the fact that she had brought us menus. Frank and Gilly had once tried producing menus but had long since given up. When all you serve is meat pies, chips, pickled eggs and crisps a menu becomes a rather embarrassing luxury.

'You've got menus?' said Patchy.

She handed us each a red plastic folder. 'Would you like to see the wine list?' she asked.

'We'll just have more of what we were drinking,' said Thumper in a very thin little voice. He looked at Patchy and then at me.

'Unless you two...'

'More of the same is fine with me,' said Patchy.

'Me too,' I agreed. 'Two pints of draught bitter and a pint of Guinness please.'

'I'll have the same,' said Thumper.

Mrs Weedon looked confused.

'Just joking,' explained Thumper quickly.

'I'll leave the menus with you for your perusal,' said Mrs Weedon. 'If you have any queries just ask Mr Weedon to let me know.'

'What's this one,' asked Thumper, who had already opened his menu. He pointed to the top item on the list.

Patchy and I opened our menus and looked at the item to which he was pointing.

Thumper read it out.

'Steaming Hot Natural Pulses Resting On A Grilled Slice From A Fresh Wholemeal Farmhouse Bloomer Generously Bathed In A Succulent Tomato Based Sauce.'

Mrs Weedon, who had already taken a few steps back towards the kitchen, turned back towards us, looked at the menu Thumper was holding and repeated what he had read out.

'Give us a clue,' said Patchy. 'What does it look like?'

'It looks like beans on toast,' said Mrs Weedon.

'It's beans on toast?' asked Thumper, incredulously.

'Some people might call it that,' said Mrs Weedon. 'But Lionel and I believe that presentation and nomenclature are very important in the restaurant trade.'

'And what's a Norway lobster?' asked Patchy.

'That would be commonly known as scampi.'

We thanked her and told her that we would probably be able to work out the rest of the menu but that if we had any more difficulty we would call her and ask her to translate for us.

After twenty minutes of careful study we asked Lionel if he would be kind enough to send Mrs Weedon back to our table.

'I'll have Norway lobster Cooked In Hot Oil With A Covering Of Crumbed Cottage Loaf And Served With Hand Fried Sliced Potatoes,' said Patchy.

'I'll have Chunky Slices Of Best Gloucester Packed Together With Succulent Pieces Of Sun Ripened Tomato Between Sliced Crusty Farmhouse Loaf,' said Thumper.

'And I'll have Steaming Hot Natural Pulses Resting On A Grilled Slice From A Fresh Wholemeal Farmhouse Bloomer Generously Bathed In A Succulent Tomato Based Sauce,' I said.

We sat back and waited. Patchy for his scampi and chips, Thumper for his cheese and tomato sandwich and me for my beans on toast.

Sitting there in the Duck and Puddle life seemed all rickety, with hardly any boo in it at all.

CHAPTER 22

'I'm glad you called in,' said Dr Brownlow. He was, if possible, even thinner than ever. The skin stretched taught over his cheekbones looked like transparent parchment. But although sunken his eyes were still bright. 'There are a couple of things I want you to do for me.'

'Anything,' I promised.

'You haven't heard what I want yet.'

'I don't care what it is. I'll do it.' He grinned. 'Risky promise.'

I shook my head.

'First, the easy one.'

'OK.'

'Look after Bradshaw for me.'

'Your butler?'

Dr Brownlow nodded.

'He's going to be my new district nurse.'

'You're still sure about that?'

'Certain.'

'What about the bureaucrats?' Dr Brownlow was right. Hiring an 82-year-old former butler as a district nurse would probably create a few problems with the local bureaucrats.

'Bugger them.'

'Just like that?'

'Just like that. They said I could choose my own nurse.'

'He's lived with me so long he's like family.'

'I know.'

'He's got nowhere else to live and he's got no relatives.' I nodded.

'He's 82.'

'I'm not surprised. I thought he was older.'

'I think he probably is. He's been 82 since 1968.'

'Then he's probably older than 82.'

'Bradshaw is a good nurse.'

'I know he is.'

'I'm leaving him the cottage the housekeeper used to have. He can live there.'

'Great. I need him now but I hope I have to wait a long time before he's free.'

'I don't think you'll have to wait long,' said Dr Brownlow, with a faint smile.

'What's the second thing?'

'Pour a couple of whiskies.'

I poured us both a whisky. A small one for me and a large one for Dr Brownlow. I added a lot of water to mine.

'One of my ambitions has always been to be bankrupt at the time of my death,' he said. 'I always rather liked the idea of popping off without leaving enough to pay the solicitor or the damned funeral people. I rather thought it would be nice to die broke, with the Government desperate to sue me for unpaid taxes.'

'A noble thought,' I said, sipping at my whisky.

'But as things stand I don't think I'm going to manage that.'

I couldn't think of anything suitable to say so I didn't say anything.

'So I want you to take this to the bank.' He picked up a white envelope from the table on his left and handed it to me.

'OK.'

'Aren't you going to ask me what's in it?'

'If you want me to know you'll tell me.'

He smiled. 'It contains a letter to the bank manager and a cheque made out to cash. The letter tells the bank manager to give you the cash to bring to me.'

'Right.'

'But I don't want you to bring me the cash.' He handed me another white envelope.

'Open that one.'

I opened it. The envelope contained a receipt, signed by Dr Brownlow. I didn't read it properly.

'This is a receipt...'

'I know what it is.'

'You realise that now that I've got the letter, the cheque and the receipt the money can just disappear?'

'That's what I thought.'

'So, what do you want me to do with it?'

'I'd like you to give it away. Do good things with it. Bilbury Mothers Wednesday and Friday Evenings Social Club. Church Organ Fund. Bilbury Boys Summer Outing. Anything you like that helps Bilbury. But don't draw attention to yourself If I just leave you this money in my Will the Government will grab a great chunk of it. But they won't spend money on helping Bilbury survive.'

Sadly, he was right. The Government (in the unpleasant shape of a bunch of NHS bureaucrats) had deliberately closed down Bilbury's only medical practice. It was only through the slightly devious efforts of the villagers that the Government had been forced to change its mind.

'Did you know that the Bilbury Mothers Wednesday and Friday Evenings Social Club now meets on Tuesdays and Thursdays?' I asked him.

'I had heard.'

'But they kept the name because they had some leftover stationery.'

He smiled.

'How much is the cheque for?'

'£50,000.'

I sipped some more whisky. '£50,000?' He nodded.

'Cash?'

'Cash.'

'Is that legal?'

'I acquired it legally. It's my money. I don't see why it isn't legal for me to take it out of the bank. They may need a day or two to get the money ready.'

'I would imagine they will. It's quite a lot of cash. What about the taxman?'

'It's money I've paid tax on.'

'I'm pleased to hear it. But will the taxman be concerned at my taking £50,000 out of the bank and giving it away?'

'You're not taking the money. You've got a receipt which shows that you gave the money to me.'

'Ah.'

'I talked to my solicitor and my accountant about this.'

'What did they say?'

'The taxman might want to question me at some point when my estate is being looked at for probate. He might feel that if the

168

£50,000 hadn't gone missing then there would have been some tax to pay on it.'

'Inheritance tax?'

'Exactly.'

I looked at him. 'They'll want to question you?'

He nodded.

'When your estate is being looked at?'

Another nod.

'After you're dead?'

'After I'm dead.'

'I would imagine you will be tempted to ignore them?'

'I would imagine I will. They will want to question me to find out what I did with the £50,000 I took out of the bank. And although you will have physically taken the cash out of the bank you, of course, will have a receipt signed by me.'

I picked up the receipt. 'This receipt.'

'Precisely. That receipt.'

'So the money will have just disappeared.'

'Like magic. The taxman can't come after you to find out what happened to the money because you will have a receipt. And he can't come after me because I'll be dead.'

'Hmmm.' I said. I sipped at my whisky and then emptied the glass. 'Do you mind if I have another whisky?'

'Please do.'

I poured myself more whisky. I added some to Dr Brownlow's glass too.

'I would suggest that you tell no one you can't trust about this little scheme of ours. You must tell Patsy, of course.'

I sipped more whisky. 'I will tell Thumper,' I said. 'And Patchy.' I thought a little more. 'And Miss Johnson.'

Dr Brownlow nodded his agreement. 'Do what you like with the money. My only suggestion is that I'd like you to spend most of it on helping the village. Feed it in here and there. Or one big splash. Whatever you think.'

'I will do that,' I promised. I was touched that he knew he could trust me not to spend it on cars, booze and fancy clothes.

'And I'm leaving the house to you,' he said.

I sipped at the whisky and said nothing for a long, long time. Neither of us said anything.

'What do you want me to do with it?' I asked him.

'You won't live in it?'

I shook my head. 'It's a beautiful house,' I told him. 'But you're my patient. I can't accept money from you.'

'Then do something with it. Just don't let anyone turn it into twelve bijou apartments for retirees from London. And don't let anyone knock it down and put up a supermarket. Use it for the village.'

'How?'

He looked at me. 'You're sure you won't live in it?'

'No. Thank you but no.'

'You don't want to sell it and keep the money?'

I smiled. 'No. Thank you but no.' I paused. 'Your son won't like not having the house, I added.'

'I don't like him and he doesn't like me,' said Dr Brownlow. 'If I leave him the house he'll have the architects in before I'm cold and they'll turn it into a corporate headquarters, a country hotel or luxury apartments. Why should I leave him the house or anything else?'

'He'll be cross.'

Dr Brownlow laughed lightly. 'He'll be very cross. Furious. And he might try to dispute the Will. But my solicitor assures me it's watertight. I had my signature witnessed by a psychiatrist and a judge so that no one could claim I was not of sound mind when I signed it.'

'Clever stuff.'

'I'm a clever fellow.'

'I know you are.'

It was his turn to smile. 'There is one thing you might consider.'

'What's that?'

'A cottage hospital.' I stared at him.

'Bilbury needs a tiny hospital of its own. Just a few beds. Nothing elaborate. Somewhere friendly and local for patients to be looked after when they're too ill to stay at home but not really ill enough to be in a proper hospital.'

'We would never get the Government to help.'

'No.'

'It would cost quite a bit to convert the house into a hospital.' He nodded.

'And then there would be running costs. Wages. Heat. That sort of thing.'

Another nod.

'The £50,000?'

He smiled. 'After paying tax £50,000 wouldn't be enough. With no tax to pay you could get the conversion work done and have some left over to pay for the running of the hospital for a year or two.'

I looked at him and saw that his eyes were closed. I got up, very gently took his hand and felt for his pulse. It was fine.

'You clever, clever old man,' I murmured. quietly, I walked over to the window and looked out at the gardens.

When I'd first seen Dr Brownlow's house I had thought it the most impressive building I'd ever seen - the most impressive house that didn't belong to the National Trust or have coach loads of day trippers parading through it. Built entirely of grey stone, softened slightly by several acres of green ivy, the house had towers, battlements and mullion windows. There was a Union Jack flying from a pole fixed at an acute angle to the front of the central tower. The front door, directly underneath the flag, and flanked by two huge stone lions, was twelve feet high and decorated with scores of very solid looking metal studs. When I'd first seen it I'd half expected Vincent Price (or a hunchbacked minion) to open the door with a good deal of creaking.

Dr Brownlow had bought the house together with his wife and it was the gardens which were his particular pride and joy. There was a formal lawn, a huge Victorian greenhouse and a large walled vegetable garden as well as several acres of woodland. Dr Brownlow loved trees in the same way that some men love cars or boats. He would take me on walks around the woodland and talk to me about them.

'See those walnut trees,' I remember him saying. 'That's the biggest group of walnut trees in the whole of North Devon.' He was very proud of them.

'Do they produce nuts?' I'd asked.

'Of course they do,' he said. 'You have to wait until they're ready to fall. You wait until the nuts are too heavy for the twig which carries them. They break off under their own weight and fall to the ground. When the tree is near to a tarmacadamed road you can hear the constant thud thud of nuts falling like stones being thrown. If you pick them too soon, as some people do, you end up with nuts which aren't properly matured. When they've fallen you let them dry out in baskets in the sunshine and then store them somewhere dry and airy. It's the fruit that are formed on the outer branches which are best. They get the most sunshine and air. The nuts at the centre of the tree are comparatively poor.'

His two dogs, now gone, used to love eating walnuts. They were only supposed to eat the ones which had broken open but they would crack the others with their teeth and then chew the nuts. Dr Brownlow had a small wooden block and a matching wooden hammer which he'd bought in a village in France in the 1930s. It was, he said, the way the French peasants used to break open their walnut shells.

'In rural France they used to use the leaves of the walnut tree too,' he told me. 'Though they probably don't bother now. They used to lay the leaves out in the sun for a while, though not long enough for them to lose their colour, and then move them into a barn. When the leaves were brittle they would rub them between their palms and put the powder into a wine bottle. They'd then cover the leaf powder with eau-de-vie spirit. They'd leave them for a fortnight and then strain the liquid through a muslin cloth, put it into bottles, add red wine and twelve lumps of sugar per bottle. They called it quinquina and it was,' he said, 'the most glorious liqueur known to man.'

Although he loved his trees he knew that occasionally they had to be felled. 'These days,' I remember him telling me, 'the so-called scientific foresters cut trees by the acre.' He shuddered. 'No sensible woodman does that,' he said. 'If you cut all the trees at once you have rows of young trees all fighting to survive at the same time. All the bugs have a field day. Instead, you should cut down each tree as its reaches its prime and then plant another in its place. And you don't cut them at ground level, like so many do these days. That leaves a stump which is terribly difficult to remove. You put a cable on a high branch and use a winch to pull the tree down in the right direction. Then while the tree is leaning you dig around the tree on the opposite side, cut off the roots and pull them out. All the time you tighten the winch, pulling on the tree and pulling out more roots. It takes much longer than just chopping through the trunk, of course, but when you've done it this way you can plant another tree in the same place. You haven't wasted the land.'

He was, I remembered, angry that modem farmers and scientific foresters (he used to say the phrase 'scientific foresters' in the same way that he would say the words 'administrator' and 'bureaucrat') would fell trees without replacing them. He compared it to using up the soil without returning the wastes to restock the minerals in the earth. He loved nature and hated those who overfished the seas or polluted our rivers. He thought oxen and horses were a great natural way to return nitrogen to the land. He hated tractors. 'They tear at the land, they cost a fortune to run, they make a great noise and a horrible smell. They give no pleasure and they return nothing to the land. A good horse or ox does its work and fertilises the land at the same time. He hated the way that country children were running off to the city, getting degrees in subjects he'd never heard of and becoming managers of fast food stores. He was depressed that so many young people couldn't do things with their hands any more.

I remember him stopping beside a huge poplar and touching the bark with his hand, as though caressing a dear friend. 'Over one hundred feet high and with a circumference of eight feet,' he said. 'Just twenty-years-old. I planted this tree. As white as a silver birch but pearly. A wonderful tree. You cut off the small side branches and the trunk continues to grow straight and true. Because there are no side branches there will be no knots in the wood. And because there are no side branches there is no shade hanging over whatever is growing nearby. He picked up a handful of twigs lying on the ground underneath the tree and made me do the same. 'Poplar twigs make great kindling,' he said. 'Almost as good as ash.'

Walnut wood and oak make the best furniture, he told me.

He said that an oak should be felled and left for years in the round out-of-doors before being cut into planks. 'Then, when it is cut the planks should be stored with strips between them so that the air can circulate. It takes 15 years for a piece of oak to season properly. These days they're in too much of a hurry. They dry the wood in a kiln. A decent carpenter will know that the wood hasn't been naturally seasoned.'

Looking through the window I saw a chestnut tree and remembered him telling me that if you put chestnuts into a box without drying them out first they will go bad within a week. 'They will sweat and heat up and be inedible,' he told me. 'You have to dry them out before bagging them.'

'Have I been dozing?'

I turned round. Dr Brownlow was awake and looking across at me.

'Just for a minute or two.'

'Sorry about that.'

'It's OK.' I paused. 'What do you want me to do with the house? You nodded off before you could answer.'

'Whatever you like. But I don't want you to give it away and I don't want you to sell it unless you have to. I'm leaving you enough extra cash to pay any death duties so the house will be yours outright.' He looked around. 'It's a nice house to live in if a little big for two.'

'Three,' I said.

He looked at me, with a raised eyebrow.

I told him about Patsy.

'Congratulations.' I could tell that he was genuinely pleased.

'Thank you.'

'Give my congratulations and my love to Patsy.'

'I will.'

'She's a sweet, sweet girl.'

'I know.'

'Kindest girl I ever met. I once told her mother that when they made Patsy it must have been the end of a week. God filled her up with all the kindness he had left over.'

I smiled.

We sat in silence for a while.

'You're leaving me everything.'

'So it would seem.'

'Why?'

'Why not?'

'That's not a very good answer.'

'It's as good as the question.'

I sipped more whisky. I would, I decided, have to walk home and then have a lot of black coffee before the evening surgery. I'd have to bicycle back and pick up the car later.

'I'm very honoured,' I said. Before Dr Brownlow could speak I held up a hand. 'Not because you're entrusting your house and a huge bundle of money to me. The house and the money are very nice but they're not all that important.' I coughed. It might have been the whisky. Or maybe the emotion. What I wanted to say was that I was pleased that he thought enough of me to do this. But I couldn't get the words out. I think he knew anyway.

Dr Brownlow smiled. 'I want you to have the Rolls as well,' he said. Dr Brownlow had an ancient black 20/25 Rolls Royce; a magnificent piece of engineering. He'd had it for over thirty years and it was his pride and his joy. 'It needs a service,' he said. 'And there's a problem with the clutch.'

I nodded.

'Surprisingly, you can take her to Tolstoy's,' said Dr Brownlow. 'As you may have noticed they aren't terribly good with modem machinery but they're pretty good with old-fashioned motors - especially anything built before the Second World War. Get them to take a look at her.'

'I will.'

'I need some more morphine.'

I reached into my pocket, pulled out a prescription pad and wrote out a prescription for two dozen ampoules of morphine. I stood up and handed him the prescription.

'Is your son arranging, er, things... for you afterwards?'

'Is my son arranging the funeral?' I nodded.

He shook his head slowly and deliberately. 'You are,' he said.

'Any special requests.'

'Get Peter to organise things. He'll make a good job of things.'

'Peter Marshall?'

'Peter Marshall. He does funerals. Thumper is making the coffin. He's a good workman when he isn't busy being jack the lad. He put a bathroom in for me once you know. And made some panelling for the library when we had an attack of woodworm.'

'If Thumper said he'll make you a coffin then he'll make you a good one.'

There was another long silence.

'Any special hymns?'

Dr Brownlow shook his head. 'Free drinks for the night at the Duck and Puddle.'

'You'll be a popular man.'

'Cheap popularity.'

'You don't have to buy people drinks to be popular,' I told him. 'And you know it. But I'll make sure Frank knows.'

I put the two envelopes into my jacket pocket. 'I'll leave my car here if you don't mind,' I told him. 'I'll come back for it after evening surgery.'

He nodded. He was almost asleep. He tired easily these days and didn't seem to me to have long to go. My visit had taken a lot out of him. I tiptoed out of the room, said goodbye to Bradshaw and walked back to Bilbury Grange. It was a dry, fine afternoon. One of those crisp days that make you want to walk for ever.

CHAPTER 23

'How did you get on in Barnstaple?' I asked Patsy later that evening.

'We found a wonderful dress,' she told me. 'But she decided it was too low cut at the front. She sa3ys men always look down on women in low cut dresses. Anyway, it was probably all a waste of time,' she said. 'Patchy has apparently found an old family dress he'd like Adrienne to wear.'

'What other wonderful things has Adrienne been up to?' I asked.

I always love hearing stories about Adrienne. She is a kind but slightly eccentric girl. She has a sweet tooth and loves food - particularly chocolate. She had once confessed that her skirts were made by Marks & Spencer but her bottom had been made by Cadbury.

'We met Patchy for lunch,' said Patsy. 'Adrienne has got Patchy in quite a whirl,' said Patsy. 'She told him that she wants a dining table with two legs.'

I looked at Patsy and raised an eyebrow.

'Patchy said that a table needs at least three legs and Adrienne wanted to know why. Patchy said because if it only has two legs it won't stand up. And Adrienne said that was silly because she's only got two legs and she can stand up.'

I laughed. 'So Patchy has got to try and find a table with two legs?'

Patsy nodded.

'Poor old Patchy,' I said.

'They're going to be fine. She loves him to bits,' said Patsy.

'He's a lot older than her,' I pointed out.

'She's worried that he isn't old enough!' said Patsy.

'That's typical Adrienne!' I said.

'She says there's an old adage that a girl should be half the age of the man she is marrying plus seven. So according to that she's a bit too old for him.'

'But she'll cope?'

'Definitely,' nodded Patsy. 'I know she's a little strange sometimes. But what's wrong with being a little strange?'

'Absolutely nothing,' I agreed.

'She says Patchy told her he is a lucky man because he'll get to sleep with a strange woman every night,' said Patsy.

'What did you say?'

'I said she's right,' said Patsy. 'I told her I get to sleep with a strange man every night and I'm very happy about it.'

'And the strange man is pretty happy about it too,' I said.

CHAPTER 24

Like all doctors I have, over the years, met a considerable number of hypochondriacs.

Dr Brownlow had taught me two important things about hypochondriacs.

First, they may not be genuinely ill but to them their fears are just as real as the fears of a patient with a genuine disorder.

Second, hypochondriacs do occasionally become really ill and so every complaint and every fear has to be taken seriously and, if necessary, investigated.

Every general practitioner has a few hypochondriacs to care for. Since mine was a relatively small practice I had relatively few genuine hypochondriacs. And mine all lived in the same household.

The Phatt family were the Bilbury hypochondriacs.

The Phatt family had moved into Bilbury about three months before I'd come out of my temporary retirement. There were four of them: Phyllis Phatt, a tall, well-built but surprisingly flat-chested woman with the physique of a rugby forward, George, her husband, a small, rather weedy little man with a wisp of gingery hair combed across a bald head and a laugh like a schoolgirl. Phyllis, who was a good foot taller than her husband, called him Clint because she thought George was rather common. She treated him like a son rather than a husband.

'How many children do you have?' I had asked when we'd first met.

'Three,' she had replied. 'Two girls and a boy.'

'How old are they?'

'The youngest girl is 14, the eldest girl is 16 and my boy is 47.' The two daughters were Phoebe (the 14-year-old one) and Pauline (the 16-year-old). Both daughters acted considerably younger than they were though both looked physically well-developed for their respective ages.

George had worked as a civil servant (he wouldn't ever tell anyone exactly which department he had worked for and since it seemed unlikely that he worked for the secret service it was generally accepted that he must have been employed by the Inland Revenue) had taken early retirement as a result of what a letter in his medical notes referred to as 'an extensive variety of stress-related illnesses'.

Phyllis Phatt had telephoned me just a few days after I'd reopened my practice. She telephoned just as I started dinner one evening. Patsy took the call and told me that a woman called Hellaire wanted to speak to me.

'Mrs Hellaire?' I said, picking up the phone.

'Hellaire?'

'Is that Mrs Hellaire?'

'No. This is Mrs Phatt,' said the caller. 'Phyllis Phatt.' It was only when she spoke that I realised why Patsy had made the mistake. The woman spoke with a fake upper class accent and sounded like an American actress trying to play a British Duchess and failing miserably. I won't try to reproduce her awful accent. It is enough to say that when she said 'hello' it came out as 'hellaire'.

'I thought I ought to introduce myself, doctor,' she said. 'We're your patients now and I expect you'll be keen to get to know all about us.'

This, of course, is just the sort of telephone call a general practitioner enjoys. Especially when it comes just as he sits down to a meal after a long, busy day. I thanked her and asked her if there was anything in particular I could do for her.

'My husband and I both have a family history of high blood pressure,' she told me. 'We both need to have our blood pressure taken regularly. We have to be careful with our health, don't we? It's such a valuable gift.'

'Do you have high blood pressure?' I asked.

'Not at the moment,' she replied. 'But I expect we will one day. I always find myself aware of the fact that we're all of us just one heart beat away from the end. Just a second or two from death.'

'Quite.'

'We're so very, very vulnerable, aren't we.'

'I suppose we are.'

'And I'm pre-diabetic.'

'Pre-diabetic?' I repeated. It wasn't a phrase I'd ever heard before.

'It means that I'll develop diabetes one day,' she told me. She made this announcement proudly, as someone might say: 'I am an Olympic athlete. I'm hoping to win a gold medal.'

She then proceeded to treat me to a long and exhaustive description of her family's medical history.

'How long will you be?' whispered Patsy, coming into the hall where I was standing. 'Do I need to put your dinner in the oven?'

I put my hand over the telephone mouthpiece. 'Heaven knows,' I whispered back. 'Could you bring my dinner out here?'

Patsy nodded. Moments later she returned with a chair. Then she returned carrying a plate. Mrs Phatt, who must have had the fittest tongue in Britain, was now going at full steam. She was describing in minute detail an operation her father had had in 1947. Gently, I put the telephone down on the hall table, sat down on the chair Patsy had provided, picked up my dinner and began to eat. Not wanting to eat alone Patsy brought out a second chair and her plate and sat with me. On the hall table Mrs Phatt chattered away. We couldn't hear everything she said but we could tell that she was still going well.

Fifteen minutes later I'd finished my dinner. I picked up the telephone. 'Hmmm,' I said, with non-committal interest. 'Very useful information.'

'I've still got my mother to tell you about,' said Mrs Phatt. 'And Mr Phatt's parents have a very interesting medical history.'

'It would help me enormously,' I said, 'if you could write all this down for me. Provide me with a sort of family tree, explaining all the family illnesses.'

'Oh certainly, doctor,' said Mrs Phatt eagerly. 'Mr Phatt and I can do that.'

'Splendid.'

'When shall we come round for our initial check ups?' she asked.

'Check ups?'

'I assume you'll want to give us all an examination,' said Mrs Phatt. 'Just so that you'll know what you're dealing with.'

'Of course,' I said, thanking my lucky stars that there was only one Mrs Phatt in the village.

'What time would be convenient for you?' she asked.

'Do you have jobs to go to? Is getting to the surgery difficult for you?'

'My husband is retired,' said Mrs Phatt. 'And I'm a houseswife.'

'Houseswife,' I repeated. 'Did you say 'houseswife'?'

'We've got a villa in Spain,' said Mrs Phatt. 'On the coast. So with two homes that makes me a houseswife doesn't it.'

'Well, just pop along to any surgery,' I told her.

There was a silence. 'With the other patients?' she asked, clearly rather shocked at the idea of being treated like any other human being.

'Oh yes, I think so,' I said.

'You don't want us to make an appointment?'

'Oh no, I don't think that will be necessary,' I said. 'Thank you for calling Mrs Phatt.'

I put the telephone down.

'Forty nine minutes,' said Patsy. I stood up and eased my back.

'I'll make you a coffee,' said Patsy.

'Put a splash of something in it, will you?' I said. I felt exhausted. Sitting through one of Mrs Phatt's monologues had been a tiring experience.

CHAPTER 25

The telephone rang. It was a call asking me to visit Les Salterton.

'I took him a chair to mend two weeks ago,' said Mrs Houghton. 'But he still hasn't mended it. That's most unlike him. He just sits there in his chair doing nothing and not saying very much. I wonder if he might have had a stroke.'

Most people in the village thought Les Salterton was in his late sixties but I'd seen his medical records and I knew better. It was nearly a decade since he'd been entitled to celebrate his seventieth birthday. (He hadn't done anything of the sort, of course. Celebrating birthdays wasn't the sort of thing he did.)

Les was a big man, well over six feet tall and beefy too, and although maybe not the brightest spoon in the drawer he was without a doubt one of the kindest.

'I am so big that it is not easy for me to be well all over at once,' he told me when we first met.

When working for a firm of market gardeners in Barnstaple he had once written to the British Olympic Committee applying for a place on the fencing team. 'I can,' he was reputed to have told them, 'put up fencing faster than anyone else I work with. I could win you the gold medal for fencing without any difficulties.'

At home Les normally wore old army boots, a pair of old wine-red corduroy trousers and the sort of shirt reputed to be favoured by Canadian lumberjacks. Whenever he came to see me he always wore his suit. This was dark blue and since it had clearly never fitted him properly I assumed he had probably bought it at a jumble sale or a junk shop in Barnstaple Like his teeth, which he normally kept in a jar of pickled eggs, he wore it only to weddings, funerals and visits to the doctor. His hair was white and long and clearly uncontrollable. It lay, or rather stood, on top of his head like one of those lap dogs which are popular with women and which are most famous for the fact that it is usually nigh on impossible to decide which end is the head end. He always wore a checked cap when he wore his suit and he would remove this before seeing me and hold it nervously in his huge, calloused fingers. He always held it in both hands as though frightened that he might drop it or that someone might try to take it away from him. The curious thing was that when he wore the hat it kept his hair compressed but when he removed the hat the hair always sprang back up again as though it was made of something much stronger and more resilient than hair. His upper lip was decorated with what had undoubtedly once been a fine moustache and although it was now stained by tobacco smoke, soup and stout it still retained the structure and design of a grand moustache. I asked him about it once and he told me that when he first grew it, just after the end of the First World War, the moustache was a symbol of manhood, respectability, family, masculinity, and a proper bourgeois sense of belonging and position. He told me that in 1918 Woolworths staffed its new Liverpool branch with clean shaven men with no moustaches. It was, he said the 'American' style. But the English people would not buy anything else from a man who didn't have a moustache.

He was at his most comfortable with a sharp tool in one hand and a piece of wood in the other and he attempted to cover his shyness and anxiety with an endearing and boyish smile.

When he was young Les had served an apprenticeship, and then worked as, a carpenter and joiner ('I don't understand why they called me a carpenter and joiner', he had once said. 'Of course I join the bits together. What do folk expect me to do? Carve 'em nicely and then leave 'em lying around loose?') and had been employed by a large firm in Staffordshire where he'd built handmade furniture for many years. Sadly, his career had rather nose dived when he had spent three weeks building a bookcase instead of a chair. 'I forgot what they asked for,' he told his employer. 'I thought a bookcase would be nice.'

After moving to Bilbury and using every penny he had to buy a former estate worker's cottage, Les had made wooden tent pegs for a year or two. The bottom had fallen out of that particular market when metal ones became popular. After that he'd made clothes pegs. This time it was the rising popularity of plastic pegs which had destroyed his business.

I'd first met him when he'd turned up at the surgery one day complaining of a sore throat. I looked at his medical records and saw that the only previous consultation he'd had had been in 1924 when he'd visited the surgery complaining of exactly the same symptoms.

'You had a sore throat in 1924,' I told him.

'I remember,' he answered hoarsely.

'Obviously a recurrent problem,' I remarked.

He nodded. Nodding was clearly easier than talking.

'The doctor prescribed hydrogen peroxide in 1924,' I said, looking at his notes again. 'But since then things have advanced a little. I can give you penicillin now.'

He looked doubtful. 'Will that be as good as the hydrogen peroxide?' he asked.

'If it isn't then I'll prescribe hydrogen peroxide,' I told him. 'But try my new fangled stuff first.'

Rather reluctantly he'd agreed.

'I'll see you in another fifty years,' I'd told him as he left.

The other notable thing about Les was that he had seven cats, all of whom he adored. I once visited him and found that he had been sleeping in a chair for two weeks. He had developed awful back pains and couldn't walk. When I asked him why he hadn't been sleeping in bed he told me that one of his cats had rather taken to sleeping on his pillow and that he hadn't had the heart to move it off. Only after finding a spare pillow in a cupboard, and putting it down on the floor beside the bed, did I manage to persuade the cat to quit the bed and Les to quit the chair.

* * *

I remembered from past experience that I would have to make some excuse for calling on Les Salterton.

However ill he was Les didn't like people interfering in his life and if he knew that I was calling in response to a telephone call from a neighbour he would have thrown me out and refused to see me.

And so I popped in the boot of the car the small table that Mortimer's sons had broken during my one time friend's ill-fated and eminently forgettable visit.

When I arrived at Les's cottage I took the table out of the boot, opened the front door and walked in.

There was no point at all in knocking on the front door and expecting a reply. (There was no bell to ring.)

The first time I'd called at Les Salterton's home I'd spent ten minutes waiting for him to answer the door. It had been Miss

Johnson who, when I arrived back at the surgery, had explained to me that Les Salterton never answered callers at his front door.

'When was the last time you answered a knock on the door and were pleased by the consequences?' he had asked me, when I asked him why he hadn't answered my knocks. 'I can't remember anyone ever banging on my door to bring me good news. How often do you answer the door and find yourself facing someone you don't want to see or receiving something you don't want? Salesmen, bailiffs and unwanted relatives all knock on doors. When people knock on the door it's invariably because they want something. By not answering when people knock on my door I avoid all these unpleasant intrusions.'

I found it difficult to argue with him and although there were some in the village who regarded him as rather more than eccentric I sometimes wondered if he wasn't the only wise one among us all.

'Hello Les, can you mend this for me?' I asked him, holding up our broken, three-legged table in one hand and the solitary leg in the other.

Les was sitting in a chair by the hearth. There was a cat sitting on his lap and another at his feet. Everywhere you looked there were cats. Even in the middle of the afternoon it was dark in his front room. The cottage had small windows, the thick curtains weren't properly drawn back, and ivy and clematis were growing over the windows. It took a minute or two for my eyes to become accustomed to the lack of light. Outside the sun was shining brightly. Inside we could well have been underground.

'Who's that?' demanded Les, peering in my direction. He seemed sleepy and had difficulty in focusing on me.

'It's the doc,' I told him. 'I've got a table that needs mending. Patsy asked me to bring it round for you to see if you can do anything with it.'

Les blinked and tried to sit up. It was clearly an enormous effort for him but I could see that both arms and both legs seemed to be working. He had been dozing and dribbling and there were damp stains down the front of his cardigan. There was skin on a cup of coffee on the table by his chair. It looked cold and undrinkable. He looked at the table I'd brought him but didn't seem to see it.

'Are you all right?' I asked him.

'Don't seem able to get going,' he told me. He gave up trying to lift himself out of the chair.

'Do you want me to have a look at you?' I asked him. 'Check you over.'

'If you like,' he replied. 'Don't mind if you do.'

'I'll just get my bag from the car.'

I popped out to the car and fetched my black bag. I'd never seen Les like this. He was normally one of the busiest men I knew - of any age. Although technically retired he worked longer hours than almost anyone I knew. Everyone who had furniture which needed mending took it along to him.

'Can I light the lamp?' I asked.

Les's cottage didn't have electricity. He had a calor gas cooker in the kitchen and relied on oil lamps for light. He had fireplaces in his living room and bedroom and lit wood fires when the weather was cold.

Les nodded. I lit the oil lamp on the mantelpiece. It filled a quarter of the room with a rich, warm, orange light.

Twenty minutes later I had gone over him systematically and methodically but had failed to find anything wrong with him. His heart and lungs were fine. His blood pressure was actually quite low. His nervous system was in tip top working order. He had lost no muscle strength. I could find absolutely nothing wrong with him.

I carefully moved a cat to one side and sat down on half of a chair opposite him. I packed my instruments away in my black bag.

'Have you finished?'

I said I had.

'Would you turn the lamp off now then, doctor.'

I got up and turned off the lamp.

'Don't need the lamp if we're just talking,' he explained. I smiled and nodded.

'You're a puzzle,' I told him.

He said nothing but just looked at me, with great sadness in his eyes. I know this may sound disrespectful but he reminded me of a trusting puppy.

'The other doctor couldn't find anything wrong with me,' said Les suddenly. It was the longest speech he'd made since I'd arrived.

'What other doctor?' I asked him, suddenly alert.

'A few weeks ago,' he replied. 'Don't know his name.'

'Before I took over the practice again?' I asked.

He nodded and stared at me silently for a while. 'Are you doctoring again?' he asked.

'Yes.'

'Are you my doctor?'

'Yes.'

He smiled and nodded approvingly.

'What did you see the other doctor about?'

'I went to see him,' he said. 'Had to go into Barnstaple Saw some chap called Dr Locum.'

'A doctor acting as a locum,' I corrected him. 'That just means he was standing in for one of the other doctors.'

'Jabbed myself in the foot with the fork,' he said. 'Needed an injection. I was doing the garden.'

'You went for a tetanus injection?'

He nodded. 'You always said I should have one if I cut myself in the garden.'

I got up from the chair, walked over to where he was sitting, bent down and examined his foot. He hadn't yet put his socks and shoes back on after my examination. There was a nicely healed scar on the top of his foot. It was quite small which was why I hadn't noticed it before. It was a few weeks old. It looked perfectly healthy.

'Did you clean the wound properly?'

'Oh yes, doctor.'

'Did he give you anything to take?'

'Just some tablets,' said Les. 'I'm nearly out of them. I need another 'description'.'

Alarm bells started ringing the moment he said this. A course of antibiotics hadn't been necessary but even if the doctor he'd seen had prescribed them it would have been for a week or ten days at the most. I had a feeling I knew what pills Les was taking.

'Where are they?' I asked him.

'In the bedroom.'

Les's bedroom was up a narrow, twisting steep staircase. It was more like a ladder than a staircase. At the top of the stairs there were two tiny rooms. One was used as a storeroom and was full of bits of furniture. The room was dominated by a six foot high double-fronted bookcase. I had no idea how he'd managed to get it up the staircase. The other room was Les's bedroom. It contained a bed and a bedside table and a small wardrobe. There was no bathroom. Les washed in the kitchen. Once a week he bathed in a tin bath outside in the garden. The toilet was fifty yards away down the garden path. There was no running water and no mains sewage. Les got his drinking water from a spring. His toilet consisted of two boards strategically placed over an old-fashioned earth closet.

There were three cats lying on the bed. One of them lifted its head when I entered the room. The other two didn't move.

The tablets, in a large brown bottle on his bedside table, were benzodiazepine sleeping tablets. The dose was enough to drug a man of Les's age. Tranquillisers had only been around for a few years but they were already some of the most popularly prescribed drugs. Many doctors, and even more patients, had become seriously addicted to them. The doctors were addicted to prescribing them (because they provided a quick and easy answer to a medical encyclopaedia of problems) and the patients were addicted to taking them partly because the drugs numbed their minds and stilled their fears and partly because the drugs themselves were ferociously addictive.

I had done some studies into these drugs and had come to the conclusion that eventually they were going to become a huge problem. The elderly seemed to me to be the most vulnerable - largely because they seemed more susceptible to the adverse effects. Many who became confused were already being wrongly diagnosed as demented and condemned to spend the rest of their lives in psychiatric hospitals or on geriatric wards.

'Did you tell the doctor you saw that you weren't sleeping properly?' I asked him when I got back downstairs again.

'He asked me how much sleep I got.'

'What did you tell him?'

'Four or five hours.'

'And he gave you the tablets to help you sleep?'

Les nodded. 'I tried to tell him that I've never slept more than that.' He shrugged. 'But he wasn't interested. He said the tablets would help me.'

'You can stop the tablets now,' I told him. I held up the bottle and let him see me put it into my pocket.

'I don't need any more of them?'

I shook my head.

'I'll come back and see you in a few days.'

CHAPTER 26

On my way home that evening I called in at the Duck and Puddle in the hope that I would find Patchy there. I wasn't disappointed. He and Thumper were playing darts. It was Thumper's turn to throw. He was holding two darts. A third dart was stuck firmly in the wall just to the right of the dartboard.

Patchy smiled rather sheepishly when I congratulated him on his engagement.

'Thumper and I are celebrating,' he said. 'You weren't here so we started without you.'

'What can I get you to drink?' I asked him.

'Whisky. Just a small one.'

I looked at him, surprised. Patchy was not a greedy man but I had never known him drink whisky in singles before.

Thumper threw his second dart. This time he managed to hit the board but not, unfortunately, with the pointed end of the dart. The dart clattered noisily to the floor.

'I thought you said you were celebrating?'

He told me that he was but that Thumper had read in his morning paper that when men toasted a lady's health in ancient Rome they would drink one glass for each letter of the woman's name. Consequently, the two of them had decided to celebrate Patchy's engagement by drinking a glass for each letter in the name Adrienne.

'It's quite a long name,' said Patchy.

'We're on the second 'n',' added Thumper. He threw his third dart. This time he actually managed to hit the board with the right end of the dart. Even more impressively the dart stuck firmly in the board. Less impressively it was in the part of the board just outside the scoring area.

'Bugger.' he said. He plucked the dart out of the board and examined the pointed end. 'These bloody darts are blunt,' he said, as though that was the reason for his failure to score.

'So you've only got one more letter to go,' I said to Patchy. 'You seem in pretty good shape to me.'

'We're doing her surname as well,' said Thumper who had put the dart down on the ledge underneath the scoreboard next to the dartboard. In doing so he had dislodged the piece of chalk which usually lived there. He did not seem to notice that the chalk had fallen to the floor. 'Kennett,' he told me, presumably in case I'd forgotten my wife's maiden name. I didn't get the impression that Thumper had been celebrating with singles.

I counted the letters off on my fingers. 'Another seven drinks to go.'

Both nodded. They didn't seem upset by this at all.

'No problem,' said Thumper. 'We'll just get even more relaxed.' He thought about this for a moment. 'Relaxation is good for you isn't it, doc?'

I agreed with him that relaxation is, generally speaking, good for both mind and body. 'Why aren't you including her middle name in the toast?' I then asked Patchy.

He looked surprised. 'I didn't know she'd got a middle name!'

'It's Christabel.' I told him.

I finished my drink and then I left.

When I got back home I asked Patsy if her sister had a middle name.

'No,' she replied, clearly puzzled. 'Both of us only have one Christian name. Why do you ask?'

'Oh nothing,' I said.

Christabel had been the longest name I could think of on the spur of the moment.

* * *

When I got home Patsy was holding her abdomen.

'Are you having pains?' I asked her.

'Very early,' she said. 'No hurry at all.'

'I should take you to Barnstaple,' I said.

'No, not yet,' said Patsy. 'They'll probably just send me home again. Then we'll spend hours driving backwards and forwards. Besides, there was an urgent call for you.' She handed me a message from Mrs Phatt. 'She said they need you urgently,' said Patsy. 'She wouldn't tell me what it was about.'

With a weary sigh I kissed Patsy, left the house, got into the car and set off for the Phatt's home.

One of the first things Dr Brownlow had taught me is that if a patient requests a visit the doctor should always go. There was, he readily admitted, some self-interest in this. 'The nicest thing people say about a doctor is: 'He will always come out." he had told me.

When they had arrived in Bilbury the Phatts had bought one of the village's smartest houses. A small but beautifully proportioned Edwardian house on the Patchole and Stonecombe road out of Bilbury. For nearly fifty years it had been home for a family who had run a smallholding on their dozen acres. Higher costs and smaller profits had made life difficult for them and very little other than essential repairs had been done to the property in the last few decades of their ownership. Upon the death of the last remaining member of the immediate family the man who'd inherited the house, a rich solicitor who worked in Birmingham, had shown very little interest in it and had put the house up for auction. The Phatts had bought it for a song. They had, it was clear, then spent a considerable sum of money restoring, improving, extending and turning the house which they had chosen into something completely different.

It was Mr Phatt who opened the front door.

'It's the wife, doctor,' he said. He spoke in a hushed tone. The sort of voice people use when there is a death or serious illness in the house. 'She's in the living room.'

Mrs Phatt was sitting on a huge white leather sofa.

'What's the trouble?' I asked her, putting my black bag down on the carpet.

'Heart attack, doctor,' said Mrs Phatt. 'I wanted Clint to call the ambulance but he said we should ring you first as a courtesy.'

I asked her to explain her pain.

'In the shoulders,' she said, rubbing her left shoulder. 'The pain goes up into my neck and the back of my head.'

'Just the left side?'

'No. Both sides.'

I took her pulse. 'I don't think it's your heart,' I told her. Her heart was beating strongly and regularly. Her colour was good. She wasn't sweating.

'Maybe it's arthritis?' she suggested. 'A frozen shoulder? A tumour with secondaries in my spine?'

'Slip your blouse off,' I told her.

'Leave the room Clint,' said Mrs Phatt. 'And you girls.' The two daughters didn't seem much interested in their mother's illness. They were both sitting watching the television. I glanced over to see what they were watching. It was a beauty competition.

'It's OK with me,' I said. 'They can stay.' I didn't particularly want to be left alone with Mrs Phatt and was happy to have the girls as chaperones. Hypochondriacs often have vivid imaginations.

'Have you been breathless?'

Mrs Phatt removed her blouse. 'It is a little difficult to breathe,' she said. She took a deep breath, immediately disproving this claim.

'Oh yes,' she said. 'That hurt.'

'Where?' I asked her.

'In my chest.'

'Have you noticed anything else wrong?'

She thought for a moment. 'I had a little diarrhoea last Thursday. I thought it might have been some prawns we ate.'

'I had diarrhoea too,' said Mr Phatt who had ignored his wife's suggestion that he leave the room.

'Anything else? Problems anywhere else?'

She gave this careful thought. 'I can't think of anything particular,' she admitted regretfully.

'Sorry I have to ask you all these questions.'

'Oh that's all right. I don't mind.'

'She likes you asking her questions,' said Mr Phatt. 'It makes her feel important. She likes talking about herself

'As if you don't!' she said. 'Ignore him. Please ask me as many questions as you like.'

On the television set the interviewer was asking a girl in a swimsuit what her ambitions were. She said she wanted world peace, a chance to work with underprivileged children and a boutique where she could sell the clothes she intended to start designing.

'I'll listen to your chest,' I told her.

'Shall I take my bra off?'

'No, I don't think that will be necessary,' I told her.

I listened to her chest. It sounded very healthy. I told her so. When I listened to her chest I couldn't help noticing that her bra straps were digging into her shoulders quite deeply.

'Your bra seems a little tight,' I said.

She fumbled with the straps. 'I think perhaps I need a bigger size,' she said. She sounded rather pleased about this.

'She's always been small breasted,' said Mr Phatt. 'There's a medical term for it. It's called micromastia.'

'There's a medical term for what you've got,' snapped back Mrs Phatt. 'Microthingy.'

Mr Phatt blushed bright red.

'What size bra do you normally wear?' I asked her, examining the small label attached at the back of her bra.

'38B.'

'Ah.' I said. 'I think we might have found the problem.' I turned to the two girls. 'Does either of you wear a 34B bra?'

The older girl looked up from the television screen. 'I do,' she said. Many teenage girls would have been embarrassed to discuss their bra size with a stranger. She wasn't. She seemed quite proud of it.

'You're wearing your daughter's bra,' I told a rather startled Mrs Phatt. 'It's too small and it's digging in and pressing on a nerve.'

* * *

When I got back home Patsy was lying on our bed in labour. Mrs Parfitt was holding her hand telling her to take deep breaths.

'It came on quicker than I expected,' said Patsy, in between deep breaths. She was sweating.

'I'll get you into the car,' I said. 'I must get you to Barnstaple.'

'There isn't time,' said Patsy.

'I'm afraid you're going to have to deliver the baby,' said Mrs Parfitt. 'I'm afraid I'm not much good at that sort of thing.' She winced. 'You know, blood and entrails and so on.'

'I hope there aren't going to be any entrails,' said Patsy. 'And not too much blood either.'

Now I was sweating too. My mind was working overtime. If I couldn't get Patsy to Barnstaple could I get a midwife over to Bilbury?

'There isn't time to bring anyone over from Barnstaple,' said Patsy, reading my mind.

And then I had an idea. 'I'll be back in just a minute,' I said, heading for the door.

I raced down the stairs and into the kitchen. From there I telephoned Dr Brownlow's home. As I had expected it was Bradshaw who answered the phone.

'How is Dr Brownlow?'

'He's sleeping peacefully at the moment,' said Bradshaw,

'Bradshaw, have you ever delivered a baby?'

'Oh yes, indeed, sir. Quite a number.'

'Can you leave Dr Brownlow for an hour?'

'Is Miss Patsy in labour?' asked Bradshaw.

'She is,' I told him. 'And too late to get her to Barnstaple We need you, Bradshaw.'

'I will be with you momentarily,' said Bradshaw. 'If you would just boil some water in preparation that would be useful.'

I put the telephone down and smiled. I felt more relaxed already. I telephoned Patsy's mother. She promised to rush round with Adrienne. I raced back upstairs.

'Bradshaw is coming!' I shouted, halfway up the stairs.

'Dr Brownlow's butler?' said Mrs Parfitt. 'What do you need a butler for?' She stopped for a moment, and thought. 'Goodness gracious! You aren't having people round to tea at a time like this are you?'

'Bradshaw is a trained nurse,' I explained. 'He's delivered lots of babies. Hundreds and thousands probably.'

I knelt down beside the bed and spoke to Patsy. 'Are you OK with that?' I asked her. I took a fresh tissue from a box beside the bed and gently wiped her face.

She looked at me and nodded. 'I rather like the idea of our firstborn being brought into the world by a butler,' she said. 'It has a certain style to it.' She grimaced and clutched at my hand as a labour pain struck.

'I've been instructed to boil water,' I said when the moment had passed.

'Good,' said Patsy. 'Will you be able to do that, OK?'

'I'll manage,' I said. 'Where's the kettle?'

Patsy aimed a weak punch at my jaw. I side slipped it easily.

'You go and boil the water,' said Mrs Parfitt. 'I'll look after your wife until Mr Bradshaw gets here.'

'Your mum and Adrienne are on their way,' I told Patsy. I went down to the kitchen, filled the kettle and three saucepans and started boiling water.

'What do you need all this boiling water for?' I asked, when Bradshaw arrived. 'I've never understood.'

'Tea,' said Bradshaw simply. 'We'll needs lots of fresh tea. Where is Miss Patsy?'

'Up the stairs, second on the left. The door is open,' I told him.

Just then Mrs Kennett and Adrienne appeared. Mrs Kennett was carrying an armful of fresh towels. Adrienne had a suitcase.

'Upstairs, in the bedroom,' I told them. 'What on earth have you got there?' I asked, pointing to the suitcase Adrienne was carrying.

'Baby clothes,' she replied. 'I learned to knit.'

I returned my attention to my water boiling.

* * *

The baby, a boy, as Patsy had predicted, and therefore a perfect excuse for me to buy a railway set, arrived just under an hour later. Bradshaw, everyone agreed, was marvellous. As planned I didn't go upstairs until Patsy was sitting up in bed with our firstborn in her arms. Her hair was neatly brushed, as she had said it would be, and she wore fresh lip tick. She looked wonderful. They both did.

And it was generally agreed that no one had ever boiled water better than I had.

CHAPTER 27

The Phatt family turned up at surgery two days after Mrs Phatt's evening telephone call.

'We waited until the end of the surgery so that you wouldn't feel bad about having to keep other patients waiting,' said Mrs Phatt.

'Oh, thank you,' I said.

I only keep two chairs in the surgery so, since there were four of them, I had to fetch a couple of spare chairs from the house before they could all sit down.

Mrs Phatt opened the small suitcase she had brought with her and took out a large, blue file. She handed it to me.

'Ah,' I said. 'Your family history.'

'That's my parents' medical history,' said Mrs Phatt. She delved into the suitcase and took out a second file. This one was yellow.

'My husband's parents,' she said, putting the yellow file on top of the blue file. 'These are yours to keep,' she said. 'We have our own copies at home.'

'Thank you.'

'My husband's medical records,' she said. She took out a red file and put that on top of the yellow file.

I nodded my thanks. Piled one on top of the other the three files were nearly a foot thick.

'This is my file,' said Mrs Phatt. She put a thick green file on top of the red file. The green file was far thicker than any of its predecessors.

'And these are the girls',' added Mrs Phatt. She put a pink file and a lavender file on top of the pile. These two files were much thinner.

'When are you going to introduce an appointments system?' asked Mrs Phatt.

'I have no plans to introduce one,' I told her. 'Most of my patients appreciate being able to pop in whenever there is a surgery. And quite a few don't have a telephone so making an appointment would be difficult.'

'Oh don't get me wrong,' said Mrs Phatt. 'I'm all for your present system. It means we can pop in whenever we feel like it.'

'Quite.'

'This is my husband, Mr Phatt,' said Mrs Phatt. 'Clint.' I shuffled through the medical records in front of me and found Mr Phatt's notes.

'He used to be George,' said Mrs Phatt. 'But he changed his name to Clint.'

Mr Phatt seemed to have found something fascinating on the carpet. He seemed shy, rather overwhelmed by his wife.

'Of course,' I said. He looked very much like a George and not a bit like a Clint.

'Not officially, of course,' muttered Mr Phatt quietly.

'And these are our daughters,' said Mrs Phatt. 'I kept them home from school so that they could come and meet you.'

'Good morning,' I said to the two Phatt daughters. They both giggled lightly but didn't say anything. One, the slightly taller one had her hair in pigtails. The other wore hers in a ponytail. Both girls wore spectacles and school uniform.

'I think I mentioned that I'm pre-diabetic,' said Mrs Phatt.

'I think you did,' I agreed.

'And pre-hypertensive.'

'Quite.'

'I also suffer from rheumatism, varicose veins, emphysema, arthritis - both main varieties - and haemorrhoids,' said Mrs Phatt.

I nodded. I wondered if her husband ever said anything. I was contemplating putting a thermometer in her mouth to shut her up for a while (Dr Brownlow had taught me that a thermometer is an essential aide when dealing with over-talkative patients and that, with a little reassurance and a stem look, one can be left in situ for up to five minutes at a time) when Mr Phatt spoke for the first time.

'I'm pre-diabetic too,' said Mr Phatt. He spoke rather surprisingly sharply. He had a curiously squeaky voice that made him sound a little like a cartoon character. 'And pre-hypertensive.'

'But not as pre-diabetic as I am, dear,' said Mrs Phatt firmly.

'I am,' said Mr Phatt.

'Oh no,' said Mrs Phatt vehemently. 'Oh no, you're not.'

'My liver is in a far worse state than yours,' said Mr Phatt emphatically. I was beginning to think I'd been wrong about Mr

Phatt. He could stick up for himself- particularly when it came to defending his medical history.

'Oh how can you sit there and say that?' demanded Mrs Phatt. 'When they took that reading of my liver enzymes the doctor said it was a miracle I was still able to walk about.' She stopped and thought for a moment. 'And then there's my mastitis. You don't have that, do you?'

'I have an enlarged prostate and two pre-malignant moles,' said Mr Phatt, attempting to match his wife's mastitis with his enlarged prostate and then trump her with the moles.

'Oh that's ridiculous,' said Mrs Phatt. She turned to me. 'I've got three and possibly four pre-malignant moles,' she said. 'When you examine him you will find that he's only got the one. And it's very pre-pre malignant.'

'I'm allergic to more drugs than you are,' said Mr Phatt. 'I'm allergic to penicillin, sulphonamide and three different types of anaesthetic.'

'The allergy to penicillin was never proven!' snapped Mrs Phatt.

'I nearly died when I had my anaphylactic shock reaction,' said Mr Phatt. 'The doctors said it was the most exceptional case they'd ever seen.'

'That was just hay fever,' said Mrs Phatt derisively.

'No it was not!' insisted Mr Phatt. 'It was a very rare example of anaphylactic shock. Far more serious than the usual variety.' He paused, clearly thinking hard. 'And I've had more operations than you have,' he added.

'Seven of yours were minor surgery,' said Mrs Phatt. 'All of mine were major.'

Listening to them was like watching a verbal tennis match. I was fascinated.

'It's a matter of opinion,' sneered Mr Phatt. 'I nearly died on the operating table twice.'

'Doctors said I was a walking miracle,' said Mrs Phatt. 'My doctor brought round a big group of medical students. They were all amazed.'

'It was a medical school,' said Mr Phatt. 'They took medical students to see everyone.'

'No they did not!' said Mrs Phatt.

'My piles are bigger than yours,' said Mr Phatt.

'That's a matter of opinion,' said Mrs Phatt. 'I'm the one who had two children.'

The two children looked embarrassed. They hadn't said a word and didn't look as if they intended to. I got the impression they never said very much. Indeed, it didn't seem likely that they ever got the chance to say much.

'And I've got an incipient prolapse,' said Mrs Phatt, as though laying down the ace of trumps. Her remark had the desired effect. Mr Phatt didn't say anything in response to this. 'Plus,' continued Mrs Phatt, 'I worry about you.'

'I worry a lot too,' said Mr Phatt, defensively.

'I know you do,' agreed Mrs Phatt. 'That's why I worry about you so much. You'll make me ill with all your worrying.' Just then there was a knock on the door.

'Come in!' I called.

'Bit of an emergency at Bunbury Cottage,' said Miss Johnson, popping her head round the door.

'Right, thank you, MissJohnson,' I said, standing up. 'Sorry about this,' I said to the Phatts. 'But I'm afraid I have to go.' I pointed to the pile of files now dominating my desk. 'Thank you so much for these,' I said.

'Don't you just want to check our blood pressure?' asked Mrs Phatt.

'Not at the moment I'm afraid,' I said. 'Emergencies have to come first.'

'Oh,' said Mrs Phatt. She sounded disappointed. Reluctantly she stood up. Once she was she standing her husband and daughters stood too. I ushered them out of the surgery, much as a mother duck will usher its ducklings in the direction she wants them to go.

'We'll see you soon!' said Mrs Phatt, leading her brood through the door.

'I'm sure you will,' I said, quietly.

'Was that a threat or a promise?' asked Miss Johnson, when she'd shut the door behind them.

I slumped back down into my chair and put my head in my hands. I knew, just as well as Miss Johnson, that there is no Bunbury Cottage in Bilbury nor, as far as I know, anywhere in the vicinity of the village.

'Thank you,' I said weakly.

'Shall I put the kettle on?' enquired Miss Johnson.

I nodded. 'And bring in some chocolate digestive biscuits, please,' I said. 'This is a time for comfort eating.'

'Shall I put these files somewhere safe?' asked Miss Johnson, picking up the files Mrs Phatt had left on my desk.

I nodded, gratefully.

CHAPTER 28

Thumper, Patchy, Frank and I were sitting in the lounge of the Duck and Puddle discussing business ventures we had come across in our time. The discussion had been triggered by the news that someone Patchy vaguely knew was opening a restaurant called The Lobster Pot. In ten minutes we managed to think of nine other restaurants with the same name. We also came up with five called 'The Captain's Table', three called 'The Hole in the Wall', seven tea shops called 'A Taste Of Devon' and six shops which their proud owners had named 'The Tackle Box' (not all of them selling fishing equipment).

When Thumper said that the wife of a chum of his had recently opened a millinery shop called The Mad Hatter's we started discussing other memorable names we had come across. We all remembered the local builder known as 'Sherlock Homes' and the travel company called 'Seymour Tours' but it was Patchy who insisted that he knew a firm of accountants called 'Limp and Grimace'.

Frank, who had joined in the discussion, said that he knew of a pair of comedians who called themselves Bitter and Twisted. Patchy said a bloke he knew had made a lot of money by selling a soap powder called CARE. He said that when women saw a label advising them to 'wash with care' on their clothes they went out and bought his product.

I said that when I was at medical school I'd heard of two businessmen who had changed their names by deed poll to 'Swifter' and 'Cheaper' so they could open a carrier service and call themselves Swifter and Cheaper without getting into trouble with the authorities for misleading advertising. Patchy said a former girlfriend of his had once run a slimming club called Waist Management. I remembered that a drug company representative had once come in to promote a sleeping tablet called Pill-O. 'The slogan that went with it was,' I added, 'the sleeping tablet that helps you get your head down'.'

Then Frank said that he'd always fancied setting up a door-to-door booze delivery service called 'Booze on Bikes' and Thumper said that 'Pissed on Pedals' would be a better name for it. After that things rapidly got out of hand. Thumper said he'd always wanted to set up an organisation called Interchip which would be like Interflora except that people could use it to ring up and have chips (and possibly but not necessarily fish) delivered to friends.

The conversation came to a rather sudden end when Patchy said that a farmer pal of his had once had a brilliant idea for making money out of flies. He said the farmer had noticed that the cow manure in his sheds always attracted a lot of flies and so, after reading that French farmers fed flies to their frogs to put meat on their legs, he had bought a huge fan, a long piece of wide rubber tubing and some old milk chums. He'd then used the fan and the tubing to suck up the flies and store them in the milk churns.

'What did he call the business?' Thumper asked.

'Dunno,' said Patchy. 'It never got off the ground. He couldn't get an export licence to sell flies to France.'

'All that brain work has made me hungry,' said Thumper, emptying his beer glass.

'You're always hungry!' I reminded him.

He shrugged, thought about it for a moment, nodded in agreement and turned to Frank. 'I'll have the Steaming Hot Natural Pulses Resting On A Grilled Slice From A Fresh Wholemeal Farmhouse Bloomer Generously Bathed In A Succulent Tomato Based Sauce,' he said.

The landlord glowered at him. 'You'll have a pie or a pickled egg and bloody like it.'

'It's good to have you back, Frank,' Thumper told him with a laugh. I looked along the counter. The jar of pickled eggs was back. A table mat had been placed on top of the jar as a stand in for the missing lid.

'I'll have a packet of crisps, please,' I said firmly. 'The ones with the salt wrapped up in a twist of blue paper please.' Just then Gilly appeared.

'What did Frank buy you in London?' Thumper asked her.

Gilly disappeared as suddenly as she had appeared and returned a moment later with a smart looking shopping bag with the Harrods logo on the side. Proudly, she held the bag up for us to see.

'Impressive,' said Thumper. 'But what did he buy you?' He leant forward a little and lowered his voice. 'What's in the bag?'

Gilly frowned. 'The bag is the present,' she said.

'Lovely bag,' said Thumper, trying to rescue the situation.

'They sell fantastic train sets in Harrods,' said Patchy. He looked at me. 'You should get one for your kid,' he said.

'I think it's a bit early,' I said.

'Oh no,' said Patchy, shaking his head. 'Give you a chance to set it all up and make sure it works properly.'

I admit I was tempted.

I've always wanted a train set.

* * *

After lunch I headed off to do my afternoon visits. As I reached my car I heard footsteps behind me. I turned to see Thumper running after me. 'Could I have a word with you, doc?' he said.

'Of course.'

'I didn't like to mention it in there,' he turned and nodded his head towards the pub, 'but my Aunt Olive has been a bit under the weather recently. I'm worried about her.'

'I'll call in before I go home,' I promised him.

'Thanks doc,' he said. 'There's no hurry, though.' And he disappeared back into the Duck and Puddle.

CHAPTER 29

I called in at the village shop to collect one or two things that Patsy had asked me to pick up. Peter was not in a good mood.

'Have you seen Gilly?' he demanded.

'Yes. I gather they had a wonderful time in London.'

'They went shopping in Harrods!' complained Peter. 'Doesn't anyone in Bilbury realise how difficult it is for a small retailer trying to make a living these days?' He paused for a moment. 'And now she's walking around with a bag advertising Harrods!'

'Well, give her a bag advertising Peter Marshall's!' I told him.

'I haven't got any,' he muttered. He thought for a moment. You could almost see the steam coming out of his ears. 'Maybe I could get some made.'

'Why not?' I said.

'I need to do everything I can to survive,' said Peter, who loved moaning almost as much as he loved making money. 'There's another new supermarket opening in Barnstaple this week.'

Knowing how much he disapproved of supermarkets I made murmuring sounds of sympathy and disapproval. No one in Bilbury ever dared let themselves be seen carrying shopping bought at a supermarket. Peter could just about bear it if he saw carrier bags from W.H.Smith or Boots in someone's car but if he saw evidence that anyone had visited a supermarket he would fly into a red-faced rage.

As I should have expected, my sympathetic sounds triggered something of an onslaught.

'I hate supermarkets!' he said. 'They're ruining our society. Go into big towns these days and all you find are supermarkets and charity shops. Both just giving things away.

You just watch! The supermarkets will lower their prices until I go bust and then they'll put their prices up again!' He waved a finger in my face.

'You're absolutely right,' I said.

'You mark my words,' continued Peter. 'I'll go out of business and then there will be no village shop. Where will everyone go to on Sunday evenings when they've run out of tomato ketchup? Village shops will be closing down left, right and centre.'

'I agree with you,' I told him.

'The village shop is the heart of any village.'

'Absolutely true.'

'Supermarkets are destroying our culture!' said Peter, warming to his eternal theme. 'And they're destroying our health.'

'Destroying our health?'

'The food they sell is rubbish,' he said. 'Packaged hamburgers. Everything double wrapped. Good old-fashioned greengrocers and butchers shops will all go under. When did you last see a proper fishmonger? And you mark my words they'll start selling books eventually and then there won't be any bookshops left.'

'You'll have to start competing with them head on!' I told him.

'How do I do that?'

I thought about it for a minute. 'You could try having one of those competitions they have where the winner gets to grab and keep as much as they· can collect in a minute.'

'How will getting people to shop quickly make any difference?' asked Peter.

'No,' I explained. 'It's a competition. The winner of the competition gets given a trolley, or in your case a basket, and then given a minute to rush around the store picking out things they want. At the end of the minute they get to keep everything they've collected.'

'I like that,' said Peter. 'I could sell a lot of stuff that way.'

'No, no. You give the stuff free to the person who is the winner.'

Peter stared at me for what seemed like an eternity but was probably no more than a minute. 'I let people fill a basket with things from the shop and I don't charge them anything?'

'That's it,' I said.

'Not a penny?'

'Not a penny.'

Peter stared at me. 'Have you just come out of the Duck?'

'Yes.'

He nodded. 'I thought so.'

'It's what the supermarkets do,' I insisted.

'And how can I compete with that?' demanded Peter. 'How can I compete if they're giving away whole baskets of stuff?'

'Well, maybe that wasn't such a good idea,' I said, abandoning the idea of explaining it to Peter. 'Maybe you just want to introduce some of those offers that encourage people to spend more money.'

'What sort of offers?'

'You could do tastings.' He looked puzzled.

'They do that in the supermarkets,' I said. 'So I'm told,' I added quickly. 'They give customers a biscuit in the hope that they'll buy a whole boxful of them. Or they give customers a glass of wine so that they are encouraged to buy a bottle of the stuff.'

Peter thought about it. 'That might work,' he agreed. 'Any more good ideas?'

'You could have a closing down sale.'

'But I'm not closing down,' he pointed out. 'Not yet anyway.'

'No, no, you don't actually have to close down. You just say you are. You put up signs saying Everything Must Go. When I arrived in Birmingham to start my six years at medical school I noticed a jewellery shop had a huge notice in the window saying 'Closing Down. Final Days. Everything Must Go.' When I left Birmingham six years later the same shop was still there with the same sign in the window.'

Peter looked puzzled. He had been running the village shop for a long time but he didn't seem to know much about the tricks employed by the retail trade.

'It's an excuse to get people to think you're selling stuff cheap,' I explained. 'None of the stuff they were selling was particularly cheap.'

Peter brightened at this. 'I don't really have to sell anything cheap?'

'Not if you don't want to. Of course, if you've got some things you are prepared to sell cheap to get rid of them then you could have a bit of a sale as well.'

Suddenly Peter's eyes lit up. 'I could have a bit of a clear out,' he said.

'Exactly!' I agreed.

'Great idea!' he said. 'Now what do you want?'

I started to read from Patsy's list and then just handed him the piece of paper. 'If you get that lot ready for me I'll pick it up later,' I said.

'Right ho,' said Peter, looking down the list and nodding happily.

CHAPTER 30

General practitioners who work in towns and cities have to contend with heavy traffic and, often, with the problem of what to do with their car when they finally arrive at a patient's home. That's the downside. On the other hand, the roads in which their patients live are usually neatly named and numbered and if they live and work in anything more than the smallest of towns there will probably be a street map of the whole area available for a modest outlay.

A GP working in a town or a city can probably expect to be able to find all, or at least most, of his patients residing within a fairly small area. And if he is lucky enough, he may be able to visit two or three of his patients within a single building. (If he's unlucky they will all be in a tall building where none of the lifts are working.)

Practising as a country GP is a very different business.

There are, of course, no flats or terraced houses in Bilbury. Indeed, there are no more than a dozen semi-detached properties in the whole of Bilbury. The vast majority of the villagers live in detached houses and cottages. And even when the lanes and tracks down which people live do have names (and, more often than not, they don't) there are certainly no such things as road signs to guide the traveller who is not content to wander where the will takes him but has, instead, some formal destination in mind. House signs, where they exist, are almost bound to have faded or to have been overgrown by ivy and other creepers. to know where most of the residents lived and, just as importantly, to know the quickest way to get to them. I knew which lane was likely to be blocked, and at what times of day, by a herd of cattle being moved to or from a milking shed. I knew at which times of year, and in which weather, certain lanes and tracks were likely to be flooded or impassable because of thick mud.

I knew exactly where Thumper's Aunt Olive lived, and the journey should have taken me no more than ten minutes. But, I was in no great hurry and it took me considerably longer than that to get to her.

People who live in towns sometimes complain that the countryside is dull and that there is nothing much to see. It's true there are no museums, art galleries, theatres or cinemas in Bilbury (though it should be remembered that the vicar does put on a film show once a fortnight during the winter months) but there are many other things to see and enjoy.

And lots of other things to keep everyone busy too.

I was about half way between the Duck and Puddle and Thumper's Aunt's cottage when I spotted half a sheep poking out into the lane. The sheep was making a considerable amount of noise but seemed unable to move. Guessing what had happened I stopped the car and parked on the grass verge.

Contrary to their reputation sheep are intelligent animals. But they are also intensely curious creatures and their lives are constantly controlled by the suspicion that the grass will always be greener (and probably tastier) on the other side of the hedge.

Since becoming a resident of Bilbury I had acquired a good deal of respect and some affection for sheep. As a town raised observer I had always assumed sheep to be rather stupid animals. That, after all, is the reputation they've been saddled with. And my ignorance about their behaviour and habits had been pretty far reaching. Within weeks of arriving in Bilbury I had rushed into the Duck and Puddle and informed the first farmer I'd seen that there were sheep in the village suffering from some terrible infection.

'What sort of infection?' he'd asked, peering at me over his pint glass.

'They've got purple spots on their backs,' I told him. 'Great purple blotches.'

The farmer hadn't laughed, though it would have been difficult to blame him if he had. He'd explained, with considerable patience, that the birds, particularly the bigger ones, the magpies, the crows, the starlings, the seagulls and so on, had been eating blackberries from the hedgerows. When I still didn't understand he asked me if I had not noticed that birds like standing on the backs of sheep. I said I had. He then asked me if I noticed that if I parked my car under a tree I was likely to find it speckled with nasty white splodges. I said that of course I had. He then pointed out that if I looked carefully I would notice that at this time of year the splodges were more likely to be purple than white. Suddenly the truth dawned on me. I bought the farmer another pint and he promised not to tell the story about how the new doctor had discovered a new and deadly epidemic of 'Purple spot' among Bilbury's sheep. As far as I'm aware he kept his side of the bargain too. That's another country truth I discovered. No one can keep a secret quite as well as village folk. (And no one can spread gossip quite as fast either.)

Gradually, over the months and years, I learned that lambs play just the same sort of games as children love. Each spring I parked my car on a piece of verge, or leant my bicycle against a tree and then stood, arms folded on the top bar of the nearest five-barred gate, and watched as lambs played tag, king of the castle and I can- get-to-that-bush-faster-than-you-can games.

When Patsy and I acquired sheep of our own I learned that sheep will learn their name and will come when called. I learned that sheep are bright enough to know how to open a gate and sneak from a field (where the only food available is grass) into a garden where there are tender shoots galore for the taking. I even saw them close a gate when, to avoid the consequences of their actions, they hurried back from garden to field. I learned that when they are happy lambs, and even sheep, will leap into the air with joy. (The Devon villagers call it pronging.) I learned that if sheep are parted from their friends they will fight to get to one another. Even years later one sheep can immediately own young lamb out of a field of a hundred. I learned that sheep hate getting wet and will always run in out of the rain (if they have somewhere to go). I learned that they hate walking through mud and will always go round a muddy patch of field if they possibly can. I learned that they can be selfish and stubborn but are often sensitive and logical. I learned that they can identify individual people, as well as sheep. And I learned that sheep get depressed in bad weather and that a depressed sheep will stand still with its head down, its ears unmoving and its eyes dull.

Like so many sheep had done before it (and just as many will doubtless do in the future) the sheep had tried to force its way through the hedge and it had got stuck. It had sealed its temporary fate by going into reverse and trying to back out of the hedge. Now it was held quite firm by a mass of brambles.

Problems of this type are so common in Bilbury that in the boot of the Morris Minor I keep a pair of thick gardening gloves. I opened the boot, took out the gloves and put them on. The sheep made one last attempt to free itself but, inevitably, succeeded only in getting itself stuck even more firmly.

It took me nearly half an hour to free the animal. I used the biggest blade on my penknife to cut through the brambles which were stuck in the sheep's wool and eventually, after a good deal of effort, I succeeded in pushing the sheep back through the hedge and into the field from which it had tried to escape. Its friends and family (including a lamb which was clearly delighted to have its mother returned to it) were waiting just a few yards away and they received it with great joy. I put my penknife away, stuffed the pieces of cut bramble into the hole the sheep had made in the hedge and removed my gloves and tossed them into the car boot. Despite having worn thick gloves my hands and my forearms were scratched and bleeding. My shirt, my trousers and my jacket were all badly snagged. I tidied myself up as well as I could and stood for a while watching the happy lamb gambolling around its mother. Then I wandered over to a nearby stretch of wooden fencing and put my arms on the top rail. I almost wished I smoked a pipe at that moment. As a poor substitute I reached down, picked a piece of long succulent grass and stuck it between my teeth.

When I'd first moved to Bilbury I would have seen very little of what was going on around me. But Patsy, Thumper and many others had taught me what to look for.

Up above the field ahead of me a buzzard was slowly circling; watching and waiting. There is something admirably serene about buzzards. They are so silent and so clearly fearless. It is easy to assume that they are harmless too. But a pair of buzzards with three young will kill 600 rabbits and 8,000 voles in a single year.

To my right a pair of bluetits hovered like hummingbirds and plucked flies out of the centre of a spider's web. The web spinner, whose lunch, dinner and supper were being taken, sat on a twig nearby. Watchful, waiting and quite possibly, and justifiably, resentful.

Swallows, just returned for the summer, raced around the field checking out their old haunts and welcoming friends as they arrived. Swallows whizz around the sky with the same joy that people would show if they discovered they could fly. Attracted, no doubt, by my sweat, two swallows swooped around me, searching for any insects which might have also been attracted by the same smells.

I heard a rustle to my right and saw a large badger emerge from the grass bank on the other side of the lane. Contrary to what most townspeople and some naturalists believe it's unusual but not at all unknown to see badgers up and about in the daytime.

The badger disappeared into the thick, long grass at the side of the lane and seemed to be struggling with something. Minutes later he was joined by a second badger. The two of them pulled and pushed and worked hard at whatever it was they were trying to move. Hesitantly, not wanting to frighten them away, I moved a little closer until I could see what they were doing. There was a dead badger lying in the long grass and the two badgers which had arrived were trying to move the body. I watched as they pulled it out of the long grass, up the bank and through a small gap at the bottom of the thick hawthorn hedge which separated the lane from the field on that side of the road. I watched as they dragged the badger's corpse across several yards of grassland and then into the edge of a nearby stretch of wood. It was clearly hard work but they didn't stop for a second. When they had managed to drag the body into the wood they dug a shallow grave, placed the body into it and then covered it with leaves and branches.

There is, truly, so much to see in the countryside if you are prepared to look.

I looked at my watch and realised that if I was going to see Thumper's Aunt Olive and get back to Bilbury Grange in time for evening surgery I'd better hurry.

* * *

Thumper's Aunt, Miss Olive Robinson, lived in a thatched cottage which had roses and clematis climbing around the door and round the windows. The traditional cottage garden is full of lupins, honeysuckle, roses, hollyhocks and delphiniums. In mid summer the garden is alive with butterflies and bees.

It is, without a doubt, one of the most beautiful cottages in Devon.

She shared it with a cat called Tinsel and a dog called Bonzo.

The cottage is, of course, a tourist attraction for holiday-makers passing through Bilbury, and Miss Robinson takes full advantage of this by selling home-made biscuits and home-made cakes. She also supplements her income by allowing foreigners to buy pieces of her furniture. To ensure that she gets top prices, her nephew Thumper somehow manages to ensure that she obtains a steady supply of small bookcases, coffee tables, trays and other items which were once the property of William Shakespeare and which are suitably marked with the initials WS and an appropriate date scratched roughly into the underside.

Thumper and Patchy Fogg, the village's resident antique dealer, long ago worked out that items of furniture small enough to be stowed inside the boot of a car, or on the back seat, are far more likely to find a buyer than pieces which will require the services of a removal company.

When confronted with a potential buyer Miss Robinson never actually says that the item of furniture belonged to Mr Shakespeare, of course. But she mentions that it has been in the family for a long, long time, hints that a distant ancestor worked with the playwright as some sort of stage manager and lets it be known that she wishes she could sell some of her belongings so that she would have enough money to pay her rates and buy a little food and fuel.

At this point she pops out into the kitchen to put the kettle on, leaving the American (German or Japanese) tourist to put two and two together and make five.

'I don't cheat these people at all,' Miss Robinson once told me. 'They think they're cheating me and they end up cheating themselves.'

It was difficult to argue with her logic and so I never tried to.

I parked the car, half on the verge and half in the lane, picked my bag off the front passenger seat, and walked up the path to Miss Robinson's front door. I knocked to let her know I was there and walked in.

She was sitting in her front parlour. I was startled by her appearance.

Miss Robinson had always been very welcoming; a very ebullient woman. She had always been a robust woman with the sort of laugh adored by television producers making weak situation comedies. No audience could have sat in silence once Aunt Olive began laughing.

Now, quite suddenly, she looked old and frail. Her hair wasn't combed or washed. And she seemed slow in everything she did. She remembered to tell me off for bothering to knock on the door rather than just walking in ('as I expect my friends to do') but she quickly showed her confusion. She asked me if she'd requested me to call and confessed that her memory wasn't what it used to be. She said she'd only just finished breakfast. And she didn't seem embarrassed about the fact that her usually immaculate living room was untidy and littered with dirty crockery, bits of clothing and newspapers and magazines.

I was glad that Thumper had asked me to see his aunt. I didn't know what was wrong but I knew at once that it was something quite serious.

'Thumper asked me to call around and see you,' I told her.

'Oh, my dear, it's nice to see you but I'm not well enough for visitors,' she said. 'My hair is a mess. Can you call back when I feel a little better?'

'It's me!' I reminded her. 'The doctor.'

'Oh dear,' she said, looking worried. 'At my age I have to keep in with the doctor.'

I smiled at her and touched her shoulder. 'How do you feel?'

'Terrible,' she said. 'If I'm honest. And at my age there isn't much point in being anything else. I look awful.' She sighed as though suddenly feeling the weight of the world on her shoulders.

'I've matured,' she said. 'Like cheese.' She thought about this for a moment. 'People think far too highly of maturity,' she said. 'It's greatly overrated. What does it mean? What's good about it?' She looked at me, as though trying to decide where she'd seen me before and then gave up the struggle. 'I've suddenly been lumbered with an old person's hair and feet,' she said with enormous sadness. 'I can't do a thing with either of them.'

'Well, let me see if I can help,' I suggested.

'Maybe you can give this hair and these feet back to the person they belong to,' she suggested.

'And get yours back for you?'

'That would be nice,' she said. 'I'll put the kettle on.' She got up and headed, with obvious difficulty, towards the kitchen. She walked with a limp and shuffled across her carpet, sounding like a boy rustling through fallen autumn leaves.

'How long have you had difficulty in walking?'

She half turned to look at me. 'Am I having difficulty in walking?'

'You seem to be,' I said.

'I suppose I am,' she admitted. 'I fell. Perhaps I sieved something. Strained something. Hurt myself I get headaches. Did you know that?'

I shook my head.

'Terrible pains in my head,' she said. 'They won't go away.'

'I think I should organise some tests for you,' I said. 'At the hospital,' I added.

Miss Robinson glowered at me disapprovingly. 'Young man,' she said, 'I am the world's leading expert on my body. It is my speciality. I know more about it than any other man or woman alive. I know more about its weaknesses, its strengths, its foibles than any of your damned specialists. And I don't care what your needles and X-rays tell you. I am telling you that I am perfectly well.'

But I knew she was wrong. And so did she.

'Can I use your phone?' I asked.

'Of course you can dear.'

I telephoned the hospital and spoke to one of the hospital doctors. I explained that I had a patient with some curious symptoms. He agreed to take her in for a few days.

'How old is she?' he asked, when I'd finished describing her symptoms.

I told him.

'We're not going to get stuck with her?'

I assured him that he was not. Like most hospital consultants he was wary of admitting elderly patients and then finding that they needed to stay in hospital for months or even years because they could not be sent home.

'No more than a week,' he said, insistently. 'We've got a massive bed problem these days.'

'No more than a week,' I agreed.

I told Olive that I wanted her to go into hospital for some more tests.

'I had some tests done,' she said. 'They said the fracture was healing nicely.'

'What fracture?' I asked.

'My arm,' she said.

'How did you break your arm?' I asked her.

'Fell off my bicycle,' she replied.

I didn't know anything about this. I made a mental note to check her medical records when I got home.

'I'll ring Thumper and ask him to take you into the hospital tomorrow morning,' I told her. 'You won't be there for long.' Then I rang Thumper.

'I've arranged for your Aunt Olive to go into the hospital tomorrow for an X-ray and some tests,' I told him. 'I could get an ambulance...'

'What time?'

I told him.

'Does she need to go in an ambulance?'

'No.'

'Tell her I'll pick her up an hour before she's due at the hospital,' he said. 'That should give us plenty of time in case we're held up on the way. Will she have to stay in?'

'Yes. I don't know how long. Just a few days.'

'Is it serious?'

'I don't have the faintest idea what's wrong with her yet,' I told him.

'Thanks for sorting out the tests so quickly,' he said.

* * *

I'd been with Thumper's Aunt for less than an hour but in that time I'd lost count of the number of cups of tea she'd poured for me. Thumper's Aunt had been brought up in a time when the quality of hospitality was measured by the amount of tea a visitor could be persuaded to drink.

'Can I borrow your toilet before I go home?' I asked her.

'It's down the garden,' she said.

'Have you not got one indoors?' I asked, surprised.

'Won't have one indoors,' she said. 'Terrible to have one indoors. People are never well when they have those things indoors.'

I headed for the back door. 'Is there a key?' I called, over my shoulder.

'A key?' said Thumper's Aunt in astonishment. 'I've been here 40 years and no one has tried to steal the bucket yet.'

CHAPTER 31

When I called in at Peter Marshall's shop on my way home I could hardly believe my eyes.

Thewords 'SHUTTING.DESTROYEDBYSUPERMARKETS.BARGAINS.SALE' were painted on the windows in whitewash.

'What do you think?' Peter asked.

'It's a bit startling,' I told him. 'But it should draw attention to the shop.'

'Great idea of yours!' he said. 'Look at this!' He pointed to a large trestle table he'd erected outside the shop. It was laden with tins and boxes.

'What on earth have you got there?'

'I looked through the old stock,' said Peter. 'There's a ton of stuff I can sell off cheaply.'

I picked up a tin. 'There's no label on this,' I said. 'It's impossible to tell what it is.'

'I call it pot luck,' said Peter. 'You buy three tins and you've got a meal.'

'But no one will know what they're eating!'

'Exactly.'

'These tins could contain anything.' Peter nodded.

'Any ideas?'

Peter shrugged. 'There's some soup. Some apricots. Some beans. Spaghetti hoops probably. Beef chunks. Dog food.'

'Do you have any idea how old this stuff is?'

'No idea at all. I found it in boxes in the shed. I've given it all a good mix. Take some tins back for Patsy. You'd be very unlucky to get three the same because I've given them a good mix up.'

'Guess how old it is,' I said. I picked up a couple of tins. They were rusty around the rims. The cans were dented. It looked as if they'd been given more than a good mix up.

'Probably twenty five or thirty years,' he said. 'This was a great idea of yours. If I can sell this lot I'll be able to pay the wholesaler.'

He rubbed his hands together and lowered his voice. 'It's only eighteen months since I paid them last time,' he confided, 'But they've been getting a bit aggressive recently.'

'If this stuff had labels on you could sell it to museums!' I told him.

'Do you think so? Maybe I can find some of the old labels.'

'What are you selling them for?'

'Twenty pence a tin.'

'But that's far more than customers would pay for tins with the labels still on!'

'Yes, I know. But I'm selling excitement and adventure aren't I?'

I put down the tin I'd been examining.

'Exciting isn't it?' said Peter.

'Yes,' I agreed.

'I'm doing tastings as well,' he said.

'Oh, right! What of?'

'Mustard and soup.'

'Mustard and soup?'

'I've got quite a lot of mustard and six cases of green pea soup,' explained Peter. 'Here you are!' He pointed to an open jar of mustard and an opened tin of soup on the trestle table and then handed me a spoon. 'Help yourself!'

'The soup is cold!' I said, peering into the tin.

'Of course it is! I can't keep soup bubbling on the stove all day, can I?'

'And how am I supposed to taste mustard?'

'You put the spoon in the mustard jar and then suck the mustard off the spoon,' Peter explained.

I looked at him and put the spoon down. 'I'll just take my shopping for now,' I said. 'Patsy will have dinner ready for me and I don't want to spoil my appetite.'

I paid him, put the shopping in the boot of the car and set off for home.

As I left Peter was trying to persuade Patchy Fogg to buy a dozen unlabelled tins of whatever for the price of twelve.

* * *

When I got back to Bilbury Grange I picked out Olive Robinson's medical records. I flicked through her notes and, in Dr Brownlow's writing, found the reference I was looking for.

220

She'd broken her left forearm in 1952.

CHAPTER 32

Now that I was a GP again I was getting used to getting up in the middle of the night.

My patients weren't a bad lot.

Unlike patients in some city practices mine hardly ever called me out unnecessarily (and never did so recklessly). But there were enough night time emergencies for me to have got used to waking up instantly when the phone went in the night.

So when the telephone went I turned on the bedside lamp and picked up the telephone and was awake within seconds.

'Hello!'

There was no one there.

For a moment I thought it was a hoax call.

And then I realised that all I'd heard since I'd picked up the telephone had been the dial tone. I was puzzling over this when the bell went again.

It was the doorbell not the telephone.

I glanced at the clock, clambered out of bed, put on my dressing gown and headed for the door. It was twenty minutes past six.

'Who is it?' asked Patsy, who was now wide awake.

'Dunno,' I replied sleepily. 'Probably a patient who doesn't have a telephone.' It was the wrong doorbell for a patient. But maybe they'd gone to the wrong door.

I tottered down the stairs and opened the front door.

'Morning doctor!' said a cheery face. For a moment I didn't recognise him. Then I realised that the caller was holding a pile of brushes in one hand and a large bag in the other. And just behind him I saw his van. It was Wilson Porter, the village sweep.

'I have a job sleeping these days,' said Wilson, putting down his bag touching his cap with the forefinger of his free hand. 'So I just pop round and visit my customers. Easier than trying to get back to sleep. Fireplace in the living room?'

'Yes,' I told him.

He picked up his bag and headed into the house. I padded after him. I was beginning to wonder if he was having a break down. Perhaps, I wondered, he was developing mania. His behaviour certainly couldn't be described as normal.

'Don't some of your customers mind you calling round in the middle of the night?'

'Oh, no,' replied Wilson. 'And the lanes are quiet. I can get round the village more easily.'

He put down his bag and brushes and took a large sheet out of the bag. He laid this down in front of the fireplace.

'Do you need me to move things out?' I asked. 'Cover things up?'

'Oh no,' he said. 'Don't worry yourself I won't make a mess.'

'It smokes,' I said. 'Actually it smokes quite a lot.'

'Always has done this one,' said Wilson.

'We did get some people in from Barnstaple,' I told him. 'Soon after we moved here.'

Wilson sucked some air in through a gap between his front teeth. 'Bet they wanted an arm and a leg?'

'We couldn't afford them,' I said.

'Wanted to rebuild your chimney?'

I nodded. 'They wanted to put in some fans.'

He laughed.

'They said the fans would help take the smoke up the chimney,' I explained.

'Probably would,' he agreed. 'But what a complicated and expensive way to do it.'

'Can you sort it out without putting in fans?'

'Of course I can,' he said. He lifted the fire basket out of the fireplace and put it on his sheet. 'Have you got any spare bricks?'

'We've got piles of them,' I told him.

'Bring me two,' he said.

I slipped on some shoes and let myself out of the house. Dawn was breaking. It was a wonderful sight. A few minutes later I was back with two ordinary house bricks.

'I've given it a poke with the brushes,' he said as I returned. 'It's clean as a whistle.' He took the bricks off me, arranged them in the fireplace and then put the grate back on top of the bricks.

'That'll sort your problem, doctor,' he said. I stared at him. 'Just that?'

He nodded. 'It'll put your fire nearer to the chimney. Plus, you'll get more air under the fire and a better draught.' He folded up his sheet and put it back into his bag. Then he picked up the bag and his brushes and headed for the door. I glanced at the clock. It was ten to seven.

'Have you finished?'

'All done, doctor!' he said. 'Call me in the morning if it's not better.' He laughed. 'There you are!' he said. 'I could have sorted it out over the phone. Take two house bricks and call me in the morning if it's not better.' He laughed a lot and clearly thought this very funny. I was still too tired to laugh.

'How much do I owe you?' I asked him.

He shook his head. 'On the house,' he said. He leant towards me. 'Just a little thank you for popping in to see my Aunt Olive,' he said.

'Olive Robinson?'

'That's the one.'

'She's your Aunt? I thought she was Thumper's Aunt.'

'She is. Thumper and I are cousins.'

'Oh.'

The endless complications of relationships within Bilbury never failed to astound me. I was always discovering that people whom I assumed were just friends were, in reality, quite close relatives. In a small village like Bilbury, most people are related to at least half the other villagers.

The sweep lowered his voice, as though about to share a secret.

'In case you're worried, I don't always do my visits at night. It's just that I'm taking the family off on holiday today. A fortnight motoring on the continent. Your missus rang me yesterday but I was booked up solid. I wanted to sort out your chimney before we go away. Hope you didn't mind.'

I stared at him and burst out laughing. 'That's very kind of you!'

He winked at me. 'You thought I'd gone bonkers, didn't you?'

I nodded. 'I did wonder,' I admitted.

'Your fireplace will be fine now,' he promised. 'Just you see.'

And it was too.

The chimney specialists had wanted over £1,000 to put it right. Wilson had done it for nothing. Total cost: two old house bricks.

224

CHAPTER 33

'It's going to be a quiet wedding. We don't want anything too big,' said Patchy. 'Just a memorable occasion with a few close friends and relatives.'

'And we certainly don't want lots of noise and dancing,' said Adrienne. 'We want our wedding to be a special, sacred occasion. We don't want one of those weddings where the women hitch up their skirts and dance round their handbags while the men drink too much beer, tell dirty stories and then start fighting.'

'Or, indeed, one of those weddings where the men dance round their handbags and the women drink too much beer, tell dirty stories and start fighting,' said Patchy.

Adrienne Kennett and Patchy Fogg, my sister-in-law and my brother-in-law to be, were sitting in the kitchen at Bilbury Grange discussing their forthcoming wedding.

'You're definitely decided on the dress?' said Patsy, who was just as excited as her sister at the forthcoming nuptials.

'Definitely,' said Adrienne.

After days spent searching the shops in Barnstaple and Exeter, Adrienne had decided that she would wear an antique lace wedding dress that had first been worn by Patchy's grandmother.

It had been altered by Adrienne's mother my mother-in-law, and the fact that the changes were invisible to the naked eye was a considerable tribute to Mrs Kennett's skills with a needle. Adrienne was taller than Patchy's grandmother and several inches larger around both the bust and the hips.

'We're getting married in Bilbury church, of course,' said Adrienne. 'But Mum and Dad aren't so sure about having the reception at the farm.'

'There isn't a lot of room there,' agreed Patsy. This was something of an understatement.

The Kennett's farmhouse was in a beautiful position and had wonderful views but a general estate agent, searching for the most appropriate bon mot, would have described the house as 'cosy'. If more than half a dozen people turned up to the reception they would be standing on one another's toes.

'They say we can have it there if we can't find anywhere else,' said Adrienne.

There was a long silence.

Patsy looked at me. I knew what she was thinking. I smiled and nodded slightly.

'You must have the reception here,' said Patsy. 'If you'd like to, of course.'

Adrienne jumped up and threw her arms around her sister. 'Oh, are you sure?' she said. 'That would be absolutely wonderful!' She turned to Patchy. 'Wouldn't that be wonderful?'

'It would,' agreed Patchy. He looked at me. 'Are you sure?'

'It'll be our pleasure,' I said. 'We can put a marquee up on the lawn.'

'I've got a pal who can let us have one at a special price,' said Patchy. Patchy always knows someone who can do things at a special price. 'Nice chap if a bit odd. He calls his business the Marquee de Sade. He also promotes rock concerts and gives lectures on flower arranging.'

'We'll pay for everything,' said Adrienne. She laughed. 'Patchy has got plenty of money.'

'Don't ever tell anyone that,' said Patchy sternly.

'But they're family!' protested Adrienne.

'Especially not family,' said Patchy. It was difficult to tell how much he was joking. Patchy wasn't as tight as Peter Marshall but he didn't like parting with money unnecessarily. I think he thought his money might get homesick if it left his wallet.

'I expect Dad will want to pay for everything,' said Patsy.

'Well, we'll let him pay for some things,' said Adrienne. She lowered her voice in that way people do when they're telling you something confidential, even though they know perfectly well that there is no chance of anyone overhearing them. 'Things have been a bit tight recently at the farm. So Patchy and I will try and grab some of the bills before he sees them.'

'Well, if it's going to be a quiet wedding it shouldn't be all that expensive,' said Patsy.

'No,' agreed Adrienne. 'Just relatives and a few very dear friends.'

'I suppose we'll have to invite these two as well,' said Patchy, nodding at Patsy and I. 'Since we're using their house.' Adrienne hit him over the head with a newspaper.

CHAPTER 34

'Do you remember a chap called Alfred Burton?' asked Patchy.

I thought hard but eventually shook my head.

'Farmer who went bankrupt. We bought his dog.'

'Lady!' I said. 'Yes, of course I remember. We paid a halfpenny each for her.'

'That's the one,' agreed Patchy. 'He moved in with his mother in a cottage in Combe Martin.'

'I remember,' I said. 'Nice little cottage.'

'His mother is dying,' said Patchy.

'Oh I'm sorry to hear that,' I said.

'She's eighty nine,' said Patchy. 'It happens.'

'Yes,' I agreed. 'I suppose it does.'

'The problem is,' said Patchy, 'that Alfred is still bankrupt.'

I waited. I couldn't see what Alfred's bankruptcy and his mother's death could have to do with me.

'The cottage goes to Alfred when his mother dies,' explained Patchy.

'Fair enough,' I nodded. 'So he can stay there.'

'Not if she dies before Wednesday,' said Patchy. I stared at him, thoroughly confused.

'Alfred's bankruptcy finishes on Wednesday,' explained Patchy.

'If she dies before Wednesday then the cottage goes to Alfred and the court will take it off him.'

'But if she dies after Wednesday Alfred gets to keep the cottage?'

'Exactly.'

'She's got to stay alive for two days.'

'Two days. Just two days.'

'I see.' I said. 'Where do I come in?'

'You're their doctor.'

'I am?' I frowned.

'Alfred and his mother used to live just outside Bilbury. They were both on Dr Brownlow's list.'

'But I don't remember ever seeing them.'

'I don't think you have. They don't bother much with doctors, lawyers or accountants.'

'I don't suppose that might possibly explain why Alfred went bankrupt? The absence of professional help?'

'I don't think you can blame yourself for that. But I suppose that good advice from a numerate accountant might have helped fend off the bankruptcy.'

I thought about things. 'I can see my future role in this drama becoming quite significant.'

'Indeed,' agreed Patchy.

'This isn't just a question of contributing a halfpenny towards buying back a sheepdog?'

'No. You need to do a bit more than that.'

'I need to keep Alfred's mother alive until after Wednesday.'

'Precisely.'

'How ill is she at the moment?'

Patchy looked at me but didn't say anything.

I closed my eyes and put my head in my hands.

'It's just the date on the death certificate that matters,' said Patchy.

'That's what's really crucial.'

'How bad is she?' I asked again.

'She's still alive,' said Patchy. He held out one hand in front of him and waved it from side to side, as though it was a raft on a choppy sea. 'Just.'

'We'd better go and have a look,' I said. 'What's her name?

'Lisa,' replied Patchy. 'Lisa Burton, nee Pinkerton.'

* * *

I called in at Bilbury Grange to have a look at Mrs Burton's medical records. Patchy came in with me.

'I've found an Alfred Burton,' I said, producing Alfred's medical records. 'He's been a bit of a nuisance,' I said, holding up the card.

'He had mumps in 1922 and a sprained ankle in 1925.'

'Clearly a hypochondriac,' said Patchy.

'But I haven't got any medical records for a Lisa Burton or a Lisa Pinkerton.'

'Try looking for Joan Burton,' suggested Patchy. I found the notes for Joan Burton straight away.

'Why did you call her Lisa if her name is Joan?'

'Everyone called her Lisa because she was such a moaner,' explained Patchy.

I looked at him and frowned. 'I don't get it.'

'Moaner Lisa.'

'Ah.'

'Have you learned anything?'

'No.' I need not have bothered going back to Bilbury Grange. Mrs Burton's medical notes were as pristine as they had been when they'd first been issued. Apart from her name and date of birth, written at the top of the card by some anonymous clerk, there was nothing at all written on her records. Leaving the useless records where they were I went back outside and told Patchy to lead the way. He had promised to introduce me to the Buttons.

Their cottage was no more than a hundred yards away from the beach, and Alfred, his mother and the dog, Lady, were all in the living room when we arrived.

Alfred looked tired and worn out. His mother, sitting in an easy chair by the fireplace, was unconscious. She was white and looked like death only very slightly warmed up. She did, however, look remarkably peaceful.

'Why didn't you call me?' I asked him.

'Didn't like to bother,' he replied. 'One of the neighbours has been helping me.' He paused. 'With the washing and so on,' he explained.

'Do you know what's wrong with her?' I asked him. Alfred looked at me and shook his head.

'What symptoms did she have?' I asked. 'Before she went unconscious?'

Alfred shrugged. 'I don't know,' he admitted. 'She wasn't very well.'

'We may have to get her into the hospital,' I told him.

'No! No!' said Patchy.

I looked at him. He made a frantic sign for me to follow him into the kitchen.

'You can't send her into hospital,' he said. The kitchen was a cockroaches' delight. Every available surface was piled high with dirty crocks.

'Why not?'

'Because she might die there!'

'She might die here.'

'Yes, but if she dies in hospital everyone will know precisely when she died. And if she dies before Thursday Alfred will be thrown out of his home. He'll end up sleeping rough.'

'What on earth are you suggesting?' I demanded. 'If she dies too soon do you really want me to ignore it and write the certificate a day or two later?'

'Yes!' said Patchy. 'Of course.'

'I can't do that!'

'Why not?'

'Because...' I tried to think of a reason. 'Because I could get into trouble,' I confessed rather lamely. 'A death certificate is a legal document.' I felt rather ashamed of myself for this feeble excuse.

'That's a bit weak as excuses go,' said Patchy.

'I know,' I admitted.

'If you send her into hospital what will they do?'

'Hopefully, they'll try and find out what's wrong with her,' I said.

'And then if they can find anything they'll try to treat it.'

'Hopefully,' said Patchy.

'Hospitals don't always try as hard as they should with elderly patients,' I admitted.

'So she probably has as good a chance - or better - if she stays here.'

'I can do some preliminary tests,' I agreed. 'But this place is a pigsty.' I looked around. 'Actually, I've seen pigsties that were much cleaner.'

'I'll get one or two people in to clean things up,' said Patchy. 'Just tidy up.'

'Can you?' I asked doubtfully.

'Definitely. And I can get one or two people to help look after Mrs Burton.'

'Who?'

'Friends. Relatives.' I nodded.

Patchy grinned. 'Good,' he said. 'Let's go back and see Mrs Burton and you can do your well-known impersonation of a doctor.'

We went back into the living room. I told Alfred to walk to the local store to buy some cleaning equipment and some black bags. He hadn't got any money so I gave him a :five pound note. Patchy went out to find a couple of women who would help nurse Mrs Burton.

And then I set about examining Mrs Burton and trying to work out what was wrong with her. I was, I suppose, hoping that I could find some simple explanation for her condition. Maybe I would be able to diagnose an easily treatable problem. Perhaps I'd be able to send Alfred or Patchy to the chemist's with a prescription and then, moments after their return, inject Mrs Burton with some magical remedy that would drag her back from the porchway in front of death's door.

But it wasn't like that.

I found out what was wrong with her within minutes.

She had a huge suppurating ulcer on her chest and a cancerous lump in her left breast that had replaced all of the breast tissue. Her lymph glands felt like golf balls, her liver felt like a boulder and there were secondary deposits in every part of her body that I could find. It was pretty clear that the kindly neighbour who had been helping to look after Mrs Burton had not invaded her privacy enough to wash anything more intimate than her face and hands.

How, I wondered, could anyone let themselves get into such a condition. How could a woman ignore a growth that had taken over so much of her body?

I would never understand but somehow I felt responsible and guilty. I was Mrs Burton's general practitioner. I should have known. The fact that I had only been her GP for a matter of months, while the cancer that was killing her had clearly been at work for years, was of no interest to me. I felt angry. I couldn't be angry with Mrs Burton and so I felt angry with myself

Alfred and Patchy came back to the house at almost the same time. Patchy brought Nelly with him. She was, he said, a relative of the family's who had done some nursing but who needed a few days work. He had, he said, agreed a fee that he would pay her. She looked to be in her early thirties. She was smartly dressed in a plain blue frock and a white cardigan. She looked efficient. I asked her where she'd trained. She told me. I asked her what qualifications she had. She said she was a State Registered Nurse. I said that was perfect.

Although Mrs Burton seemed to be unconscious I always assume that patients can hear what I am saying even when I strongly suspect that they cannot and so I took the three of them into the tiny kitchen. I told them the blunt truth.

'No hope?' said Alfred.

'No hope, I'm afraid,' I said. 'No one can do anything for your mother - except make her comfortable and make sure that she doesn't suffer.'

Many doctors don't realise it but in medicine 'nothing' is often the best thing to do.

Alfred nodded his understanding. 'I'll go and sit with her,' he said. He left the three of us alone.

'So, how long do you think she'll last?' asked Patchy.

'She could go at any time,' I said. I sighed and looked at Patchy questioningly. 'Midnight on Wednesday?'

Patchy nodded.

'Midnight between Wednesday and Thursday?' I asked, making sure.

Patchy, understanding my caution, nodded again.

I looked at my watch and did some quick calculations. 'We've got 46 hours,' I said.

'Should we move her upstairs?' asked Nelly. 'Into her bedroom?'

I shook my head. 'She's comfortable where she is. If we try moving her we could kill her. I've never seen such a terrible case of metastatic cancer. It's spread everywhere.' Patchy paled. 'Don't tell me any more,' he begged. 'I'm not terribly good with illness.'

I smiled at him weakly. 'Who has been coming in to help Alfred?' I asked.

'Just an old woman who lives a few doors away,' said Patchy. 'Not really a friend. She was just helping out.'

The door from the living room opened and Alfred came back in. 'Do you mind if I take the dog for a walk?' he asked. There were tears in his eyes.

'Good idea,' I told him. 'Have you got anywhere that you can stay for the next day or two?'

Alfred shook his head.

'He can stay with me,' offered Patchy.

'Your mum could go at any time,' I told him. 'Do you want to be with her when she goes?'

He looked at me uncertainly.

'Would you rather say goodbye now?' I asked him. 'And go and stay with Patchy?'

Alfred nodded.

'Then take him with you,' I said to Patchy. 'Nelly and I will look after Mrs Burton.'

When they'd gone I turned to Nelly. 'Do you understand what's happening here?'

She nodded. 'Patchy explained.'

'Are you entirely happy about being part of it?'

'Absolutely,' she replied. 'Definitely. Alfred's farm was taken by the bank. They were the only people to whom he owed money.

They could have let him work off his debts but they wouldn't. If they'd waited a few months and let him sell the year's crops he would have been OK. And they'll take his mother's cottage if we don't help. Of course I'm happy about being part of it.' She nodded. 'Most definitely,' she said. She paused. 'Alfred is my uncle,' she added.

'Right,' I said. 'Then we keep this to just the two of us. And we take it in turns to sit with her. We need a shift system.'

'And if she dies before Thursday we just keep coming in and out as if she was still alive?'

I nodded.

'And, whatever happens, we don't ring the undertaker until Thursday?'

There are times in life, I was discovering, that doing the right thing means doing the wrong thing.

Mrs Burton died on Thursday.

CHAPTER 35

Patsy was in Barnstaple at the post natal clinic and so I popped into the Duck and Puddle for a cheese sandwich and a pint of shandy.

'What are you getting Patchy and Adrienne for their wedding?' Thumper asked me when I'd ordered.

'I don't think we've really thought about it,' I admitted.

'Anne and I are getting them a toaster,' said Thumper. Anne Thwaites is his girlfriend and the mother of his child.

'Ah,' I said. 'Hmmm.' To be honest this didn't sound very original to me.

'Ask Frank what he and Gilly are getting them,' said Thumper.

Frank was pouring my shandy. 'What are you and Gilly getting the happy couple?'

'A toaster,' replied Frank instantly. 'Peter Marshall bought a whole pile of them from a bankrupt wholesaler in Bristol. They were made in Korea. He's selling them very cheap. Only three quid each.'

I looked at Thumper. He was grinning. 'We'll get them something else as well,' he said. 'But I thought that if we all bought them a toaster - and exactly the same model toaster - it might be rather fun.'

'How many of us are there?'

'Peter's got twenty three toasters.'

'Do you know twenty three people all prepared to buy a toaster?'

'Oh yes! There are only three left. But I told Peter to put one aside for you. I knew you wouldn't want to be left out.'

'Do they all work?'

'No idea. Does it matter? Out of twenty three toasters there is bound to be one or two that work.'

'I'll call in on the way home,' I promised.

'We're all going to wrap our toasters up,' said Frank. 'And try to make them look different.'

'Adrienne will be thrilled,' I said, picking up my sandwich and taking a bite. I knew that Patchy would appreciate the funny side of being presented with twenty three cheap Korean toasters but I couldn't help wondering if Thumper might not be over-estimating the bride-to-be's sense of humour.

CHAPTER 36

I called in to see Les Salterton the next morning.

It was a beautiful day and he was working outside in his garden. He often did that. 'The wind blows the shavings away,' he once explained. 'No sweeping up to do when I finish work.'

He saw me coming and stood up from his work bench. He straightened his back and smiled in welcome. 'I've finished mending your table,' he said. 'Good as new now.'

'Thanks. How do you feel?' I asked him.

'Fit as a fiddle,' he said. 'That course of tablets did me a power of good.' He leant closer and lowered his voice. 'I'd been feeling a bit low,' he confided.

I didn't tell him that it was the tablets that had made him feel low and that it was stopping them that had made him feel good again.

'There's a pair of green woodpeckers down the lane,' he said.

'Want to see?'

Of course I did.

Before we set off, Les bent down and popped a brick in between the front door and the frame to stop it closing completely. 'I have to leave the door open so that the cats can get in and out.' He paused and frowned. 'Besides,' he added, 'I don't think I've ever had a key.'

We wandered down the lane and spent half an hour watching the green woodpeckers digging holes in trees as only woodpeckers can.

'Did you know that green woodpeckers were once regarded as vermin?' he asked me quietly.

Surprised, I said I didn't.

He told me that in the 18th century the green woodpecker had become unwanted because of its habit of hammering its way through the wooden shingle roofs of country homes. 'The church oversaw their destruction,' he told me. 'But unlike the red kite and the raven, species which were also regarded as vermin and which were wiped out, the green woodpecker survived.'

As we wandered back up the lane towards his house and my car I wondered how many city GPs get to spend a guiltless half an hour bird watching in the middle of a working day. It occurred to me too that in towns and cities people measure time by minutes and seconds. In the country people measure time in hours and days.

Not for the first time I was pleased that I'd chosen to live in Bilbury, and grateful that I'd been given the opportunity.

CHAPTER 37

It was three days since Olive Robinson had been to the hospital and I still hadn't heard about the tests that had been done. After lunch I telephoned the hospital. I spoke first to the pathology laboratory. They had found nothing noticeably abnormal in any of the tests they'd done. Then I dialled the direct number of one of the hospital radiologists; a fellow I had known at medical school. He was the only doctor I knew who still smoked and his small office at the hospital was always thick with cigarette smoke. Smoking had been banned in the rest of the hospital but the administrators had failed to persuade him to pop out into the hospital grounds every time he needed to top up his nicotine levels.

'Funnily enough I've just put her skull X-ray back up on the light box,' he told me, thoughtfully. He was using the speaker phone on his desk and it made him sound as though he was talking in an echo chamber. 'It's a bit of a puzzle to be honest. Her ventricles are dilated but they look a bit odd. I can't quite decide why. Is she showing signs of dementia?'

I told him that she was.

'That could be it,' he said. 'Brain tissue deteriorating. Ventricles enlarging.' There was a pause and I heard a match strike as he lit a fresh cigarette. 'How old is she?'

'Seventy two,' I told him.

'That's probably it then.' He coughed for a few moments.

'When are you going to give those things up?' He laughed. 'Don't you start.'

Neither I nor anyone else could understand why a radiologist, of all people, should smoke. Every week he viewed the chest X-rays of people with lung cancer caused by smoking. But it didn't seem to bother him. 'Got to die of something,' he said merrily.

'It doesn't seem like simple dementia,' I told him. 'She has become confused,' I told him. 'But it's all happened very quickly. Far too quickly for a simple dementia. And she's also having difficulty in walking. She drags her left leg.'

'I know it's a pretty obvious thought but you're sure she hasn't had a stroke?'

'Pretty sure. I can't find any evidence of one. And there's another thing: she's complaining of constant headaches.'

'What sort of headaches?'

'Just a general headache. All over her head. She complains it feels as though her head is about to explode.'

There was silence at the other end of the phone. 'You still there?' I asked.

'Yeah,' said the radiologist. 'It's a puzzle isn't it. Anything show up on the blood tests.'

'Nothing interesting.'

'Let me think about it a bit more,' he said. 'Maybe I'll come up with something. Maybe you ought to get her in for a few days so that we can keep an eye on her.'

CHAPTER 38

'I'm still no nearer getting a diagnosis for Olive Robinson,' I told Dr Brownlow.

I wanted to talk to him. Dr Brownlow was the best diagnostician I'd ever known.

Making a clinical diagnosis is like solving a puzzle. Sometimes the solution is easy. The clues are easy to spot. But too often the clues are hidden, the evidence confusing and contradictory and the conclusion debatable.

When Dr Brownlow had learned his profession, a doctor had to rely very much on his own eyes and ears for the information with which he would make a diagnosis.

In the 1960s, when I was trained, doctors had vast quantities of equipment available to them. 'Too much information can mask the diagnosis,' Dr Brownlow once told me. 'Doctors forget that their laboratory tests and X-rays and so on aren't always right. Too many young doctors - and a good many older ones - make the mistake of ignoring the patient and listening only to the bits of paper they get from the laboratory. They then compound their error by treating what they suspect the diagnosis to be, rather than treating the patient.'

He was right. I learned a lot from Dr Brownlow.

'When the patient talks he is telling you the answers,' Dr Brownlow once said. 'He probably doesn't realise he's telling you the answers, of course. Finding the answer from what he tells you is your job.'

Dr Brownlow would often just sit quietly and let his patients ramble on. 'Doctors should shut up and listen more,' he told me. He believed that collecting information was more important than a physical examination. And he was right about that too.

'Some diseases are rare,' he said. 'But to the people who get them they aren't rare at all. Put together all the information a patient gives you and you will sometimes suddenly see that the condition you thought was impossibly rare will suddenly become quite obviously certain.'

When I was a young assistant and we were working together I remember a patient appearing at the surgery with a fever. Dr Brownlow diagnosed malaria. 'How on earth did you make that diagnosis?' I asked him afterwards, greatly impressed. 'I would never have thought that a patient in Bilbury might have malaria.' Dr Brownlow had simply shrugged. 'It was obvious. He told me he'd just come back from a trip to Africa,' he said. 'And I didn't know he was going so I knew he hadn't taken any prophylactic medicine.'

We were sitting in the living room with the French windows thrown wide open. Sunshine and birdsong filled the room. Bradshaw was tidying up. When I'd arrived he'd offered to leave and finish tidying the room later but both Dr Brownlow and I had told him that there was no reason for him to leave. Since Bradshaw was going to join me as Bilbury's district nurse he would soon get to know whatever medical secrets there might be in the area. And Bradshaw had, in any case, long ago proved himself to be the soul of discretion.

'Nothing else from the tests?'

I shook my head. 'They even did a lumbar puncture to see if she had raised cerebrospinal fluid pressure.'

'Nothing odd?'

'Absolutely normal.'

'How is she?'

'Steadily deteriorating.'

We sat in silence for a few moments. The silence was broken only by the sound of birds singing and Bradshaw wheezing very lightly as he put books back into the bookcase. Dr Brownlow had been looking through his books before I'd arrived; taking leave of some old and much valued friends as he'd put it.

'So tell me again, what's wrong with her.'

'She's gradually developing dementia, she complains of constant headaches and she's losing power and function in one leg –s o much so that she can't walk without help. Her memory is going, she's constantly tired and she's incontinent.'

We stared at one another, neither speaking.

'Definitely hasn't had a stroke?' I shook my head.

'Blood pressure?'

243

'Normal.'

'And the dementia isn't just senile dementia?'

'No. It's developing too quickly for that. Just last week she was doing the crossword in the paper. This week she just can't pay attention long enough to do one clue. Her judgement seems to have gone and there are daily changes in her moods and behaviour. And then there are the physical problems which you don't get with dementia. Her legs are weak and she's terribly unsteady. Sometimes her feet seem to freeze to the floor and she has great difficulty in taking the next step. Instead of walking she shuffles - she walks in a strange, wide-legged sort of way and she's fallen twice recently.'

'And she's incontinent?

'Urine only.'

'And a headache you say?'

'Constant. Nothing seems to make it go away. And she has difficulty in focusing her eyes.'

Dr Brownlow sighed. 'Poor Olive,' he said.

'They've brought in several consultants to look at her,' I said.

'Every time a neurologist or consultant physician comes up from Exeter they get him to take a look.'

'No ideas?'

'Oh, lots of ideas. But nothing useful.' Suddenly there was a cough. I turned.

'I hope you don't mind my saying something, doctors,' he said.

'But I couldn't help overhearing what you were saying about Miss Robinson.'

'If you've got any ideas Bradshaw they will be welcomed,' said Dr Brownlow. 'We're both stumped. And so, it seems, are the bright boys at the hospital.'

'Well, sir, when I was in the army in India, we once saw a patient who had similar symptoms to those currently being experienced by Miss Robinson,' said Bradshaw. It was one of the longest speeches I'd ever heard him make.

'And...?' said Dr Brownlow.

'Eventually a diagnosis of normal pressure hydrocephalus was made,' said Bradshaw.

Dr Brownlow looked at me. 'What on earth is that?' he asked.

I shook my head. I'd never heard of it either.

'What's that?' Dr Brownlow asked his butler.

'I believe it to be a rare neurological condition,' said Bradshaw. 'As I understand it, the condition develops when the fluid surrounding the brain, the fluid which normally surrounds and protects the brain tissue...'

'You're talking about the cerebrospinal fluid?' said DrBrownlow.

'Exactly so, sir. The cerebrospinal fluid is normally reabsorbed if there is too much of it. But in this particular condition the reabsorption does not take place as it should and the increasing amount of fluid around the brain puts pressure on the delicate tissue, resulting in a unique form of dementia - very much, I think, like the type currently suffered by Miss Robinson. The patient whom I saw had very much the same sort of symptoms - even including the wide-legged walk and considerable instability.'

'Good heavens, Bradshaw!' said Dr Brownlow. 'It sounds as if you could have cracked the case.'

'I do hope that I have been able to help, sir,' replied the butler. 'I have always been fond of Miss Robinson. A true lady, I've always felt.'

'Exactly so,' said Dr Brownlow. 'Is there any treatment for this condition? Can we do anything to help Miss Robinson?'

'Oh, I believe so, sir,' said Bradshaw. 'If the excess fluid were to be removed from around the brain by the installation of a drainage tube...'

'A shunt?' I suggested.

'Precisely so,' nodded Bradshaw. 'With the aid of a shunt it should be possible to reduce the amount of fluid pressing on the brain.'

'And the symptoms will disappear?' asked Dr Brownlow.

'Judging by the incident I remember there should be a noticeable improvement in Miss Robinson's condition if this were to be done,' said Bradshaw.

Dr Brownlow looked at me. 'I'll ring the hospital now,' I said. 'I'll have a word with the doctor looking after Olive and then I'll drive into Barnstaple and make sure that they are doing everything they can.'

'Congratulations Bradshaw,' said Dr Brownlow, turning to his butler. 'Pour yourself a large whisky. You've earned it.'

'Thank you, sir,' said the butler.

'And pour another one for me. And one for the young doctor while he rings the hospital.'

Seven minutes later I put down the telephone. 'They hadn't thought of normal pressure hydrocephalus,' I told Dr Brownlow and Bradshaw. 'But the consultant agrees that this could well be what is causing Miss Robinson's problems. They're going to get on with it straight away.'

As I sipped the whisky Bradshaw had poured I could not help reflecting that if he had not overheard our conversation Olive Robinson would have probably never been diagnosed.

Many patients regard medicine as a science. It isn't. Accurate diagnoses are often missed. And, far more often than doctors like to admit, they are made by chance.

* * *

When I got back to Bilbury Grange, Patsy met me at the door and whispered to me that Adrienne was in the kitchen and on the warpath.

'She says she's got a bone to pick with you,' said Patsy.

I couldn't think of anything I'd done that could have possibly upset my sister-in-law. I wandered into the kitchen convinced that I had done nothing wrong.

Adrienne was holding our baby. He was wrapped in a blue shawl. I kissed his forehead. Just looking at him I could tell he was going to be wise, handsome and honest; a man looked up to and admired by everyone who knew him. None of this was mere paternal pride but would have been obvious to anyone who looked at him. I gazed at him adoringly. He had Patsy's eyes. I wondered how long it would be before I could buy him a bicycle. 'Why did you tell Patchy that my middle name is Christabel?' she demanded.

Ah.

'It's a long story,' I told her, turning round and heading back for the door. 'And I've just remembered I've got someone I must call in on.'

That's one of the advantages of being a country GP. There's always a good reason to be somewhere else in a hurry.

'I'll be in the Duck and Puddle,' I whispered to Patsy as I left.

'Give me a call when your sister has gone.'

I found Thumper in the Duck and Puddle. I told him that Bradshaw might well have diagnosed his aunt's illness.

246

'You mean Bradshaw made the diagnosis even though all the doctors were stumped?'

I nodded.

'When I heard he was going to be the new district nurse I was a bit apprehensive,' admitted Thumper. 'But this changes things a bit doesn't it?'

'I hope so,' I agreed. 'I hope the rest of the village feels the same.'

'They will,' said Thumper firmly. 'Oh, they will.'

I was convinced.

* * *

The doctor at the hospital telephoned me the next day.

'Great news!' said the consultant. He sounded quite excited. 'Dr Brownlow's butler has shown us all a thing or two.'

'You think Olive has got normal pressure hydrocephalus?'

'Definitely!' said the consultant. 'We put in a shunt and lowered her cerebrospinal fluid pressure. It's amazing. She's a different woman. She's still a bit slow but she says the headache has gone and she can walk pretty well normally.'

I thanked him, told him I'd be in to see her soon, and put down the telephone.

'Olive?' asked Patsy when I walked into the kitchen.

'She's going to be fine,' I told her. We hugged one another and cried with joy. We were both very fond of Thumper's aunt.

And then, while I sipped the tea Patsy had made, I telephoned Thumper to tell him the good news.

Thumper is the toughest guy I know.

He burst into tears when I told him the news.

It was one of those moments when it feels really good to be a village doctor.

CHAPTER 39

It was, at last, the morning of the big wedding. Three men working for Patchy's chum had erected a huge white marquee on our back lawn.

(It had the slogan 'Marquee de Sade' stitched into the canvas just beside the entrance. 'Oh, I've heard of him,' said Mrs Kennett when she saw the slogan. 'Isn't he foreign? Fancy him making tents and bringing them all this way from abroad.')

Adrienne, Patsy and their mother had spent much of the previous week preparing food for the feast which would follow the ceremony. By noon the twelve trestle tables which had been put up in the marquee were so laden with plates of food that they were beginning to creak.

It had been decided to have a cold buffet and there were hundreds of different types of pie and pasty on display. There were three whole salmon, six huge plates of cold meats and a tureen full of cold soup which Adrienne had prepared from nettles and dandelions which she had collected herself There were slices of chicken breast, a huge side of cold beef and what looked like several hundred home made mushroom vol au vents. There were enough sandwiches to keep an army marching for a week. The three-tier wedding cake, which took pride of place at the far end of the marquee, had been made by Adrienne's aunt, and to keep the sweet-toothed happy before the cutting of the cake ceremony there were numerous dishes full of sherry trifle (sponge fingers, red jelly, yellow custard, mixed fruit and fresh cream topped with multi-coloured hundreds and thousands and little silver balls) half a dozen sponge cakes and a vast array of fairy cakes, scones, profiteroles, cream horns, cream-filled brandy snaps, jam tarts and home-made biscuits. Olive Robinson, Thumper's aunt, had been out of hospital just one day but had, nevertheless, managed to make a fruit cake, a carrot cake and a Victoria sponge. She was looking good. I learned from Thumper that there had been some doubts in the village about Bradshaw becoming my district nurse but that these doubts had now disappeared entirely.

The wedding presents were piled high on a trestle table just inside the entrance to the marquee. They were positioned there so that the bride and groom could open them in full view of their guests. The twenty three toasters which had been purchased from Peter Marshall's shop had all been neatly wrapped and although some attempts had been made to disguise the contents it wasn't difficult to guess that a lot of presents were items which came in neat, oblong boxes.

The men who had brought the marquee had offered to set up some portable lavatories on one of our smaller lawns but we had decided that this wouldn't be necessary. We had, instead, put up one notice inviting lady guests to use the lavatory in the surgery - the one provided for patients - and another notice pointing to a rather overgrown area behind three large oak trees and a stretch of beech hedge. Thumper, who was Patchy's best man, had prepared a special sign which said, simply, 'USED BEER DEPARTMENT'.

'I thought it was going to be a quiet wedding,' I whispered to Patsy. We were standing alone in the garden. The calm before the inevitable storm. We had rushed back home from the church so that we would be ready to welcome the bride and groom and their guests.

The ceremony had been dignified and beautiful. Patsy, who had been the bridesmaid, was still wearing the beautiful pale yellow dress with a lot of frills which her mother had made for her. She vowed that she was not going to change out of it all afternoon since she was unlikely to get another chance to wear it.

We had both been able to go because Mr Parfitt, who said he wasn't terribly interested in weddings but who I knew couldn't bear to see his lawn being trampled by a lot of strangers wearing high heels, had volunteered to sit by the telephone for me in case there were any medical emergencies. His wife had promised to look after the baby. I didn't think Mr Parfitt would have to take too many calls since most of the villagers were likely to be in the tent on our back lawn and anyone who needed me wouldn't need a telephone.

'I think the guest list grew a bit larger than they had anticipated,' replied Patsy.

'How many people are coming?' I asked.

'Patchy says they kept it down to a minimum.'

'How many people are coming?'

'Around two hundred.'

'Two hundred!' I was astonished. 'Where are they all going to park?'

'My Dad has moved the cows out of one of his fields,' said Patsy.

'There's a sign up saying Free Parking.' I looked at her.

'He wanted to charge a shilling for the day,' admitted Patsy who knew what I'd been thinking. 'But Adrienne and I managed to persuade him not to.'

'Don't forget to keep two pieces of cake,' I told her. 'One for Dr Brownlow and one for Bradshaw.'

'Of course I won't.'

Dr Brownlow had desperately wanted to attend the wedding but he was sinking fast. He had, however, sent a splendid wedding present (an envelope stuffed with fivers) and had asked for a piece of cake in return.

'Everything looks well under control,' I said recklessly. The truth is that I was bursting with pride and far too pleased with the world around me to realise just how much I was tempting fate. Patsy looked beautiful and thoroughly regal. Bilbury Grange looked absolutely magnificent. And our new baby (being looked after by a very elegantly dressed Mrs Parfitt) was, of course, a microcosm of perfection.

From the driveway there were the sounds which told us that the principal players and their guests were arriving. Patsy, full of excitement, hurried forward to greet them.

I wandered into the marquee, picked up a jam tart and crammed it into my mouth before I joined her.

* * *

An hour later the wedding party was in full swing.

It was not, perhaps, the quiet and low key wedding 'just for a few close friends and relatives' which I seemed to remember the happy couple talking about in our kitchen. But it was, at least, a dignified wedding. No one had fallen over or disgraced themselves and although it was clear that there were going to be enough pies and cakes left over to feed the proverbial five thousand (without the aid of any miracles of enhancement) the organisation seemed faultless.

The opening of the twenty three toasters had started things off well.

I think Patchy had guessed that something was up when he saw the huge array of similarly sized boxes awaiting them. He clearly knew what was going on after the first three packets had been opened to reveal identical Korean toasters.

'Splendid!' he cried, holding up one of the toasters and pointing to the other two. 'Fresh toasters for Monday, Tuesday and Wednesday. Let's just hope we get toasters for Thursday and Friday too.'

And of course, they got toasters for Thursday and Friday. And for the weekend and for the next fortnight too.

'Marvellous!' cried Patchy. 'I've always thought it's a wise idea to buy spares when you find something you really like.'

'These came from Peter,' muttered Frank gloomily. 'You'll probably need all the spares to make one piece of toast.'

If Adrienne was disappointed by this apparent lack of proper planning among her friends she managed to hide it well. And when the huge pile of toasters were stacked in a comer of the marquee and replaced by the real presents any residual disappointment she might have felt disappeared entirely.

So, even Thumper's practical joke had, it seemed, been well received.

And you can't ask for much more at a wedding than that the best man's practical joke goes down well.

* * *

Looking through the retrospectoscope (a medical instrument much favoured by a tutor of mine at medical school which enables the user to examine events with the inestimable benefits of hindsight) it is clear that I should have realised something odd was happening rather earlier than I did. Sadly, I did not, though, to be perfectly honest, I doubt if events would have been any different if I had.

Bizarre things were occurring everywhere.

Peter Marshall was attempting to climb up one of the main poles holding up the marquee. Anne Thwaites was trying to juggle with scotch eggs (and judging by the tell-tale debris at her feet proving to be not very good at it) and an uncle of Patchy's from Huddersfield was standing on a wooden trestle table (from which he had thoughtfully removed the table cloth) and preparing to prove that he could fly. A cousin of Patchy's was lying flat on his back snoring very loudly. Samuel Houghton and his wife were dancing the polka (or, at least, their own version of as much of a polka as can be danced in an area about four foot square) and Harry Burrows had taken one of the toasters out of its box and was trying, unsuccessfully and inexplicably, to cram a Cornish pasty into the slit at the top of the toaster.

(We were later to find that Harry would have been just as unsuccessful if he'd tried to insert a slice of bread. Sadly, the opening in the top of the toasters wasn't wide enough to take a whole slice of bread. Remarkably, although Patchy and Adrienne were the proud owners of 23 toasters, they were only able to make a full round of toast by spearing a piece of bread on a toasting fork and holding it in front of the fire.)

'Do you think they're all drunk?' asked Patsy. Even for Bilbury this was more than vaguely eccentric behaviour. She and I had been kept busy ensuring that the wedding guests were adequately fed and watered and had not, as yet, managed to eat or drink anything.

'They seem drugged to me,' I said, staring in astonishment as, no more than six feet away from where we were standing, the vicar and his wife started to undress one another.

Patsy stared at me. 'Are you serious?'

I nodded. 'I'm afraid so. If the vicar had had enough to drink to banish his inhibitions to that extent he'd be flat on his back and incapable of unbuttoning his own trousers.'

We stood and stared in astonishment as the vicar did indeed remove his own trousers. He did this nimbly and gracefully. I had never expected the vicar to be a man who favoured underwear decorated with cartoon characters. Having removed his trousers the vicar gave out a great whoop and flung them skywards.

'If you ever wear boxer shorts like those I may divorce you,' said Patsy.

'You need have no worries,' I assured her.

The first clue as to the cause of all this mayhem came when Samuel Houghton shuffled over to ask if there were any more mushroom vol au vents.

'I'm afraid not,' Patsy told him. 'All the ones we had were out.'

'Pity,' said Samuel.

'Did you know that your trousers were around your ankles?' I asked him

'The vicar's wife unfastened my braces,' he told me proudly. 'Stout woman.' And he shuffled off, examining abandoned plates as he did so. Occasionally, he found an abandoned mushroom vol au vent and when he did so he popped it straight into his mouth.

'Who made the mushroom vol au vents?' I asked Patsy.

'Have you tried them? Are they all right?

'I haven't tried one. But they seem popular. They've all gone. Who made them?'

'Adrienne.'

It was the answer I'd expected. 'I don't suppose she picked the mushrooms herself?'

Patsy, rather pale now, nodded.

And then I knew.

'Do you think there is something wrong with the mushrooms?' asked Patsy.

'I think Adrienne has made her vol au vents with magic mushrooms.'

Patsy actually lifted one hand and placed it across her mouth, just in the way people are supposed to do when they are shocked by news they've been given.

I looked around to see if I could find Adrienne. I had hoped to be able to ask her about the mushrooms she'd used but it was at this point of the wedding celebration that things really started to get out of hand and suddenly the mushroom vol au vents were only part of the problem. There was an even bigger problem to deal with.

* * *

Two weeks earlier the father of the bride (and, coincidentally of course, my father-in-law) had read an article in a farming magazine in which the author had claimed that he had found that it was possible to increase the milk yield of a herd of dairy cattle by playing them music.

Ever anxious to increase his income, and hopefully his profits, Mr Kennett had borrowed an old portable tape recorder of mine and an Elvis Presley tape belonging to his daughter Patsy in order to see if his cows responded in a similar way.

To his (and everyone else's) astonishment he had discovered that his cows did produce far more milk after they had spent a few hours listening to the rocking and rolling of Elvis Presley than they did when they had spent their time listening to their more usual rustic auditory diet of birds tweeting, leaves rustling and one another mooing. Mr Kennett had discovered that a herd of happy rockers

253

produced noticeably more milk than a herd of cows who knew nothing of blue suede shoes.

Mr Kennett had generously made it clear that since his cows lived in the field adjacent to our garden, he did not plan to play music during the wedding celebration.

This was not quite as generous a gesture as it first appeared for even if Mr Kennett had wanted to continue with his experiment he wouldn't have been able to because Patsy and I had borrowed back the tape recorder and the Elvis Presley tape. We wanted them so that we could provide music in case any of the wedding guests wanted to dance.

But what we had all overlooked was that Mr Kennett's cows were chewing the cud in the field next to Bilbury Grange.

And we were playing music.

Moreover, we weren't just playing music we were playing exactly the Elvis Presley tape which the cows loved so much and which had proved to have such a dramatic influence on their mood that it had actually resulted in a measurable, and profitable, increase in milk production.

If we had thought about this a little more we might have realised that there might be consequences. In our defence all I can say is that there were a lot of other things to think about.

It was, I think, Gilly Parsons who first noticed that the cows in the next field were taking a more than usual interest in what was going on in the marquee in the garden at Bilbury Grange. However, although she had lived in Bilbury for many years Gilly had never really become a country girl; she remained a city dweller at heart.

Having enjoyed a few glasses of champagne her reaction was not to cry out something useful such as 'Help! Help! Cows have got into the garden and are trying to get into the big tent!' but to totter unsteadily towards them crying 'Here pretty cows, here pretty cows!', making the sort of kissy kissy noises which town dwellers who have little understanding of the animal world usually consider appropriate for attracting cats and small dogs, and holding out a large plate containing three of Mrs Kennett's scones, two ham and pickle sandwiches, a fresh tomato, a boiled egg, two large pickled gherkins and a large dollop of sherry trifle. She had lost her blouse in her tussle with Frank but had, I am relieved to be able to report, managed to retain full ownership of her brassiere.

254

I know all this because I saw her.

Embarrassing as it is to have to admit it, I saw her and I did nothing.

My excuse is that I was, at the time, torn between trying to decide whether to persuade Ben to take his teeth out of the photographer's trousers or to dissuade Sophie, who was clearly making plans to try to jump onto the top tier of the wedding cake.

(I never did find out why Ben, a normally obedient and docile dog, had taken a dislike to the photographer - though it may well have been that Ben had at some point Hoovered up the fallen remains of a mushroom vol au vent and that his behaviour had, therefore, been transformed by what he'd eaten. Sophie, on the other hand, has always had a habit of leaping up onto things regardless of the consequences so her intentions came as no surprise at all.) I suspect that I wouldn't have been able to do anything anyway for things then happened very quickly.

'The cows are trying to get into the tent!' yelled Thumper Robinson. And in less time than it took him to say this the first few cows had managed to force their way into the tent.

'It's a marquee!' shouted Patchy who was, for some reason, quite touchy about it being called a marquee and not a tent. He and Adrienne were circulating among the guests and offering thanks. Thanks for coming. Thanks for the card. Thanks for the best wishes. Thanks for the toaster. Patchy was shaking a lot of hands and Adrienne was getting kissed a good deal. Not surprisingly, not many people seemed to want to kiss Patchy.

'OK! The cows are trying to get into the marquee!' shouted Thumper.

I turned and you didn't need an honours degree in animal husbandry to work out that his diagnosis was absolutely spot on. The cows were trying to get into the marquee and they were proving to be quite good at it.

There were four reasons why I realised precisely why the cows had come into the marquee.

First, they weren't interested in any of the food on offer.

Second, they all headed for the corner of the marquee where the cassette player was sitting.

Third, they all started swaying. It was, I suppose, their way of showing their appreciation of the King's music. They weren't exactly dancing, not in a Fred Astaire sort of way, but they were definitely swaying.

Fourth, Mr Kennett explained things to me.

'It's the music,' he said, having hurried over to where Patsy and I were standing. 'They like your music.' He explained.

'So let's turn it off,' suggested Thumper, who'd hurried over to see what we wanted to do.

It seemed an easy solution.

We turned off the tape recorder and, dutifully, Mr Presley stopped singing.

The cows stopped swaying but they didn't go away. They looked disappointed. One of them mooed in protest. I had never before realised just how much a moo sounds like a boo. Two cows chose the moment to provide ample proof that they had not been house trained. Or marquee trained either. I was glad Mr Parfitt wasn't there to see what was happening to his lawn.

'They're not going to go,' said Patsy in a tiny voice.

'No,' agreed Mr Kennett.

The cows stayed where they were. One of them turned round and knocked over a table. Several platefuls of sandwiches fell on the floor. I instinctively checked to make sure that there were no mushroom vol au vents among them. The last thing we needed was a marquee full of cows who'd eaten magic mushrooms.

'Maybe we can use the fact that the cows will go where the music is,' I suggested. 'If I take the cassette player out of here and turn it on maybe I can get the cows to follow me.'

'Like the pied piper of Hamelin?' said Patsy.

'Exactly.'

'Can you get them to back out of the tent and back into the field?'

I shook my head. I didn't think I wanted to try to get them to force their way back out through the side of the marquee. It had been a miracle that they hadn't done any damage to the canvas when they'd forced their way in. I walked across the tent and picked up the cassette player. Then I walked briskly out of the marquee before turning it on. I turned the volume up as high as it would go. The lead cow responded immediately (there is always a lead cow in a herd) and began to move in my direction. Slowly, I headed for the driveway. The lead cow followed me and the other cows followed the lead cow. Elvis finished 'Hound Dog' and started singing 'Heartbreak Hotel'. The cows didn't seem to mind.

Within minutes- I was in the lane and behind me the cows were swaying out of our driveway. As they swayed one way their udders swayed the other way. It would, I thought, take me no more than a quarter of an hour or so to lead them round to the gateway leading into the field from which the cows had escaped. I would then find the gap they'd used to get into our garden and block it with a piece of corrugated iron. There isn't a field in North Devon that doesn't have a spare sheet of corrugated iron lying around in it somewhere.

As Elvis finished 'Heartbreak Hotel' and started on 'Jailhouse Rock' I looked back. The cows were still there. More surprisingly, so were most of the wedding guests. I really had become the pied piper of Hamelin.

'Play 'All Shook Up!',' suggested Patchy. 'Maybe we'll get milk shakes.'

Naturally, things didn't go quite as smoothly as I had hoped. Someone, presumably one of our guests, had parked their car in the gateway leading into the field where I wanted to take the cows.

And so, knowing that I would eventually come to another suitable field, I kept walking.

Just Elvis and I impersonating the Pied Piper of Hamelin.

The swaying lead cow was just behind me. The other cows were just behind the lead cow. The dancing guests followed them.

It was a mile and a half and forty five minutes later before I found a suitable empty field which had a gate I could open. By that time the procession I was leading consisted of two dozen cows, fifty wedding guests, a car towing a caravan (driven by a woman whose command of the expletive was impressive), three cars, a tractor towing a trailer full of silage and a boy on a bicycle who presumably had no sense of smell or else he would have surely overtaken the tractor towing the trailer full of silage.

When I'd shut the cows into their new field, and let the caravan, the three cars, the tractor and the anosmic boy on the bicycle go on their way, I led the guests back to Bilbury Grange. I turned off the cassette player lest this encourage the cows to break out of their new field but the guests, who presumably knew the contents of the tape by now, kept dancing anyway.

By now the effects of Adrienne's magic mushrooms had largely worn off. Some of the guests, in particular the vicar and his wife, were looking tired, puzzled, confused and rather sheepish.

'Excuse me,' said the vicar, sidling up to me as we arrived back at Bilbury Grange. 'I don't suppose you've seen my trousers have you?'

I told him where I'd last seen them. He seemed grateful. I leant a little closer and whispered. 'Nice boxer shorts. I've always been fond of Donald Duck.'

He looked down, thanked me and blushed.

* * *

'Where did you get the mushrooms from?' I asked Adrienne later that day. She and Patchy were changed and ready to leave for their honeymoon in south Devon. They had a suite booked in the Victoria Hotel in Sidmouth.

'Oh just here and there,' said Adrienne. 'They were really fresh. I picked them the day I made the vol au vents. They can't possibly have gone off.'

'I'm sure they were fresh,' I said. 'I don't think there's any question of that. Can you remember what the mushrooms looked like?'

'They were very pretty,' said Adrienne. 'Much prettier than ordinary mushrooms.'

Patchy stared at her open-mouthed in horror.

'You could have poisoned everyone!' he said.

'Oh no,' said Adrienne. 'I didn't make enough vol au vents for everyone.'

'You must have picked magic mushrooms!' Patsy told her.

'Oh well,' said Adrienne dismissing everyone's concern with a shrug. 'People seemed to have a good time didn't they?'

We all agreed that everyone seemed to have had a good time.

'When we get back from our honeymoon,' said Patchy. 'I'll pick my own mushrooms if you don't mind.'

'Oh, OK,' said Adrienne. She put her arm around her new husband. 'You're not cross with me, are you?'

Patchy looked at her, shook his head and sighed.

No one ever manages to stay cross with dear Adrienne for long.

CHAPTER 40

The telephone call I had been expecting, and dreading, came at 3.37 a.m. one cold, wet, windy morning. I turned on the bedside light and picked up the telephone.

'Can you come, please, doctor. I think it's time.'

I recognised the voice and there was no need for me to ask where I should go or what it was time for. I said I would be there as soon as I could, swivelled out of bed and picked up the trousers, lying ready on the floor, to pull over my pyjamas.

'Who was it?' asked Patsy sleepily.

'Bradshaw.'

She sat up, as instantly awake as I had been. 'Dr Brownlow?'

'Bradshaw says he's going.'

Patsy reached out and touched my arm.

Dr Brownlow was just conscious when I got there. I held his hand. He was in no pain and there was nothing whatsoever that I could do for him now. I was there as a friend as much as I was there as a doctor.

He drifted in and out of consciousness and then gradually the moments when he was conscious became shorter and the moments when he was unconscious became longer.

Bradshaw left us alone for much of the time. You could see that he was exhausted. He had been looking after his master for many months without a break. I made a mental note to make sure that he had a rest before starting work as district nurse. He wouldn't want to. But I would make sure that he did.

For some of the time Dr Brownlow and I sat quietly. Neither of us saying a word. Occasionally, I spoke. I told him about some of the clinical problems I was puzzling over. I told him how our new baby was doing. (He had been delighted when Patsy and I had taken the baby round for him to see. And even more delighted when we'd told him that we were naming the baby after him.) I told him about Patchy and Adrienne's wedding. He was conscious when I told him about the cows. He smiled and nodded a lot. He enjoyed the story.

Eventually he stopped smiling and stopped nodding and his hand started to go cold and the light started to break through the trees outside and a new day had begun and Dr Brownlow had gone.

I found Bradshaw and told him to go to bed and told him that I would see to the immediate arrangements.

As I drove home the clouds started to appear and the sun disappeared and then the rain came.

It was as it should have been.

It was not a day for sunshine.

* * *

We buried Dr Brownlow in the garden next to his wife. Bradshaw and I put his stethoscope in the coffin with him. The whole village turned out. I looked around the church during the service and couldn't see a dry eye anywhere. Dr Brownlow had been immensely popular. He had been an excellent country doctor but, more than that, a great human being, To me he had been a mentor and a friend. He had been a guide and a father figure.

* * *

Hours after Dr Brownlow had been buried I went back to sit beside his grave in what had been for so long his garden. I took a small silver hip flask he had once given me. It was filled with his favourite malt whisky. From time to time I took a sip from it and from time to time I poured a few drops onto the fresh earth on top of his grave. I wanted to ask him if he minded my going to him from time to time when I needed help and advice. He said that would be fine.

When I'd finished I leant the hip flask beside his gravestone. It would, I knew, be there whenever I went back.

It was late when I got home. Patsy had been keeping dinner warm for over an hour.

'I'm sorry,' I said. 'I went to talk to Dr Brownlow.'

'I thought you had,' she said. I looked at her. 'I guessed,' she said.

'I asked him if he minded if I popped along there when I had tricky clinical problems.'

'What did he say?'

'He said he'd be delighted to see me.'

'Good old Dr Brownlow,' said Patsy. 'He never said 'No' to anyone, did he?'

'Never,' I agreed.

* * *

In the days that followed Dr Brownlow's GP son complained bitterly about the will. He even consulted a lawyer who sent me a venomous letter announcing that his firm would be taking legal action to overthrow Dr Brownlow's wishes. But Dr Brownlow's preparations stalled any attempts to overthrow the will. When the lawyer saw the letters Dr Brownlow had prepared he gave in. There was no apology, of course. Just the apology of silent withdrawal.

Dr Brownlow had managed to stymie the tax man too.

A mean, ferret-faced man in a cheap suit turned up one day from the Inland Revenue. He said he was investigating the disappearance of a considerable amount of cash from Dr Brownlow's account and asked me if I knew anything about it. I showed him the receipt that Dr Brownlow had arranged and refused to answer more of his questions on the incontestable grounds of patient confidentiality. He didn't seem particularly happy but he went away again and I lost no sleep over his misery.

Gradually, I got used to driving Dr Brownlow's old Rolls Royce. I didn't want to sell it but it was truly a most impractical car. It was so big it felt like driving a small country. Thumper said that whenever I set off the radiator would always be half way to my destination.

I had intended to keep it in a barn and use it only for special occasions. But I grew to like it. And the villagers liked to see it being driven around the village. It was a tangible link with Dr Brownlow, whom they had all loved so much. And so I started to use it for my visits to patients and for trips into Barnstaple It cost a fortune in petrol but the mechanics at Tolstoy's Garage loved looking after it so the maintenance and repair bills were very reasonable.

CHAPTER 41

A month or so later I was sitting in my study staring at a blank sheet of paper.

It was, I had decided, time to start another book about life in Bilbury.

I had two problems.

First, so much had happened that I really didn't know where to start.

Second, there was so much still happening that I was finding it difficult to look backwards and put the recent past into perspective.

I still missed Dr Brownlow, of course. There was a huge void both in the village and in my life. It felt strange to know that he had gone and would never be coming back.

But I still spoke to him at least once a week.

I would cycle round and sit by his graveside and talk to him. I would ask him about patients who were puzzling me. And he would listen.

There was a lot to be done and a lot I needed his help with.

There was, for example, the conversion of Dr Brownlow's old house into a small cottage hospital for Bilbury. I'd already talked to Thumper about hiring workmen who would be prepared to work for cash -with no questions asked. It would not, he said, be difficult. The cash was still hidden in a safe place. I would have to find an explanation for the way the building work had been funded. But Thumper and I had already worked out a way to do that.

The telephone rang.

Reluctantly, I picked it up.

It was Mortimer.

'I thought it was about time we caught up with one another,' he said. 'It's been some time since we saw you.'

'It has.'

'Sorry I haven't got round to writing or ringing. We've been terribly busy. We managed to get planning permission to put another bedroom over the garage. You can't imagine the chaos. And then we

263

bought a new dining room suite. White leather. We'd only had it a week when one of the kids got orange crayon on one of the cushions. Strewth! Clarice went clear through the roof We had three different specialists round to try and get the mark out of the leather. And it took us seven weeks to get the insurance company to pay up.'

I muttered something suitably sympathetic.

'What else? Oh yes, a very, very good friend of ours called Maurice, died. We were utterly devastated. He lived in the Lake District. Near Kendal. A long drive for the funeral. We decided to stay over a few days and make a short holiday of it so that the trip wouldn't be entirely wasted. We found a nice little hotel. It was very reasonably priced, though the room was rather small and the view disappointing. The family held the funeral in the afternoon, which we thought was rather thoughtless because we wanted to take a boat ride down Lake Windemere. Consequently, we had a heart breaking decision to make. The boys had never been on the Lake and in the end we decided that Spotty wouldn't have minded and so we gave the funeral a miss. All things considered I suppose the weekend didn't turn out too badly. We were lucky with the weather.'

He paused to breathe. 'What else has happened?' he asked himself There was another quiet moment while he thought. 'Oh, Clarice lost another half a stone and changed her hairstyle. I had a huge row at work over parking space allocations. You simply can't believe how petty-minded some of these people can be. Oh, and you won't believe this but some bastard cut the wires to the headlamp washers on the Volvo. Would you believe it? I'm pretty sure I know who it was. One of the administrators. I've got his card marked. I tell you, it's been a pretty devastating few months. You and Patsy simply wouldn't have coped with it. Clarice and I often think of you two just muddling along down there in Bilbury. No worries. No stresses.' He paused, for the first time. 'I expect it's been as quiet as ever down there.'

I stared out of the window.

I had gone back into practice. Patsy and I had had our first baby. Dr Brownlow, my friend and mentor, had died. Patchy Fogg and Adrienne Kennett had got married at Bilbury Grange. A baby, a wedding and a funeral. It didn't seem to me to have been an entirely uneventful year in Bilbury. But I realised that none of these were things I wanted to share with Mortimer.

'You still there?'

'Yes.'

'Silly question. What am I saying? Nothing much ever happens in Bilbury, does it?.'

'No,' I agreed. 'Nothing much has happened. Quiet as always.'

We said goodbye and promised to keep in touch. I put the telephone down. Outside a squirrel raced up an oak tree. Ben, who'd been chasing it across the grass, stared up rather forlornly. Emily, who was asleep by the window, opened an eye, watched for a moment and went back to sleep. Sophie, who was lying beside her stood up, arched her back, yawned and then walked two paces to her left. She then sat down on the blank sheet of paper I'd been staring at and started to lick her bottom.

There was a gentle tap on the half open door. I turned. Patsy was standing there with a cup of coffee. There were two bourbon biscuits in the saucer.

'I thought you might like a break.'

I pointed to Sophie sitting on the blank piece of paper in front of me.

'Underneath that cat there is a blank sheet of paper. I haven't started yet.'

'Oh.' She brightened. 'Never mind. Come and have a look at that old junk room next to the nursery.'

'Oh no!' I said. 'You don't want it clearing out do you?'

'The nursery is a bit small,' she said. 'I wondered if we could get Thumper to take down the wall dividing the nursery from the junk room and make the nursery bigger.'

I looked at her, puzzled. 'What's wrong with the size of the nursery? It's a perfect size for a baby's room.'

'It's perfect for one baby.'

'Exactly.'

'But not really big enough for two.'

'I suppose not but what...' I stopped, looked at her and started to grin.

'Careful!' she said, smiling, as I put my arm around her and pulled her onto my lap. 'I'll spill your coffee.' She put the cup and saucer down on my desk and put her arms around my neck.

'It's definite?' She nodded.

'Then I suppose I'd better clear out the junk room,' I said. 'Most of it can be thrown out. I'll have a bonfire this evening. And when I've cleared it out I'll ring Thumper and get him to take down the partition wall.'

Patsy started laughing.

'Do you think we should redecorate? When's it due? What are we going to call it? Do you think it will be a boy or a girl?'

'What about your book?'

I helped Patsy to her feet and then stood up myself 'It'll have to wait,' I said. 'I need to clear out that junk room.' I picked up my coffee and took a sip. It had cooled. I drank half of it. I offered the biscuits to Patsy.

'You'd better have one of these,' I told her. 'You need to start eating for two.'

Patsy took a biscuit. I popped the other one into my mouth. Sophie, who had finished licking her bottom, turned round three times and lay down on my blank piece of paper. I stroked her back, tickled Emily under the chin and headed for the junk room.

There would, at least, be an excuse for another bonfire.

Nothing much else ever happens in Bilbury.

* * *

If you enjoy the Bilbury books you may enjoy other books by the same author including `Mr Henry Mulligan', `It's Never Too Late', `Second Innings', `Mrs Caldicot's Cabbage War' and `Mrs Caldicot's Knickerbocker Glory'. For full details of over 100 books by Vernon Coleman please see his author page on Amazon or http://www.vernoncoleman.com/

Reviews of previous books in the Bilbury series of novels

THE BILBURY CHRONICLES

"I am just putting pen to paper to say how very much I enjoyed *The Bilbury Chronicles*. I just can't wait to read the others." (*Mrs K., Cambs*)

"I have just finished reading *The Bilbury Chronicles* and I would like to take this opportunity to congratulate Mr Coleman on writing such a wonderful book which is both entertaining and touching. I now enclose an order for Bilbury Grange." (*A.L., Ballymena*)

"I am writing to tell you how much I enjoyed reading your book *The BilburyChronicles*. Thanking you sincerely for giving me so much pleasure." (*Mrs A. H.,Ramsgate*)

BILBURY GRANGE

"I found the book to be brilliant. I felt as though I was part of the community. Please keep me informed of any more in this excellent series." (*I.C., Cleethorpes*)

"A cornucopia of colourful characters help to weave a rich tapestry of village life subtly tempered with gentle humour ... the mixture of rural beauty, human nature and the odd whisper of nostalgia combine to make this book a real delight." *Western Gazette*)

BILBURY REVELS

"Settling down with Vernon Coleman's latest novel set in the fictional Devonshire village of Bilbury is one of the best restorative treatments I know for relieving the stresses and strains of modem living." (*Lincolnshire Echo*

BILBURY COUNTRY

"This fourth novel in the series describes what happens to Bilbury and its villagers when a newspaper story turns a trickle of visitors into a flood. Full of charm and humour." (*News & Star)*

"...thank you for your latest Bilbury book. I have read it with deep interest and enjoyed it." (*Mrs C., St Albans*)

BILBURY PIE

"I have just read Bilbury Pie recommended by a local library. I enjoyed it so much I read it like 'eating a box of chocolates' 2 or 3 chapters at a time to make it last and savour its flavour. I thank you for giving people pleasure and plenty of smiles." (*Mrs G., Banbury*)

BILBURY PUDDING

``Colourful characters, rural reflections and a nostalgic look at country life.'' *North Devon Journal*

Printed in Great
Britain
by Amazon